Ian McEwan's *Enduring Love*

Ian McEwan is one of Britain's most inventive and important contemporary writers. Also adapted as a film, his novel *Enduring Love* (1997) is a tale of obsession that has both troubled and enthralled readers around the world.

This guide to McEwan's haunting novel offers:

- an accessible introduction to the text and contexts of *Enduring Love*;
- a critical history, surveying the many interpretations of the text from publication to the present;
- a selection of new and reprinted critical essays on *Enduring Love*, by Peter Childs, Rhiannon Davies, Paul Edwards, Sean Matthews, Martin Randall and Kiernan Ryan, providing a range of perspectives on the novel and extending the coverage of key critical approaches identified in the survey section;
- cross-references between sections of the guide, in order to suggest links between texts, contexts and criticism;
- suggestions for further reading.

Part of the *Routledge Guides to Literature* series, this volume is essential reading for all those beginning detailed study of *Enduring Love* and seeking not only a guide to the novel, but also a way through the wealth of contextual and critical material that surrounds McEwan's text.

Peter Childs is Professor of Modern English Literature at the University of Gloucestershire.

Routledge Guides to Literature

Editorial Advisory Board: Richard Bradford (University of Ulster at Coleraine), Shirley Chew (University of Leeds), Mick Gidley (University of Leeds), Jan Jedrzejewski (University of Ulster at Coleraine), Ed Larrissy (University of Leeds), Duncan Wu (St. Catherine's College, University of Oxford)

Routledge Guides to Literature offer clear introductions to the most widely studied authors and texts.

Each book engages with texts, contexts and criticism, highlighting the range of critical views and contextual factors that need to be taken into consideration in advanced studies of literary works. The series encourages informed but independent readings of texts by ranging as widely as possible across the contextual and critical issues relevant to the works examined, rather than presenting a single interpretation. Alongside general guides to texts and authors, the series includes 'Sourcebooks', which allow access to reprinted contextual and critical materials as well as annotated extracts of primary text.

Already available:*

Geoffrey Chaucer by Gillian Rudd
Ben Jonson by James Loxley
William Shakespeare's The Merchant of Venice: A Sourcebook edited by
    S. P. Cerasano
William Shakespeare's King Lear: A Sourcebook edited by Grace Ioppolo
William Shakespeare's Othello: A Sourcebook edited by Andrew Hadfield
William Shakespeare's Macbeth: A Sourcebook edited by Alexander Leggatt
William Shakespeare's Hamlet: A Sourcebook edited by Sean McEvoy
John Milton by Richard Bradford
John Milton's Paradise Lost: A Sourcebook edited by Margaret Kean
Alexander Pope by Paul Baines
Mary Wollstonecraft's A Vindication of the Rights of Woman: A Sourcebook
    edited by Adriana Craciun
Jonathan Swift's Gulliver's Travels: A Sourcebook edited by Roger D. Lund
Jane Austen by Robert P. Irvine
Jane Austen's Emma: A Sourcebook edited by Paula Byrne
Jane Austen's Pride and Prejudice: A Sourcebook edited by Robert Morrison
Byron, by Caroline Franklin
Mary Shelley's Frankenstein: A Sourcebook edited by Timothy Morton
The Poems of John Keats: A Sourcebook edited by John Strachan
The Poems of Gerard Manley Hopkins: A Sourcebook Edited by Alice Jenkins
Charles Dickens's David Copperfield: A Sourcebook edited by Richard J. Dunn
Charles Dickens's Bleak House: A Sourcebook edited by Janice M. Allan
Charles Dickens's Oliver Twist: A Sourcebook edited by Juliet John

* Some titles in this series were first published in the Routledge Literary Sourcebooks series, edited by Duncan Wu, or the Complete Critical Guide to Literature series, edited by Jan Jedrzejewski and Richard Bradford.

Charles Dickens's A Tale of Two Cities: A Sourcebook edited by Ruth Glancy

Herman Melville's Moby-Dick: A Sourcebook edited by Michael J. Davey

Harriet Beecher Stowe's Uncle Tom's Cabin: A Sourcebook edited by Debra J. Rosenthal

Walt Whitman's Song of Myself: A Sourcebook and Critical Edition edited by Ezra Greenspan

Robert Browning by Stefan Hawlin

Henrik Ibsen's Hedda Gabler: A Sourcebook edited by Christopher Innes

Thomas Hardy by Geoffrey Harvey

Thomas Hardy's Tess of the d'Urbervilles edited by Scott McEathron

Charlotte Perkins Gilman's The Yellow Wallpaper: A Sourcebook and Critical Edition edited by Catherine J. Golden

Kate Chopin's The Awakening: A Sourcebook edited by Janet Beer and Elizabeth Nolan

D. H. Lawrence by Fiona Becket

Joseph Conrad by Tim Middleton

The Poems of W. B. Yeats: A Sourcebook edited by Michael O'Neill

E. M. Forster's A Passage to India: A Sourcebook edited by Peter Childs

Samuel Beckett by David Pattie

Richard Wright's Native Son by Andrew Warnes

J. D. Salinger's The Catcher in the Rye by Sarah Graham

Ian McEwan's Enduring Love by Peter Childs

Arundhati Roy's The God of Small Things by Alex Tickell

Ian McEwan's *Enduring Love*

Peter Childs

Routledge
Taylor & Francis Group

LONDON AND NEW YORK

First published 2007
by Routledge
2 Park Square, Milton Park, Abingdon, Oxon OX14 4RN

Simultaneously published in the USA and Canada
by Routledge
270 Madison Ave, New York, NY 10016

Routledge is an imprint of the Taylor & Francis Group, an informa business

© 2007 Peter Childs

Reprinted 2009

Typeset in Sabon and Gill Sans by RefineCatch Limited, Bungay, Suffolk
Printed and bound in Great Britain by
the MPG Books Group

British Library Cataloguing in Publication Data
A catalogue record for this book is available from the British Library.

Library of Congress Cataloging in Publication Data
Childs, Peter, 1962–
    Ian McEwan's Enduring love / by Peter Childs.
        p.   cm – (Routledge guides to literature)
    1. McEwan, Ian. Enduring love.   I. Title.
    PR6063.C4E5335   2006
    823'.914–dc22

                                    2006022255

ISBN 10: 0–415–34558–8 (hbk)
ISBN 10: 0–415–34559–6 (pbk)
ISBN 10: 0–203–56710–2 (ebk)

ISBN 13: 978–0–415–34558–3 (hbk)
ISBN 13: 978–0–415–34559–0 (pbk)
ISBN 13: 978–0–203–56710–4 (ebk)

Contents

Acknowledgements

The editor and publishers would like to thank Rodopi for permission to reproduce an extract from Rhiannon Davies – 'Enduring McEwan', *Posting the Male: Masculinities in Post-War and Contemporary British Literature*, edited by Daniel Lea and Berthold Schoene, Amsterdam: Rodopi, 2003, pp. 105–23.

Notes and references

Primary text

All references to the primary text are taken from *Enduring Love*, Ian McEwan (London: Vintage, 1998). References will be in parentheses in the body of the text, stating the chapter and page number, e.g. (Ch. 12, p. 99).

Secondary text

References to any secondary material can be found in the footnotes. The first reference will contain full bibliographic details, and each subsequent reference to the same text will contain the author's surname, title and page number.

Footnotes

All footnotes that are not by the author of this volume will identify the source in square brackets, e.g. [Baldwin's note].

Cross-referencing

Cross-referencing between sections is a feature of each volume in the Routledge Guides to Literature series. Cross-references appear in brackets and include part titles as well as the relevant page numbers in bold type, e.g. (see Text and Contexts, pp. 21–2).

Introduction

This study aims to give a well-rounded introduction to one of Ian McEwan's most intriguing novels by offering a broad set of perspectives informed by a range of critical opinions. The reader will find here a summary of the reviews, reactions and many ways of reading *Enduring Love*, as well as several newly written essays offering fresh angles and insights. After this introductory discussion, the book is arranged into five parts.

Though *Enduring Love* is a novel contemporary with McEwan's early period of writing it, one of the interesting facets of the narrative is that it makes few references to when it is set. As David Malcolm has noted, 'the social and historical aspects of characters' lives are almost completely ignored', and in many ways the novel aims instead to deal with timeless concerns, such as morality and love, subjectivity and objectivity, psychology and epistemology (theories of know-ledge).[1] Part 1, Texts and contexts, therefore looks at the contemporary context of the book not so much by sketching its socio-political background as by offering ways of approaching its subject matter through four sections. The sections focus on, first, themes and structure; second, Ian McEwan's career as a writer; third, the references, allusions and antecedents that the novel draws upon; and, finally, the ways in which *Enduring Love* engages with social understanding, scientific know-ledge and cultural beliefs.

Part 2, Critical history, provides an extended analysis of the novel in the light of the reviews, essays and other works of criticism that have appeared in the years since *Enduring Love*'s publication. McEwan's novel has yet to develop a con-siderable body of criticism – and this is one of the exciting aspects of studying contemporary texts – so the readings included in this chapter are less summaries of critics' interpretations than discussions of the main aspects of the novel that have interested commentators to date.

Part 3, Critical readings, brings together a number of readings of the novel by different critics who have all followed McEwan's career closely and who each approach the text from a different angle. These essays illustrate how such a rich story can be studied at length by concentrating on a particular facet of its multilayered narrative. The diversity of readings illustrates that literature cannot

---

1 David Malcolm, *Understanding Ian McEwan*, Colombia, South Carolina Press, 2002, p. 171.

be pigeonholed as a textual elaboration of just one subject, but that several aspects of its construction can profitably be foregrounded to illuminate a particular component of its concerns.

Enduring Love was made into a film in 2004. Though not the first adaptation of McEwan's fiction for the screen, it was the most widely distributed cinematic version of one of his works. Part 4, Adaptations, thus looks closely at the ways in which the book was adapted and discusses some of the most important aspects of the film's re-reading of the novel.

The final short part, Part 5, provides an annotated guide to the criticism of the novel to date. It provides a guide to the books, articles, essays, reviews and interviews that should be consulted when studying the novel.

Finally, it is important to note that *Enduring Love* is such an admired book by readers not only because it has an engrossing and compelling plot, but also because it attempts to consider some of the most fundamental human questions about the meaning of love and the purpose of life. This is an aspect to McEwan's work that either attracts or repels. He is a deeply serious writer, even when writing in a comic vein, and either has to be celebrated for his interest in what might colloquially be called the 'big questions' or criticised for believing that postmodernism and its rejection of such universal questions has not changed, or perhaps superseded, those questions.

McEwan's most recent novel before *Enduring Love*, *Black Dogs* (1992), was a study of evil through which he hoped to approach a sense of what we mean when we say that something is good. *Enduring Love* similarly is a study of love through an examination of an extreme form that more closely resembles its mirror opposite (and so leads to life-threatening violence). While *Enduring Love*'s obvious theme is love, it is clearly as much concerned with how love can be obsessive and intimidating as it can be supportive and redeeming. It is especially concerned with the ways in which lovers and others can be self-deluding. Like several of McEwan's novels, it has a marriage in crisis at its centre: a couple whose union is threatened by the sudden appearance of a third, unwanted 'lover'.

In briefest outline, McEwan's plot describes how a social misfit, Jed Parry, fixates on the novel's narrator, Joe Rose, following their meeting in a moment of emotional intensity: a five-man attempt to hold down a hot-air balloon in danger of flying away with only a child aboard. The reader is never quite sure until late on whether Parry is indeed stalking Joe, or, as his partner Clarissa suspects, Joe is to some degree fabricating the story. Through these doubts and interpretations, *Enduring Love* develops as a novel about the different narratives, theories and beliefs people use to interpret events in their lives. Though the plot can be accused of being overly schematic, as arguably are those of several of McEwan's books, *Enduring Love* is in many ways a compelling and chilling study of an individual who has to endure a love that is unreciprocated but unswerving and which, like a runaway balloon, threatens quickly to get out of control and into danger.

1

Text and contexts

The text

In terms of subject matter, McEwan's book is to many readers most clearly a novel about endurance, or survival, and love in its several forms: romantic, familial, idealised, obsessive, jealous. It is additionally both about the forces that are destructive of love and about love as a destructive force. As Joe mentions, while Hollywood films show how love can be forged or strengthened by shared intense experiences, in fact 'sustained stress is corrosive of feeling. It's the great deadener.'[1] In terms of story shape, with *Enduring Love* McEwan also wants to break free from the formulas of romantic convention, in which marriage or reconciliation supplies a satisfying but artificial narrative closure. The novel form conventionally follows an arc of beginning, middle and end, moving from stasis through complication, crisis and confrontation to a new stasis, but McEwan shapes the trajectory of his story to include a recognition that life does not come to an end the way a narrative concludes on its final page.

This irresolution or resistance to closure is a feature of much twentieth-century experimental literature, but it is also a part of the thematic tissue of *Enduring Love*. The novel has not one but three endings, signalling different viewpoints on the events Joe has narrated. The twenty-fourth chapter concludes not with Joe and Clarissa's story but with a visit to the Logan household, which is only a moment in the couple's attempt to see if their lives can be pieced together again. The first appendix turns their experience of Jed Parry into a case history of the kind that Joe might wish to research if he could resuscitate his academic career. It concludes that Parry's 'case' involves 'a most lasting form of love, often terminated only by the death of the patient' (Appendix I, p. 242). Disallowing this termination, Parry's death itself is not encompassed by the novel and instead his voice surfaces again in the second appendix to affirm continuity and continuance, three years after the main events of the novel. Previous events have themselves taken place over only a small space of time, a few weeks, and the breathless pace of the narrative is suggested by its arrangement into twenty-four chapters, like the hours of one day.

---

1   Ian McEwan, *Enduring Love*, London: Vintage, 1998, Ch. 22, p. 213. All subsequent references will be given in the body of the text.

In terms of distinctiveness, the aspect of the novel most praised by reviewers on the book's publication was the gripping opening chapter. These scenes immediately throw the characters into a situation of crisis, which appears initially not to be in the lives of the protagonists, Joe Rose and Clarissa Mellon, but in the lives of others. That the balloon incident proves also to be an important moment for Joe and Clarissa brings immediately into focus some of the key questions McEwan is interested in with regard to self-preservation and cooperation. The selfish response to this event would be merely to ignore or observe it. From the point of view of the individual's principal evolutionary drive to survive, the logical and natural response would seem to be to avoid a situation that can place the self in danger. Yet, humans also have an altruistic component to their psychological make-up, and they frequently seek to help others who are in danger, sometimes to the extent of endangering their own safety, as happens at the start of McEwan's novel.

McEwan has described the several effects on the reader he was trying to achieve in the pivotal opening chapter: first, that he wanted to suggest immediately a particular, highly organised materialist cast of mind in his use of Joe's narration; second, that he sought to create a chapter concentrating on the visual and on the detailed imagination of the spatial relationship between a group of individuals; third, that he wished to fashion a dramatic incident that would work as a moment of intensity in which Jed could become emotionally attached to Joe; and fourth, that he aimed to grab the reader's attention in a situation 'that involves morality, involves instinct, involves an adaptationist account of why we are what we are, quite distinct from the deist account that Jed is going to espouse'.[2]

In another interview, McEwan explains that the story of the balloon was not the genesis of the book, but a device to bring disparate people together to explore issues he had been researching.[3] He says that, when he heard about a balloon accident in Germany,

> What immediately struck me was the dilemma of knowing that if you all hang on, you can bring this balloon down to earth. But as soon as anyone breaks rank, then madness follows. The issue is selfishness. And that seems to me to be the underlying basic moral factor about ourselves. We're descended from generations of people who *survived*, who acted successfully. But who also cooperated successfully; so we clearly need to save our own skins and look out for own interests, but we're social animals and we need other people dearly.[4]

When planning *Enduring Love*, McEwan found himself most interested in the way contemporary scientists were starting to write about human nature

---

2   Margaret Reynolds and Jonathan Noakes (eds), *Ian McEwan: The Essential Guide*, London: Vintage, 2002, pp. 15–16.
3   McEwan has since written the introduction to David Hempleman-Adams's *At the Mercy of the Winds* (2001), Bantam, the story of the first man to fly to the North Pole by balloon.
4   Quoted in Dwight Garner, Interview with Ian McEwan, 'Salon Interview', *Salon* (31 March 1998). Available at <http://archive.salon.com/books/int/1998/03/cov_si_31int.html>. (Accessed 11 October 2005.)

and the links between biology and psychology. He was also interested in the anthropological turn from studying human difference to observing human sameness:

> [O]ne of the things you'll find in all humans is that people stand around and talk about each other and judge each other and take great delight in examining their motives. [. . .] We identify ourselves by it, our group-ings, and we bring to bear all that emotional intelligence, talking about someone's motives or how they crossed the line of acceptability or how they didn't pull themselves back from disaster. Novels, in a focused and more articulate way, do many of the same things.[5]

With respect to the catalytic force driving the dramatic events in the novel, McEwan wanted to stage a trial for the faculty of reason. His rational protagonist was to be faced with 'the most irrational thing' McEwan could conceive:

> a man who not only has fallen in love with him and believes that Joe loves him back but is persuaded, as are a number of schizophrenics, that he's receiving messages and the endorsement of God in this pursuit and that he must bring this materialist, this atheist, into the lap of God.[6]

McEwan also wanted his narrator to be doubted by the reader, not just by Clarissa and the police:

> I wanted a man at the centre of this who was a clear thinker, who appears to be right but then perhaps is wrong, but in fact is right [. . .]. I wanted, in other words, to write a book somewhat in praise of rationality which I think gets a very poor showing in western literature.[7]

The men that McEwan assembles at the balloon at the start of the story can be considered from a number of angles. To begin with, they are a disparate group in terms of employment and age: Joe Rose, a forty-seven-year-old freelance science writer; John Logan, a forty-two-year-old Oxford family doctor; Joseph Lacey, a sixty-three-year-old farm labourer; Toby Greene, a fifty-eight-year-old farm worker; James Gadd, a fifty-five-year-old advertising executive; and Jed Parry, a twenty-eight-year-old unemployed man. Aside from Gadd, the pilot, Logan is the only one who has children, and his sacrifice to save Gadd's grandson has to be considered with this in mind, because children serve in this childless novel as a means to bring people together, from the first scenes to the last.

The purpose of the tragedy is not simply to bring Joe and Jed together. All of the men are assigned a role in the narrative. James Gadd is guilty of losing control of the balloon, and this is anticipatory of all the guilty actions and thoughts that

---

5   Quoted in Dwight Garner, Interview with Ian McEwan.
6   McEwan in conversation with James Naughtie, Radio 4's *Book Club* programme (1 October, 2000). Transcript at <http:www.bbc.co.uk/arts/books/club/enduring/transcript.shtml>. (Accessed 10 February 2004.)
7   McEwan in conversation with James Naughtie, *Book Club*.

occur throughout the book. Toby Greene breaks an ankle at the site, while John Logan of course loses his life, and Joseph Lacey will be the key figure in finding the people who can explain what happened before the fall of Logan. None of the men is unaffected by the accident.

The situation the rescuers find themselves in is neatly summarised by Joe: 'A child alone and needing help. It was my duty to hang on, and I thought we would all do the same' (Ch. 1, p. 13). Yet, seconds later he is thinking 'The child was not my child, and I was not going to die for it' (Ch. 1, p. 15). Underlying the entire scene is the question of the degree to which individuals have an obligation towards others, which is an issue again at the end of the novel when James Reid and Bonnie Deedes step forward out of a sense of obligation – and in doing so 'save', or at least redeem, John Logan. Though it may not seem so at first, this is intricately tied to the other key elements of the novel, and is important in terms of: Joe's obligation towards Jean Logan; his 'right' to buy a gun to protect himself and Clarissa from Jed Parry; the extent to which Joe and Clarissa have obligations of trust and understanding towards each other after their seven-year relationship; and the question of the degree to which Jed has any right to involve himself in Joe's life or to which Joe has any obligation towards Jed. 'When are you going to leave me alone?' (Ch. 10, p. 91) is a key concern in the novel between these last two people, but on the occasion this question enters the text, it is asked by Jed. Joe has earlier summarised the social issue of human interaction in these terms: 'our mammalian conflict – what to give to the others, and what to keep for yourself. Treading that line, keeping the others in check, and being kept in check by them, is what we call morality' (Ch. 1, p. 14).

For McEwan, exploring morality is something that can best be done at the extremes of human experience. For this reason, his subject matter is often harrowing, such that, even at the start of his career, he appeared to reviewers to be in the vanguard, with Martin Amis, of a new generation of writers emerging in the late 1970s and 1980s, including Pat Barker, Julian Barnes and Graham Swift. Like other novelists, including Amis, McEwan has subsequently been repeatedly upbraided as an immoral or amoral writer, when in fact his interest in the horrific, the marginal and the perverse has precisely been aimed at defining ethical limits. The contemporary novelist Michèle Roberts wrote about him in a review of *Enduring Love*:

> Ian McEwan is always described as writing about gore and nastiness, perverse philosophies, machismo metaphysics – and very fed up he must get with this, too. Just because he wrote one story about things that go bump in bell-jars doesn't mean he should be typecast forever as baddish and laddish.[8] In fact, his novels are sheep in wolves' clothing.
>
> Under their dark, bristling, thrillerish surfaces lurk explorations of the way we love now: men and women mostly, but parents and children too. His world appears a naturalistic one, but is also metaphorical, as in a romance. He illuminates inner states as well as outer ones, though his

---

8   The reference here is to 'Solid Geometry' in McEwan's first short-story collection *First Love, Last Rites*.

landscapes are always realistic and noir-ish enough to satisfy the butchest of readers.[9]

This seems to be a fair assessment of McEwan's writing, and it is one I will return to as part of the discussion of the adaptation of *Enduring Love* to film (see Adaptations, **p. 135**), yet it is a judgement that most critics only arrived at with the publication in 2001 of *Atonement*. *Enduring Love* was primarily greeted on release as a psychological thriller in the context of McEwan's previous career, to which I will shortly turn.

First, to end this introductory section, I want briefly to sketch the particular ingredients of the novel that make it a unique mix of concerns centred on questions of human interaction. There are five aspects to be mentioned here. The first is psycho-sexual. On *Enduring Love's* publication, many reviewers thought that McEwan had made up the term 'de Clérambault's syndrome', but this is not the case. The condition is named after Gaëtan Gatian de Clérambault, a French psychiatrist (1872–1934) who published his detailed work, *Les Psychoses passionelles*, on the subject in 1921. A person suffering from de Clérambault's maintains, like Jed, an unwavering delusional belief that another person, usually of higher social status, is in love with them. This form of erotomania, which may be a feature of paranoid schizophrenia, was originally described by de Clérambault as having a phase of hope followed by one of resentment. It is an extreme form of erotic or emotional attachment that is peculiar for having no basis in a relationship between the two people involved. In *Enduring Love* McEwan is interested in the syndrome as another example of bonds that can tie strangers together, metaphorically figured in the balloon ropes that Jed and Joe grasp, but he is also concerned with the connections between an extreme psychological state, de Clérambault's, and the everyday phenomenon of being in love.[10]

A second aspect to the novel's concern with human interdependence and attraction is literary and draws its relevance from Clarissa's research interests. The Romantic poet John Keats (1795–1821) is associated less with love poetry than love letters, and the posthumous publication of his correspondence outraged sections of Victorian society. Keats became obsessed with a young woman he met in London called Fanny Brawne and wrote her letters of passionate intensity, but his love remained unconsummated at the time of his death in Rome from tuberculosis. The elements of ardent love, impassioned correspondence, obsession and illness all provide contexts for discussion of *Enduring Love*, as will be explored below.

Third, at the end of *Enduring Love* there is an acknowledgements page which states McEwan's indebtedness to several books and authors. Aside from two biographies, one by Robert Gittings on Keats and one by Stephen Gill on Wordsworth, the books listed are nearly all, broadly speaking, works that have had an impact on the field of evolutionary biology, an area of study which, among other things, advances the gene rather than the individual or species as the unit of (natural) selection. Evolutionary biology is still controversial but gained a foothold in

---

9 Michèle Roberts, Review of *Enduring Love*, *The Times*, 23 August 1997.
10 See G. G. de Clérambault, 'Les Psychoses passionelles', in *Oeuvres psychiatriques*, Paris: Presses Universitaires, 1942, pp. 315–22.

university biology departments in the 1970s and 1980s. These books will be considered in further detail later (see Text and contexts, **pp. 23–7**) but for now it is worth signalling that McEwan is interested in evolutionary psychology and socio-cultural evolution in *Enduring Love*. For example, if love is unique to humans, what part does it play in the individual's survival or the species' endurance? Also, if evolution promotes the survival of the fittest, what role do altruism and collaboration play in self-preservation?

A related area to evolutionary biology is that of microbiology, the discovery of DNA, and the Genome Project that Jocelyn briefly talks about with Joe and Clarissa (Ch. 19, pp. 164–5). In the 1940s, DNA (deoxyribonucleic acid) was identified as the transforming principle responsible for transmitting genetic information, and in the early 1950s Francis Crick and James D. Watson (Ch. 19, p. 165) published their breakthrough work on the structure of DNA, based on the research of Rosalind Franklin and Maurice Wilkins (Ch. 19, p. 165), thereby reorienting the understanding of evolution as a molecular process. The brooch of human DNA, two gold bands 'entwined in a double helix' (Ch. 19, p. 163), which Jocelyn presents Clarissa, is another example in the book of patterns and of interlinkages: a material representation of chemical connections that underlie emotional ties. It is also an object of beauty linking the realms of art and science, aesthetics and empirical truth. It is DNA that contains the genetic blueprint dictating the biological development of all cellular life forms, and Joe is reminded of the connections between all living things when the animal urge to defecate forces him to crouch in the woods:

> Some people find their long perspectives in the stars and galaxies; I prefer the earthbound scale of the biological. I brought my palm close to my face and peered. In the rich black crumbly mulch I saw two black ants, a springtail, and a dark red worm-like creature with a score of pale brown legs. These were the rumbling giants of this lower world, for not far below the threshold of visibility was the seething world of the roundworms – the scavengers and the predators who fed on them, and even these were giants relative to the inhabitants of the microscopic realm, the parasitic fungi and the bacteria – perhaps ten million of them in the handful of soil, and therefore the plants, the trees, and the creatures that lived among them, whose number had once included ourselves. What I thought might calm me was the reminder that, for all our concerns, we were still part of this natural dependency.
>
> (Ch. 22, pp. 206–7)

As soon as Joe reflects on this 'natural dependency' he recollects how unnatural modern human life is, and he then considers an angle to a fifth aspect that needs to be borne in mind when reading *Enduring Love*: 'It was our own complexity that had expelled us from the Garden' (Ch. 22, p. 207). This reminds us of Jed's religious perspective and of the Garden of Eden, but it is also a reference to the Earth as a garden – as an ecological world from which humans have expelled themselves through pollution, mineral exploitation and over-farming. Whether it be a metaphysical or a terrestrial paradise that humans can inherit, the selfish drive to preservation, of the individual, the species, or the gene, means that people rarely think of this grand scale of life which lies so far beyond their own immediate concerns, such as: 'my de Clérambault, and my threatened loved one' (Ch. 22, p. 207). Joe might also say *my* story here as *Enduring Love* is very much a narrative told from his perspective, and if there is one aspect to McEwan's novel that requires particular attention, it is the fact of Joe Rose's narration, as will be discussed extensively in the essays that comprise Critical readings (see **pp. 41–121**).

The author

Born in Aldershot in 1948, the son of a soldier in the British army and his wife, McEwan spent many years of his childhood abroad, in Singapore and Tripoli. He attended eight different schools before being sent at age eleven to Woolverstone Hall boarding school in Suffolk. He took his first degree, in English Literature and French, at Sussex University, and then graduated in 1971 with a masters in modern fiction and creative writing from the University of East Anglia. His book-length debut was a collection of short stories he worked on during his MA, *First Love, Last Rites* (1975). Though the collection won the Somerset Maugham award, the volume immediately earned McEwan's writing the label 'literature of shock', mainly because of its preoccupation with sexualised children and violent abuse. Though the stories were highly praised in many quarters, to a majority of reviewers the settings seemed sordid and bleak, the narratives lurid and morbidly compelling: stories of incest, a severed penis, child murder, a man who wants to return to the safety of the womb. Yet the collection was also widely recognised as an extraordinary first publication from a new literary voice. At this time, long-established novelists dominated literary fiction and comparatively few major new writers of fiction had come to prominence in the time immediately before McEwan and Martin Amis emerged in the mid-1970s. Both these writers presented a fresh, challenging view of the modern world, markedly different from the dominant novelists of the time, such as Doris Lessing, Iris Murdoch and William Golding.

First Love, Last Rites was followed by McEwan's second collection, *In Between the Sheets* (1978). These stories shared concerns with those of the first collection – sex, violence, disturbance – and created a particular kind of reputation for McEwan that has taken many years to fade. The preoccupations of *In Between the Sheets* can be suggested from the stories' subjects: a father who feels sexually tempted by his daughter and her friend; a two-timing, sexually diseased man castrated by the nurses he has been deceiving; a man who falls in love with a shop-window dummy; a woman writer who keeps an ape as a lover. It is only the final story, 'Psychopolis', written after a trip to the USA, that hints at the possibility of McEwan's writing developing in new directions.

Yet it would be several years before McEwan explored these wider possibilities. His first novel, *The Cement Garden* (1978), about two brothers and two sisters surviving in their house together after the death of their parents, seemed to most reviewers to continue the preoccupations of the short stories. Indeed, as a novella itself, it could be considered a survey at greater length of familiar McEwan territory, including sibling rivalry, claustrophobic lives, taboo sex, infantilisation and disguise. With a small cast of barely more than six characters in the novel, there is as strong a sense of intimacy and insularity as in the earlier stories, but at its core the narrative is about the ways in which a family of orphaned children stick together. Its narrator is the second oldest of the four children, Jack, a fourteen-year-old whose Oedipal desires come true when his father collapses and dies of a coronary while building the cement garden of the title. When their mother dies shortly afterwards, Jack and his three siblings do not report the death to the authorities but simply bury her corpse in cement in the basement. Each of the four children responds to their loss and subsequent fragile independence differently, but the dominant movement is one of regression. The story ends with Derek, the boyfriend of Jack's older sister, Julie, breaking into the mother's concrete tomb and the police arriving at the house immediately after Jack and Julie have sex for the first time, as though installing themselves as the new parents in the family home.

The Comfort of Strangers (1981) is narrower again in its range of characters and is markedly different from *The Cement Garden* in that it is concerned with how people behave in an unfamiliar environment. Apparently set in Venice, *The Comfort of Strangers* tells the story of a tourist couple, Colin and Mary, who become involved with a local man, Robert. When they meet Robert's wife Caroline, Colin and Mary learn that the older couple are involved in a long-standing sadomasochistic relationship, in which they believe Caroline is trapped. The book draws parallels between the two couples but builds towards Robert's premeditated murder of Colin. Through the course of this simple narrative McEwan explores the way in which travellers are at the mercy of others when holidaying in alien surroundings. In several ways, McEwan's second and equally short novel appears to share the interest in isolation and incest evident in his first, largely because the central couple of *The Comfort of Strangers* are almost like brother and sister and are so wrapped up in their own world they sometimes find it difficult to remember they are separate individuals. Reminiscent of the children's behaviour in the earlier novel, Colin and Mary sleep in the afternoon, talk little and do not even have the energy or motivation to tidy their hotel room. Where Jack and Julie in the earlier novel are adolescents who prematurely become adults in the familial home, Colin and Mary are adults (she divorced with children) who revert to a child-like state, reliant on their hotel maid to look after them in the unfamiliar temporary home of a foreign hotel. In both *The Cement Garden* and *The Comfort of Strangers* there is an almost claustrophobic feel to the lives of the main characters, a family and a couple into whose midst strangers come in search of sex and power. In each novel, too great a closeness creates its own problems for the protagonists, and they are presented as deeply vulnerable to outsiders who can expose the dangers of, and prey upon, their intimacy. *The Comfort of Strangers* was shortlisted for the Booker Prize in 1981 but was a controversial novel on publication because McEwan had chosen to explore sadomasochistic relationships. He has said in interview about the couples in the story:

> Robert and Caroline were for me simply a sort of comic drawing of a relationship of domination, and when this decently liberal and slightly tired couple, Colin and Mary, come in contact with that relationship they find it has a sway over their unconscious life, and they begin to act out – or rather speak to each other – these incredible masochistic and

sadistic fantasies while they are making love ... because they haven't ever addressed the matter at a deeper level of themselves; they've always seen it as a social matter.[11]

The Child in Time (1987), McEwan's third novel, is thematically linked to his first two. As in *The Cement Garden*, there is a male protagonist whose maturation is central to the narrative, but as in *The Comfort of Strangers* there is a fundamental concern with a couple in crisis. Once more, childhood is a major preoccupation, as are gender relations. However, McEwan's third novel marks a considerable change from his earlier fiction in certain other respects. Informed by the experience of writing for television and film, and after a six-year gap since his last novel, *The Child in Time* has a wider social and political purview than either *The Cement Garden* or *The Comfort of Strangers*. For many critics this revealed McEwan to be one of the foremost novelists of his generation though for others it proved he was best writing about couples and families in near-claustrophobic situations. The story of *The Child in Time* takes place over a few years in a projected future of the late 1990s, in a London of beggars licensed by the government and schools offered for sale to private investors. The central storyline focuses on a married couple, Stephen and Julie, who grow apart after their only daughter goes missing. The second-string plot concerns the composition and publication of a government childcare manual. These two strands of narrative are brought together not just through events in Stephen's life but also via his concern with the idea that a generation or society can be appraised by its attitude towards the nurturing and education of children.

McEwan's following publication is a Cold War spy story that has at its heart the preoccupations of many espionage novels, such as deception, duplicity, ignorance, aggression and the loss of innocence that accompanies the acquisition of knowledge and experience. As suits the genre, *The Innocent* (1990) is more complexly plotted than McEwan's previous fiction and the prose is heavily symbolic at times. The story works as an allegory of how strong countries impose their wills on weaker ones, and *The Innocent* is the first of McEwan's books to intimate a European dimension to his interests. The story is set in Berlin at the time of Operation Gold, the attempt by the British and American military to tunnel into the Soviet sector to infiltrate its communication systems in 1955–6. As well as focusing on the actual tunnel built by MI6 and the CIA, McEwan also breaks the fictional frame of the narrative by introducing the real figure of George Blake, the double agent who betrayed Operation Gold before the tunnel was even started. *The Innocent* is concerned with the way the post-war Western world divided into factions aligning themselves with the mutually suspicious superpowers, and so foregrounds the opposed political philosophies of the USSR and Euroamerica, but it is also a story about the end of the British Empire and the rise of American global cultural domination. The novel is set at the time in British politics of the confusion and humiliation of the Suez Crisis in 1956 when US condemnation of the Anglo-French naval attempt to reopen the Suez Canal to their shipping lines revealed Britain's post-imperial dependence on American support for its foreign

---

11 John Haffenden, *Novelists in Interview*, London: Methuen, 1985, p. 179.

policies. *The Innocent* details the loss of Britain's leading international role, together with its assumption of a secondary position in the new world order and also concerns the transition to the Cold War signalled by the division of Berlin, whose carving-up is imaged in the literal dismemberment of a body in the novel's middle section.

McEwan's next novel, *Black Dogs* (1992), is presented as the memoir of an orphan fascinated by the families of others. This early loss of his parents when he was eight years old has led Jeremy to seek parental figures with authority but compassion, solutions but sympathy. A preface provides the reader with Jeremy's background, concentrating on his relationship with his sister and his protective love for her daughter. Yet, in several ways the principal figures in the novel are Jeremy's parents-in-law, June and Bernard Tremaine, a separated couple who met as communist sympathisers but whose experiences and temperaments have taken them in diametrically opposed philosophical directions. This concern with ideological differences continues a theme from *The Innocent*, with which *Black Dogs* shares an interest in the construction and destruction of the Berlin Wall. In *Black Dogs*, the pulling down of the wall in 1989 is symbolic of the breaking down of a barrier between June and Bernard's seemingly irreconcilable perspectives. June is a spiritual being, an intuitive believer and a natural communicator, while Bernard is a logical rationalist and unswerving materialist. She searches for the 'hidden truth' of the universe and argues that she would not take the life of another no matter what the benefit, while he believes there is no truth that science cannot ultimately reveal to humanity and argues that he would countenance the death of hundreds of people if it were to save the lives of thousands (arguments that can be considered in the light of the dilemma facing the men at the start of *Enduring Love*). In the opening section of the novel after the preface, June is dying from leukaemia at a nursing home in 1987, where Jeremy visits her. While he makes notes from the stories June tells him and reflects upon his conversations with Bernard, Jeremy starts to consider himself the intermediary between this alienated couple. As he learns more of their background and the circumstances of their marriage, Jeremy also increasingly becomes an image of the novelist, of the observing outsider trying to make sense of the lives and opinions of others. The narrative of the novel does not proceed chronologically but leads up to an incident in 1946: an encounter June had in France with two predatory dogs, which brought her to a belief in God. June understands the dogs to be embodiments of evil, exemplars of a persistent malignant force that can arise anywhere at any time. The events of the book, from the assault on Bernard at the Berlin Wall in 1989, through Jeremy's visit to the Majdanek concentration camp in Poland, to his disturbing experience in France of the violent forces in himself, can all be considered from this perspective. Against the metaphysical explanation of events, Bernard would rationally argue that all examples of 'evil' are historically specific incidents of violence that could be eradicated by improved social and political systems. Though McEwan himself is atheistic, Jeremy ultimately leans more towards June's understanding of the universe than Bernard's, believing there are spiritual forces at work that the rationalist mind will never comprehend. An episodic novel, *Black Dogs* is at heart a meditation on the nature of moral forces. The book uses the dogs of its title, which have supposedly been trained by the Gestapo not only to attack but to rape, as an emblem or manifestation of a primal evil that will periodically surface in Europe (McEwan's 1993 film script for *The Good Son* is also exercised with modern Western society's refusal to countenance the existence of evil). The narrative is thus concerned with the secular meanings of 'evil' and 'good', the latter figured as the redemptive power of love. Taking his cue from the poet W. H. Auden, McEwan forces on the reader the conviction that, whatever one takes them to be symbols of, the 'black dogs' can, and indeed will, arise again in the future, and only love can in some sense overcome the violent tragedies of history.[12]

In his 1994 study, Kiernan Ryan notes that McEwan felt constrained by the 'Ian Macabre' tag and had deliberately attempted to turn away from his previous preoccupations with his play *The Imitation Game* in the early 1980s. Ryan notes McEwan's lament that he 'had been labelled as the chronicler of comically exaggerated states of mind', but of course McEwan's next novel was to return to one of these 'states of mind' very forcibly in the figure of Jed Parry.[13] The difference is that by this stage of his career McEwan could present mental extremity alongside a rationalist point of view he had explored in recent novels, such as *Black Dogs*.

Enduring Love was McEwan's next novel in 1997, and *Amsterdam* appeared only a year later. While two of *Enduring Love's* reference points are Keats's odes (discussed in Critical history, p. 19) and Jed's final assertion that 'faith is joy' (Appendix II, p. 245), the climax of *Amsterdam* occurs when one of its twin protagonists discovers that his millennial symphony has been unconsciously plagiarised from Beethoven's 'Ode to Joy'. *Amsterdam* won the Booker Prize in 1998, but for several commentators this was seen to be a case of the right author winning for the wrong book, because *Enduring Love* is generally considered superior. *Amsterdam* is a little different from McEwan's earlier novels. Read as another serious exploration of themes of responsibility and rivalry, it doesn't match the high standards of McEwan's previous work; however, read as a black comedy, the novel's 'faults' (predictability, melodrama, over-coincidence) appear to be entirely within the genre of social satire and to reveal a new strand to McEwan's writing. The plot centres on three men gathered together at the funeral of a woman to whom they have all been lovers. Following a series of bizarre plot twists and misunderstandings, two of the men, supposedly best friends, travel to Holland while secretly planning to kill one another. Unknown to the other, they each intend to do this under the guise of voluntary euthanasia as Holland's relaxed laws allow this to be done legally in certain circumstances. The third man, husband to the dead woman, appears at the end of the novel to rise from being a foolish cuckold to the orchestrator of the others' doom. Set in 1996, the book shows McEwan's continuing skill at giving macabre twists to debates over contemporary social issues as the narrative explores the dubious morality of the well-off portion of a generation brought up in the post-war era. It suggests that the ruling political and cultural elite since the Conservative Party returned to government in 1979 has become increasingly marked by a politics of sleaze and greed, epitomised by the scandals associated with Tory MPs Neil Hamilton and

12 'We must love one another or die' is a famous line from Auden's poem 'September 1, 1939', *Another Time*, London: Faber & Faber, 1940.
13 Kiernan Ryan, *Ian McEwan*, Writers and their Work, Plymouth: Northcote House, 1994, p. 2 (the quotation is from Haffenden, *Novelists in Interview*, p. 173).

Jeffrey Archer.[14] Perhaps most appropriately seen as a witty diversion, *Amsterdam* reads like a potboiler in between McEwan's more important novels and can best be enjoyed as his first attempt at social satire.

McEwan's subsequent novel, *Atonement* (2001), was another foray into new fictional terrain, in that, for the first time, he set a novel mostly before his own birth. Though it ends in the present, the narrative begins in the mid-1930s and hinges on a child's disastrous misinterpretation of the sexual desires of an older sister and her lover. Briony Tallis misunderstands the passion between her older sister Cecilia and her new lover Robbie Turner, an old friend, for something much more sinister. Filtering events through her over-active, fiction-fuelled imagination, Briony accuses Robbie of a sexual attack that results in his imprisonment and Cecilia's ostracisation of her family. The novel's middle section is an intense rendering of the retreat of British soldiers to Dunkirk in May 1940, an event in which McEwan's father took part, which broadens out the book's concern with questions of guilt, responsibility and reparation. An intricate story, the entire narrative itself proves to be the central character's attempt at finding atonement and regaining some semblance of harmony before her death: Briony's/McEwan's title word comes from the Middle English 'at onement' and signals her desire to regain peace by atoning for her false accusation of Robbie. The book received some of McEwan's best reviews, partly because it suggested he was engaging in a complex and allusive way with the canon of English literature and, particularly, with a much-discussed strand: the country-house novel that often examines the state of the country in microcosm and includes diverse works across the centuries such as Jane Austen's *Northanger Abbey* (1818), Henry James's *The Spoils of Poynton* (1896) and Kazuo Ishiguro's *The Remains of the Day* (1989). However, *Atonement*'s virtues are those of the very best literature with every sentence well turned and with a complex use of intricate imagery. McEwan's next book, *Saturday* (2005), was written in the same clear, direct prose as *Atonement*. Set on 15 February 2003, McEwan's ninth novel is a day-in-the-life narrative that tracks the movements of one character, a neurosurgeon, from the early hours of Saturday morning to the dawn of Sunday. It is an introspective, contemplative book that is clearly a narrative focused on one Western individual's domestic happiness but deep uncertainty about the world's future given the 'war on terror' that has marked the beginning of the twenty-first century. However, from another perspective, *Saturday* is principally about consciousness and mental states, including the degenerative effects of Alzheimer's and Huntington's disease. The political issue that hangs over the book is the Iraq war. Surgeon Henry Perowne is a liberal who wavers between uncertainties over the war when he discusses the impending attacks with his no-nonsense American squash partner and pro-invasion convictions when he gets into an argument with his daughter Daisy who has participated in the march against the war. Yet Perowne's belief in the invading task force is akin to a negative vote because he is not at all sure what the invasion of Iraq will bring about other than the deposition of Saddam Hussein, of whose brutal regime he has heard stories at first hand from an Iraqi professor of Ancient History. By

14 For a discussion on how the word 'sleaze' entered British politics in the 1990s, see the BBC web site at <http://news.bbc.co.uk/1/uk_politics/600178.stm>. (Accessed 26 April 2006.)

the close of the book, Perowne is far less sure that the war is for the best. The attack that a motorist, with whom he has had a car accident that morning, has mounted against his family has left him fearful and enervated, unsure of the right thing to believe. His sense of separation from the violence of the world has been shattered and Perowne ends the book a still-contented but now anxious man.

Alongside his novels and short stories, McEwan has produced a variety of other work. The first of his several film and television scripts was written in 1974 but aired in 1976. A half-hour confrontational dinner-party drama directed by Mike Newell, the play, entitled *Jack Flea's Birthday Party*, was considered a part of the stories assembled for *First Love, Last Rites* by McEwan. In 1979, an adaptation of one of his best short stories in the debut collection, 'Solid Geometry', was halted by the BBC following concerns over its sexual subject matter, but the story was eventually made by an independent film company into a short television drama directed by Denis Lawson in 2002. In 1980 McEwan had his second original television script produced: *The Imitation Game*. Directed by Richard Eyre as a BBC *Play for Today*, and set in the government code-breaking head-quarters at Bletchley Park, this is a story of sexual politics within English patriarchy during the Second World War (the title comes from the test for whether a machine can think set by mathematician and Enigma-code breaker Alan Turing). McEwan's subsequent scripts have been for film: *The Ploughman's Lunch* (1983), an anti-Thatcherite story set at the time of the Falklands, again directed by Eyre; *Soursweet* (1988), a faithful adaptation of Timothy Mo's 1982 novel about a Chinese family in 1960s Britain; and, ten years later, *The Good Son*, a dark thriller about a seemingly angelic boy whose cruel, destructive impulses are only recognised by his bereaved cousin. In 1983, McEwan's Audenesque oratorio about the threat of nuclear war, *Or Shall We Die?*, was performed at London's Royal Festival Hall with a score by Michael Berkeley. McEwan has also published a novel for children, *The Daydreamer* (1995). He was created a fellow of the Royal Society of Literature in 1982, given an honorary D.Litt. by his Alma Mater, the University of Sussex, in 1989, and awarded a CBE in 2000.

Literary contexts

> 'But the more Keats saw of Wordsworth himself, the more critically, as his letters show, he came gradually to look upon him. . . . The fullest expression of this critical attitude occurs in a letter written to Reynolds at the beginning of February. Keats is for the moment out of conceit with the poets of his own time; particularly with Wordsworth, whom he had always devoutly reverenced from a distance . . .'[15]

Enduring Love is a novel with one narrator but it is also a story with three central protagonists who all have a different understanding of human reality. Joe Rose is

---

15 Sidney Colvin, *John Keats*, Chapter 8, 1917. Available at <http://englishhistory.net/keats/colvinkeats.html>. (Accessed 13 October 2005.)

a rationalist who thinks science reveals facts about existence and the universe. Though she might not disagree with this standpoint, his partner Clarissa Mellon feels that art, beauty and happiness, not facts, are at the centre of people's relationships and that these are the important things that underpin life and love. Jed Parry believes that God underpins reality. The three of them thus begin from different premises: cognition, emotion and faith. It is worth considering that these three perspectives also relate to significant periods of Western cultural history. The view that God was at the centre of life was incontestable in Europe up to the Renaissance, after which time, through the influence of art and classical civilisation, human interests became more important; since the eighteenth-century Enlightenment, rationalism and science have dominated our understanding of the world, though the Romantic period at the turn of the nineteenth century reasserted the importance of nature, emotion and imagination.

These three perspectives all have their correlatives in the novel. The book's use of evolutionary science will be discussed in the next section and Clarissa's interest in the Romantic poets of the late eighteenth and early nineteenth centuries will be considered below (these include Wordsworth and Keats, as well as poets such as Byron and Shelley, William Blake, Samuel Taylor Coleridge and Anna Laetitia Barbauld). McEwan's incorporation of Jed's religious viewpoint is most clearly present in the book's religious allusions, especially in its opening scenes when parallels with Eden and the Fall, from the first book of the Bible, are suggested. It is also there, however, in small parallels between the suffering and sacrifice of Jesus and that of Joe and John Logan. Each aspect also has its literary connections within the novel: in the nineteenth-century narrative turn in science discussed by Joe (Ch. 5, pp. 48–9),[16] in the references to Clarissa's search for Keats's missing letter (Ch. 24, p. 221) and in the allusions to John Milton's seventeenth-century epic poem of the Fall, *Paradise Lost* (while the first chapter concludes with, 'I've never seen such a terrible thing as that falling man' [Ch. 1, p. 16], a direct quotation from *Paradise Lost* follows shortly: 'Hurl'd headlong flaming from th' Ethereal Sky' [Ch. 3, p. 29]). Kiernan Ryan's essay later in this volume provides a fascinating discussion for considering McEwan's use of the 'fall' motif (see Critical readings, **pp. 45–54**), but for now I will concentrate in this section on other literary contexts and the theme of Romantic love.

When Joe first brings de Clérambault's syndrome to mind, he recognises that

> for there to be a pathology there had to be a lurking concept of health. De Clérambault's syndrome was a dark, distorting mirror that reflected and parodied a brighter world of lovers whose reckless abandon to their cause was sane. . . . Sickness and health. In other words, what could I learn about Parry that would restore me to Clarissa?
>
> (Ch. 15, p. 128)

Joe makes the connection between Jed's love and other kinds, but he is not able to admit a resemblance beyond that between the diseased and the healthy – between

---

16   See Gillian Beer's book *Darwin's Plots: Evolutionary Narrative in Darwin, George Eliot and Nineteenth-Century Fiction*, London: Routledge, 1983.

the recklessly sane and the recklessly insane. Yet, he does see Jed's love for him as a distorted reflection of his own love for Clarissa. Joe's description of Parry's behaviour is indeed sometimes deeply reminiscent of what might be regarded as a 'normal' state of being in love: 'teasing out meanings, imbuing nonexistent exchanges with their drama of hope or disappointment, always scrutinizing the physical world, its random placements and chaotic noise and colours, for the correlatives of his own emotional state' (Ch. 17, p. 143). There is here a reminder that romantic love is itself a contested phenomenon. For evolutionary scientists it is practically a universal feeling, evident in almost all societies.[17] For social scientists, love has not been seen as a constant fact of human life but as a Western cultural concept that should be historicised. For example, Morton Hunt writes in *The Natural History of Love* that it is 'a pattern of love that is essentially Western, strongly Anglo-Saxon, and relatively new on earth. Western love, in a manner scarcely to be found in earlier history, attempts to combine sexual outlet, affectionate friendship and the procreative familial functions, all in a single relationship.'[18]

What is not open to question is that the modern understanding of love in the West has been informed by Romanticism, and by poets such as Keats, and is today so important that it has become a key measure of individual happiness and a pervasive ingredient of popular culture, in which the metaphorical register has shifted from 'my love is like a red, red rose', one origin of Joe's name, to kinds of (sexual) dependency: 'Love is the Drug' and 'Addicted to Love.' At one point, Joe muses on drink, drugs and mind-altering substances, which he does not explicitly link to love, but which appear to have similarities and which can have beneficent effects but can also lead to addiction and worse: 'these are the consequences of simple abuse which flow, as surely as claret from a bottle, out of human weakness, defect of character' (Ch. 20, p. 187). Another aspect of this passage is the renewed suggestion that Joe is resistant to losing control, that he is intolerant of people who allow desire to overwhelm reason: 'You can hardly blame the substance,' he concludes (Ch. 20, p. 178).

Joe is hostile to the narratives of literature in which Clarissa believes, as we find when he laments the 'derisory' science collection at the London library: 'The assumption appeared to be that the world could be sufficiently understood through fictions, histories and biographies. Did the scientific illiterates who ran this place, and who dared call themselves educated people, really believe that literature was the greatest intellectual achievement of our civilization?' (Ch. 4, p. 42). It is not hard to imagine this mental comment directed at Clarissa, who devotes her life to studying literature and who, in the months before the balloon accident, has been taken away from Joe for much of her sabbatical by her devotion to another man: Keats.

One of the purposes of the novel's open-to-doubt account of what occurred at Keats's meeting with Wordsworth in December 1817 (Ch. 19, pp. 167–8) is to remind the reader that stories are often perpetuated because they are memorable and appealing rather than because they are true. When questioned by Wallace at

17 On this subject see the work of David Buss in *The Evolution of Desire*, London: Basis Books, 1995, and *The Dangerous Passion*, London: Bloomsbury, 2000.
18 Morton Hunt, *The Natural History of Love*, New York: Knopf, 1959, p. 342.

the police station over whether the Keats–Wordsworth anecdote is rooted in fact, Joe replies 'the only account we have is unreliable' (Ch. 20, p. 179).

Deciding on whether an account is reliable or unreliable is not necessarily straightforward and can frequently be a matter of perspective. It is a dilemma the reader faces through most of the book with regard to Joe's narrative because his is the only account available. Reliability can also be subjective and is often a matter of trust rather than of the 'facts' that Joe would prefer to rely upon. A story might also be factually incorrect but emotionally true: 'It isn't true, but we need it. A kind of myth,' says Jocelyn of the Keats and Wordsworth story; 'It isn't true but it tells the truth,' says Clarissa (Ch. 19, p. 169). The story of the two poets also parallels Joe's relation with Jed, since Wordsworth (at forty-seven, the same age as Joe) dismisses his admirer's poem because he is 'unable to endure any longer this young man's adoration' (Ch. 19, p. 168). Keats, we are told by the 'unreliable' witness Haydon, felt the rebuff deeply and never forgave Wordsworth (Ch. 19, p. 168), just as Jed's inability to forgive Joe's rejection of him is about to be demonstrated in this scene by the restaurant shooting.

McEwan cites two texts that would have provided information on the first meeting between Keats and Wordsworth. The first of these, Robert Gittings' biography of Keats, is referenced in the novel (Ch. 19, p. 169), but the second, Stephen Gill's *William Wordsworth: A Life*, is only mentioned in the acknowledgements.[19] In a phrase that could apply to Joe Rose, Gill says of the two poets' meeting: 'Perhaps more than on any other occasion in Wordsworth's life one longs for a reliable witness to what actually happened.'[20] Instead, there is only the word of the painter who introduced them, Benjamin Haydon. The words 'pretty piece of Paganism' are reported by Haydon and it is he who decides that this was an insult for which Keats never forgave Wordsworth. Yet Gill points out that 'pretty' was not for Wordsworth a derogatory term. And Gittings observes that Haydon's account was given thirty years later when his 'megalomaniac tendencies' were bordering on 'insanity'.[21] McEwan is not choosing the anecdote about Keats just for its example of a grievance felt by a younger man against an older, but because of its parallel case to the restaurant scene with regard to the difficulty surrounding the reliability and objectivity of witness accounts. (Gittings says that 'What followed [when Keats met Wordsworth], though often repeated in various forms, is still open to doubt'.)[22] Interestingly, what in many ways undermines Joe's account of the restaurant shooting is his 'daydream' about the poets' meeting triggered by the words '*By then Keats was dead*' (Ch. 19, p. 170).

In relation to Keats, the theme of enduring love surfaces again in the novel's last chapter. Clarissa has been in touch with a Japanese scholar who has read a reference to a letter Keats wrote but never posted. It was addressed to his fiancée Fanny Brawne and contained a 'cry of undying love not touched by despair' (Ch. 24, p. 221). In a strand of the narrative that runs parallel to Joe's attempt to divert Parry's love through rational analysis, Clarissa is determined to track down

---

19 Robert Gittings, *John Keats*, Harmondsworth: Penguin, 1971 and Stephen Gill, *William Wordsworth: A Life*, Oxford: Clarendon, 1989.
20 Gill, *William Wordsworth*, p. 326.
21 Gittings, *John Keats*, p. 251.
22 Gittings, *John Keats*, p. 251.

further proof of Keats's ardent love for Fanny: of something undying at the moment of Keats's death. Her quest is as driven as Joe's, and just as his is partly rooted in guilt, hers is partly rooted there too: in her desire to affirm that love endures after death, a belief that is arguably all the more important to her because she cannot conceive and so will not endure through her children. Joe says she wants her 'ghost child' to 'forgive her' despite the fact that she is guilty of nothing (Ch. 3, p. 32), just as Joe wants expiation for Logan's death despite the fact he has 'nothing to be ashamed of' according to Clarissa (Ch. 23, p. 217).

The relevance of Keats to the three protagonists of *Enduring Love* is suggested by the references in the restaurant scene to his poems *Endymion* and 'Ode on a Grecian Urn'. While one of the closing lines of the ode is quoted in the novel, 'Beauty is truth, truth beauty' (Ch. 19, p. 166), it is complemented by the equally famous line, 'A thing of beauty is a joy for ever', which are the opening words of Book I of *Endymion* (1818). When connected to the closing sentence of McEwan's novel – Jed's assertion that 'Faith is joy' – the lines help to draw the different values but linked terms of the novel's love triangle. Joe adheres to the notion of truth's importance above everything else, even though he is aware of the near impossibility of objectivity. Clarissa, the Keats scholar, places greater trust in Keats's view of love and beauty – joys that endure (on 13 October 1819 he wrote in one of his letters to Fanny that 'Love is my religion'[23]). For Jed, such joy is to be found in faith.

Keats's odes have themes that are relevant to *Enduring Love*:[24] the difference between the transient and the permanent, the inextricable ties between joy and pain, the contrasts and similarities between nature and art, knowledge and imagination. Keats's 'Ode on a Grecian Urn' contrasts life, with its trials leading only to death, to the permanence of beauty in art, represented by the figures on the urn. Textual connections between the ode 'Ode on a Grecian Urn' and *Enduring Love* are easy to trace, most clearly in Keats's phrase 'For ever wilt thou love', but there is also, for example, the second line's reference to the urn as a 'foster-child', bringing to mind Joe and Clarissa's adoption of a child. Similarly, *Endymion* has many phrases that strike the reader of McEwan's novel as bearing on the same theme: '. . . if this earthly love has power to make / Men's being mortal, immortal. . . .'[25] Keats' poem is an allegory of the search for love, based on the Greek myth of Endymion, which tells the story of the moon goddess, Cynthia, who falls in love with the shepherd boy Endymion, tending his flock on Mount Latmos. She is so besotted by his beauty that she descends from heaven to be with Endymion in his dreams – Endymion begged youth, sleep and immortality from the gods so he could dream forever. The poem is a fine example of Keats's ability to luxuriate in sensuous description, though it is often deemed also to have faults of excessive digression and tedious narrative exposition.

Keats is renowned not only for his poetry but also his letters, which were described by the eminent twentieth-century poet T. S. Eliot as the most important in all literature. Clarissa's belief that 'love that did not find its expression in a

---

23 *Letters of John Keats*, ed. Robert Gittings, Oxford: Oxford University Press, 1970, p. 334.
24 Two years after *Endymion*, Keats wrote the following odes in 1819: 'To Psyche', 'On Indolence', 'To a Nightingale', 'To Autumn', 'On a Grecian Urn' and 'On Melancholy'.
25 John Keats, *Endymion*, Book 1, ll. 843–4.

letter was not perfect' (Ch. 1, p. 7) has to be considered in this light, though it would be impossible to resolve the question of what 'perfect love' might be, other than God's. The relationship between Keats and Fanny Brawne, the 'girl next door' at Wentworth Place he fell in love with, is well known as one of the greatest examples of a love affair in letters (though none of Fanny's survives), but it was a relationship in which Keats greatly feared his love was unrequited. It is thus a comparison and contrast to the love affair Jed seeks to conduct with Joe through his 1,000 letters (while Keats suffered, and died, from tuberculosis before he could marry Fanny, Jed suffers from a very different kind of illness). Joe's intense scanning of these letters for clues about Jed is meant directly to parallel Clarissa's literary analysis of Keats. Her search for the last unsent letter from Keats to Fanny finds its correlative in the final letter of *Enduring Love*, which is an unsent letter (the last one as far as the novel is concerned) from Parry declaring his undying love for Joe. While Clarissa says that she detects a similarity between Jed's writing and Joe's in the letters, a thematic comparison would be made with the Keats correspondence. Jed's letters make declarations and accusations similar to phrases found in Keats's letters to Fanny Brawne, in one of which he even declares that 'You will call this madness' (May 1820).[26] Three examples from Keats can suffice: 'Ask yourself my love whether you are not very cruel to have so entrammelled me, so destroyed my freedom' (letter dated 1 July 1819);[27] 'I cannot exist without you – I am forgetful of everything but seeing you again – my Life seems to stop there – I see no further. You have absorb'd me' (13 October 1819);[28] and 'Do not live as if I was not existing. . . . You must be mine to die upon the rack if I want you' (May 1820).[29]

If we move now to a further literary context, *Enduring Love* can be also considered in the light of the major preoccupations of McEwan's other works outlined in the previous section. For example, *Atonement* (2001) emerges at the end of its narrative as an extended exercise in attempted reparation and expiation. It is presaged in the earlier novel's concern with forgiveness: Joe is seeking forgiveness for his part in John Logan's death, Clarissa wants her unborn children to forgive her (Ch. 3, p. 32), Jed asks Joe for 'forgiveness' (Ch. 22, p. 212), and the novel ends with James Reid and Jean Logan each seeking forgiveness (Ch. 24, p. 230). The book ends before the appendices with Joe and Clarissa needing to forgive each other but unable to see the other person's point of view. Another related theme of *Enduring Love* is that of innocence and guilt and this features strongly not just in *The Innocent*, but also in both *Saturday* and *Atonement*, while the presence of unconventional love triangles is again notable in *The Innocent*, but also in *Amsterdam*.

Also, it has been noted many times in reviews that children and childhood are an abiding concern of McEwan's fiction from the short stories onwards. His first novel *The Cement Garden* features children almost exclusively, while even those that centre on adults, such as *Black Dogs*, *Saturday* and *The Child in Time* are clearly concerned with the responsibilities of one generation towards another.

26 Gittings, *Letters of John Keats*, p. 377.
27 Gittings, *Letters of John Keats*, p. 263.
28 Gittings, *Letters of John Keats*, p. 334.
29 Gittings, *Letters of John Keats*, pp. 375–6.

There are also many novels that feature orphans or in which adults either mourn the removal or regret the absence of children from their lives.

Certainly one of the most remarked-upon aspects to several of McEwan's novels is a focus on couples at a major crossroads in their relationship, as in *The Comfort of Strangers* and *The Child in Time*. The latter novel's main storyline concentrates on Stephen and Julie, a husband and wife who, through the disappearance of their only child, become estranged, but appear to be reconciled with the birth of a new baby at the close of the narrative. The movement from estrangement to tentative reconciliation in scenes associated with children has a distinct parallel in *Enduring Love*.

Lastly, one of the major elements of *Enduring Love* that features in the next section, science, was a much-debated interest of *The Child in Time*. In that novel the protagonist Stephen has a vision across time, which is a phenomenon that can be explained from the perspectives of art, religion or science, like the three endings of *Enduring Love*. McEwan had been interested in science since childhood and in the years before the publication of *The Child in Time* he continued to read books on Newtonian physics, quantum mechanics and relativity theory. By the time of *Enduring Love*, McEwan's focus has of course shifted from theoretical physics (in *The Child in Time* there is a physics lecturer, Thelma, who challenges the importance of literature much as Joe does in *Enduring Love*) to evolutionary biology, but both novels underline McEwan's belief that we live in a 'golden age' of scientific discovery and popular explanation (in books like the British theoretical physicist and cosmologist Stephen Hawking's *A Brief History of Time* [1988], the American psycholinguist Steven Pinker's *The Language Instinct* [1994] and the British evolutionary biologist Richard Dawkins' *The Selfish Gene* [1976]). The importance of certain aspects of contemporary science to McEwan's novel means that the next section, on cultural contexts, will focus on aspects to *Enduring Love* that are often downplayed by critics but that are crucial to an understanding of the author's aims.

Cultural contexts

> This was the love he should have felt for every soul in the world: all the fear and the wish to save concentrated unjustly on the one child.
>
> (Graham Greene, *The Power and the Glory*, quoted as an epigraph by Robert Wright, *The Moral Animal*)[30]

Analyses of *Enduring Love* are most usually interested in its presentation of Keatsian Romantic love, in its treatment of stalking and 'madness' and in its depiction of a couple in crisis. If social science is discussed, it is most often in the context of Jed's psychopathology, yet McEwan's equal if not stronger interest is in evolutionary psychology, the study of how the Darwinian principle of natural

---

30 Robert Wright, *The Moral Animal: Evolutionary Psychology and Everyday Life*, London: Abacus, 1994.

selection continues to affect our mental processes and behaviour to serve the ends of survival and reproduction. (The English naturalist Charles Darwin [1809–92] is most famous for formulating the theory of evolution by natural selection in his books *On the Origin of Species* [1859] and *The Descent of Man* [1871].) Critics have shown little inclination to explore this aspect to the novel, preferring to dismiss it as another example of fiction unwisely overstepping its boundaries, like McEwan's concern with theoretical physics in *The Child in Time*. This is partly a matter of science and art remaining largely separate spheres, of 'two cultures' operating in education and society in parallel to each other but with little contact, understanding or cross-over.[31] A feud over this matter famously surfaced in C. P. Snow's much-debated Rede lecture of 1959 entitled 'The Two Cultures',[32] but was restarted around the time of McEwan's novel. Consequently, in his 1998 book *Consilience: The Unity of Knowledge*, E. O. Wilson claims that the gulf between the two cultures of the sciences and the humanities not only continues to exist today but remains substantially unexplored and unexplained.[33]

There are thus two areas of social science that are of particular interest when studying *Enduring Love*. The first can be discussed by drawing on Paul E. Mullen and Michelle Pathé's article, 'The Pathological Extensions of Love', from which McEwan quotes (Appendix I, p. 242). The authors maintain that unrequited love that doesn't wither either continues without demanding return, or: 'The other way forward from a lonely idiopathic erotic fixation is to resort to fantasy or delusion to replace the lack of response from the beloved.'[34] It is this second case that is encompassed by erotomania, which is described by Mullen and Pathé as an 'autistic mode of being'.[35] One example offered in the article is of a man who

> doggedly pursued his 'God chosen bride' over several years. His life became dominated by the quest, and all his other interests were subordinated. He created chaos for the object of his affections, put the lives of others in danger, and totally destroyed the fabric of his own life, culminating in long-term incarceration.[36]

This has echoes in Jed's case, of course, as does the contention that 'we do not

---

31 For an extended discussion see Raymond Tallis, *Newton's Sleep: Two Cultures and Two Kingdoms*, London: St Martin's Press, 1995.

32 C. P. Snow, *The Two Cultures and the Scientific Revolution*, Cambridge: Cambridge University Press, 1959, debated and responded to in F. R. Leavis, *Two Cultures: The Significance of C. P. Snow*, London: Chatto, 1962. Also see F. R. Leavis, 'Two Cultures? The Significance of Lord Snow' in *Nor Shall My Sword: Discourses on Pluralism, Compassion and Social Hope*, New York: Barnes & Noble, 1972.

33 E. O. Wilson, *Consilience: The Unity of Knowledge*, London: Vintage, 1998. In the book, Wilson argues that 'the love of complexity without reductionism makes art; the love of complexity with reductionism makes science', (p. 59). McEwan's review of *Consilience* was published as 'Move Over Darwin', *The Observer*, 20 September 1998, p. 13.

34 Paul E. Mullen and Michelle Pathé, 'The Pathological Extensions of Love', *British Journal of Psychiatry*, 165, 1994, pp. 614–23, p. 614.

35 Mullen and Pathé, 'The Pathological Extensions of Love', p. 614. The mention of autism in relation to Jed might provoke the question of the extent to which it also, for different reasons, applies to Joe, who retreats into himself and fixates on one subject. See the discussion by Matthews in Critical readings, **pp. 97–8**.

36 Mullen and Pathé, 'The Pathological Extensions of Love', p. 617.

love someone because they give us pleasure but because we experience joy';[37] 'joy', as written by Jed, being the final word of McEwan's novel. Reviewing sixteen cases in all, Mullen and Pathé conclude that the 'boundaries between the normal and the pathological [are] ill-defined.'[38] And this is the sentiment with which McEwan closes his own essay in Appendix I of *Enduring Love* by quoting the final lines of Mullen and Pathé's article (Appendix I, p. 242).

McEwan's novel, like the Genome Project, is also interested in the connections between humanity and animality, but it is especially intrigued by humans' simultaneous civilised distance from and animal closeness to their evolutionary past. This is not just at the level of Joe's scientific papers or the issues at stake in the balloon accident, because McEwan adds incidents throughout the book to underline this theme. For example, Joe contemplates the relationship when he is reduced to squatting in some trees to defecate, driven only by fear and the desire to survive and protect (Ch. 22, p. 207). It is also there in little touches such as Leo Logan's appearance in striped face paint: 'I'm not a tiger, I'm a wolf' (Ch. 24, p. 223). If one wants to investigate these issues beyond the covers of the novel, there are pointers at the end of *Enduring Love* where McEwan acknowledges that he is indebted to a number of authors and books on aspects of evolutionary science: E. O. Wilson, *On Human Nature* (1978), *The Diversity of Life* (1992) and *Biophilia* (1984); Steven Pinker, *The Language Instinct* (1994); Antonio Damasio, *Descartes' Error: Emotion, Reason and the Human Brain* (1994); Robert Wright, *The Moral Animal: Evolutionary Psychology and Everyday Life* (1995); Walter Bodmer and Robert [*sic*] Mckie, *The Book of Man: The Human Genome Project and the Quest to Discover our Genetic Heritage* (1995) (Acknowledgements, p. 247). In the rest of this section I shall therefore look briefly at the likely significance of each of these writers to McEwan.

Wilson is a particular touchstone for McEwan, who has said of him, 'I do not know of another working scientist whose prose is better than his. . . . He is a superb celebrator of science in all its manifestations, as well as being a scourge of bogus, post-modernist, relativist pseudo-science, and so-called New Age thinking.'[39] Wilson is responsible for the theory of 'gene-culture co-evolution', which argues both that culture has biological roots and that culture and genetics interweave to evolve humanity's diversity (e.g., the incest taboo is a cultural prohibition which supports cross-fertilisation: biological exogamy). Most important to Wilson's development of sociobiology (the theory that animal and therefore also human behaviour is amenable to analysis through an evolutionary lens in the systematic study of the biological basis of social interaction[40]), and in some ways most important to McEwan's novel is the insight of the evolutionary biologist William Hamilton into kin selection. Until Hamilton, no one had been able convincingly to offer an explanation of Darwin's observation that in an ant colony only the queens reproduce yet all work cooperatively and altruistically for the

37 Mullen and Pathé, 'The Pathological Extensions of Love', p. 621.
38 Mullen and Pathé, 'The Pathological Extensions of Love', p. 621.
39 Quoted by Ed Douglas, 'Darwin's Natural Heir: Guardian Profile', 17 February 2001. Available at <http://www.guardian.co.uk/Archive/Article/0,4273,4137503,00.html>. (Accessed 13 October 2005.)
40 E. O. Wilson published the foundational book on *Sociobiology* in 1975 (an abridged edition was published by Belknap Press in 1980). Wilson deals with human beings in a short final chapter only.

good of the colony. Hamilton's answer, still in Darwinian terms of natural selection, was that siblings would sacrifice themselves for the propagation of the genes
they share.[41] From this, Wilson was able to argue that the focus of evolution is on
the preservation of, not the individual but, the gene.

McEwan says of Wilson that he is:

> a scientific materialist who warmly embraces the diversity of human
> achievement – including religion and art, which he sees in evolutionary
> terms. One of his tasks has been to further the Enlightenment project of
> absorbing the social sciences into science proper; another has been to find
> a sound ethical basis for ecological thinking. He is fundamentally a ratio-
> nal optimist who shows us the beauty of the narrative of life on earth.
> He is living proof that materialism need not be a bleak world view.[42]

That narrative of life on earth is arguably what Joe begins at the end of the
novel in his story for Rachael and Leo (one of the goals of *Enduring Love* is to
convey the value of viewing human evolution and existence as part of and in
terms of the planet's natural world). The import of this can be found throughout
Wilson's work, as in the concluding chapter of *The Diversity of Life*: 'The more
closely we identify ourselves with the rest of life, the more quickly we will be able
to discover the sources of human sensibility and acquire the knowledge on which
an enduring ethic, a sense of preferred direction, can be built.'[43]

In *The Language Instinct* (1994), Steven Pinker proffers the theory that language is biologically woven into the human mind, thus challenging the view that it
is primarily a cultural development. He thus sees language as one of the many
Darwinian instincts that, in humanity, has adapted and evolved to solve problems
in its environment. In similar vein, Antonio Damasio, a professor of neurology,
puts forward the theory in *Descartes' Error* (1994) that emotion plays a crucial
role in the exercise of reason, challenging the implications of many of the French
seventeenth-century rationalist philosopher René Descartes's statements, such as
'[reason is] the only thing that constitutes us men and distinguishes us from the
brutes'.[44] Damasio concludes that, instead of reason and emotion occurring in
different parts of the brain, feelings are enmeshed in rationality's networks at the
level of its neural (relating to the nerve system) underpinnings, just as Freudian
psychoanalysis earlier argued that humans were creatures motivated by desires
and drives that underlie consciousness and undermine rationality. Damasio's
argument is in part derived from case studies. Referring to one of these, he says in
the Introduction:

> I had before my eyes the coolest, least emotional, intelligent human
> being one might imagine, and yet his practical reason was so impaired

41 Ed Douglas, 'Darwin's Natural Heir: Guardian Profile'.
42 Quoted by Ed Douglas, 'Darwin's Natural Heir: Guardian Profile.' Also, see McEwan's article
    'Evolution of a Life's Work', *The Financial Times*, 12 July 1997, p. 5.
43 E. O. Wilson, *The Diversity of Life*, Harmondsworth: Penguin, 1994, p. 332.
44 *Discourse on the Method of Rightly Conducting One's Reason and Seeking the Truth in the
    Sciences*, in *The Essential Descrates*, ed. Margaret D. Wilson, trans. Elizabeth S. Haldane and
    G. R. T. Ross, New York: Meridian, 1983, p. 107.

that it produced, in the wanderings of daily life, a succession of mistakes, a perpetual violation of what would be considered socially appropriate and personally advantageous.[45]

Jed Parry can be considered in some ways a case study in literature along similar lines, while Joe's attempt to separate reason from emotion is exposed by Damasio's theory because it illustrates how successful human interaction is not entirely logical or rational but rooted in mutual understanding and sensitivity to feelings. Though it may not have been published early enough for McEwan to draw on for *Enduring Love*, Mark Turner's *The Literary Mind* (1996) is a key text for appreciating aspects to the novel. In his study, Turner argues that story comes before grammar, and that language is a product of humans' 'literary' mind:

> The literary mind is not a separate kind of mind. It is our mind. The literary mind is the fundamental mind. Although cognitive science is associated with mechanical technologies like robots and computer instruments that seem unliterary, the central issues for cognitive science are in fact the issues of the literary mind.[46]

These issues are projection, parable and story, the last being the basic principle of mind for Turner. Damasio has described Turner's book as an 'elegant bridge between two worlds', effectively delineating a connection between the 'two cultures'.[47]

More recently again, Damasio has published a book on consciousness, *The Feeling of what Happens* (1999), in which, echoing Turner, he asserts the primary importance of imagination to the functioning of the mind, as it is this ability that allows humans to foresee possible futures, to synthesise parts of their existing knowledge to create new thoughts and to imagine themselves into the position of others. This last matter is something McEwan famously discussed in his articles for *The Guardian* newspaper soon after the 9/11 attacks on the Twin Towers of New York's World Trade Center in 2001.[48] For McEwan, the crucial empathic aspect of the imagination is that it enables individuals to alter their actions in the light of envisaging the world from different perspectives. While McEwan thought that most people watching the television broadcasts would have been so affected, precisely because they would have imagined themselves into the position of the victims of disaster, this was what the hijackers had refused to imagine, because otherwise their actions would be unthinkable. For McEwan, imagination is linked to compassion, but *Enduring Love* also reveals the danger of an overactive imagination that is all too mistakenly certain of how the other feels.[49]

---

45 Antonio R. Damasio, *Descartes' Error*, London: Picador, 1995, p. xi.
46 Preface to Mark Turner, Introduction to *The Literary Mind*, Oxford: Oxford University Press, 1996.
47 For an overview of *The Literary Mind*, see <http://markturner.org/lm.html>. (Accessed 10 October 2005.)
48 These are 'Beyond Belief', 12 September 2001, and 'Only Love and then Oblivion', 15 September 2001. Both are available at <http://www.ianmcewan.com/bib/articles>.
49 Ian McEwan, 'Only Love and then Oblivion: Love Was All They Had to Set Against their Murderers', Special Report: Terrorism in the US, *Guardian*, Saturday 15 September 2001. McEwan

Robert Wright's *The Moral Animal* (1995) is an overview of evolutionary psychology, with this basic premise: 'Altruism, compassion, empathy, love, conscience, the sense of justice – all of these things, the things that hold society together, the things that allow our species to think so highly of itself, can now confidently be said to have a firm genetic basis.'[50] One of the pertinent subjects it discusses is 'reciprocal altruism' (which Wilson labels in *Sociobiology* a kind of 'bartering' stretched out over time).[51] Wright explains this by analogy with the game-theory example of 'the prisoner's dilemma'. In this hypothetical case, if police with insufficient evidence to convict two prisoners of more than a minor crime offer them separately the opportunity to have the minor crime dropped if they betray the other, then the option seems attractive. In terms of self-protection, Prisoner A would be wise to inform on Prisoner B. But Prisoner B would also appear best served by betraying Prisoner A, and here the dilemma arises if the prisoners take each other's position into account. An understanding of the other's identical circumstances means that the prisoners, who could end up both convicted of a major crime, might realise that their best choice is not betrayal but 'sticking together'. Evolutionary psychologists believe that a principle of this kind is built into the make-up of successful species, whose members will trust and support each other in a spirit of mutual, beneficial cooperation, unless they have reason not to: 'The logic that would lead to cooperation in an iterated prisoner's dilemma is fairly precisely the logic that would lead to reciprocal altruism in nature.'[52] The argument is thus that humans' benevolent and cooperative impulses are rooted in their most basic inclinations, because the best overall strategy to secure help for oneself when in need is to help others when they are. Taken to its most valued human limit, this would be the evolutionary logic behind 'romantic' love after the initial sexual attraction has diminished, and the reason why it might endure. Wright also argues something similar about marriage:

> That divorce does grow less likely as more children are born is sometimes taken to mean that couples choose to endure the pain of matrimony 'for the sake of the children'. . . . But it's at least possible that evolution has inclined us to love a mate more deeply when marriage proves fruitful.[53]

This is interesting in terms of Joe and Clarissa's childless relationship, but the most intriguing test case for evolutionary psychology that McEwan introduces is their adoption of a child (an act that can make little sense in terms of traditional Darwinian readings or of selfish genes but might be an extreme example of reciprocal altruism).[54]

---

wrote two articles for the *Guardian*, on 12 and 15 September. On 8 July 2005, McEwan also wrote for the same paper a follow-up article on the London tube and bus bombings of the day before, *Guardian*, G2, pp. 3–4.

50 Wright, *The Moral Animal*, p. 12.
51 See Note 43.
52 Wright, *The Moral Animal*, p. 193.
53 Wright, *The Moral Animal*, p. 130.
54 It is worth noting that many thinkers oppose the notion of selfish genes, for numerous and wide-ranging reasons. The French philosopher Gilles Deleuze, for example, considers the drive of life to be the pursuit of difference and variation, not selfishness.

Finally, Walter Bodmer and Robin Mckie's *The Book of Man* (1994) is an overview and discussion of the Human Genome Project which has informed McEwan's presentation of the conversation in the restaurant in *Enduring Love* (Ch. 19, pp. 163–4), the significance of which is partly to bring to the fore of the novel the importance of genetics to human action and emotion.[55]

A last interest of the novel to mention here is in fate and coincidence (other terms can be used – each one implying a particular understanding of reality). The balloon accident that brings Joe and Jed together makes their meeting precisely that – accidental. Yet, to Jed it is fate. The shooting of Colin Tapp at the restaurant, who is also seated in a threesome and has been attacked before, is to the police entirely straightforward, but to Joe it is simply a coincidence – it was meant to be me, he argues (Ch. 20, p. 175), in the same terms that his guilty conscience may have accused him over John Logan's death. The fact that Jean Logan believes her husband was having an illicit affair is also a kind of coincidence inasmuch as there were two people in his car at the time of the balloon accident who were having a clandestine relationship. Clarissa also says that Jed's 'writing's rather like yours' (Ch. 12, p. 100) to Joe. This is a matter of chance and perception, but the implication is profound for their relationship, because the statement intimates something more: that Clarissa considers it possible that Joe has written the letters himself. In terms of the theme of obsession, this is allied to Clarissa's search for Keats' lost letters, and could suggest that she is so devoted to her quest that she sees epistolary connections where there are none. As Joe has said of Keats's letters: 'I'd had the idea that Clarissa's interest in these hypothetical letters had something to do with our own situation' (Ch. 1, p. 7). A final 'coincidence' occurs at the Logans'. Leo and Rachael are entwining themselves in the curtains and playing a game of a king and queen signalling to another (Ch. 14, p. 123). This reminds Joe of the man who treated a woman who believed George V was signalling to her through the curtains at Buckingham Palace: de Clérambault. From here it is a small step to take for Joe to decide he has gained an insight into Jed Parry's obsession, yet it takes him no further in terms of the book's major unasked question: why does Parry fall for *Joe*?[56]

And so, as I mentioned at the start of this chapter, we can say that *Enduring Love* has two central interests, one of which is to do with romantic love and deep emotional attachment and the other of which is concerned with the reasons for human endurance. This latter draws on game theory to suggest that, while people are genetically inclined to be selfish, the species has survived so successfully because of the inclination to trust and cooperate with each other – with not just friends and family, but also with complete strangers.

---

55 According to the National Human Genome Research Institute web site, the Human Genome Project is 'an international research effort to sequence and map all of the genes – together known as the genome – of members of our species, *Homo sapiens*. Completed in April 2003, the HGP gave us the ability, for the first time, to read nature's complete genetic blueprint for building a human being.' See <http://www.genome.gov/HGP>. (Accessed 30 April 2006.)

56 It occurs to Joe to think of this question with regard to Clarissa, but the mystery of Jed's love for Joe remains just that.

2

Critical history

Enduring Love was first published in 1997 and critical commentary on the novel to date is limited. In this chapter, I will nonetheless summarise key points from the reviews, essays and books that have offered up fresh readings or provided insights into the workings of McEwan's sixth novel, beginning with comments by the author himself and some of the most influential early press reviews before moving on to consider also later and longer criticism. *Enduring Love* was generally well received from the start and its reputation has not declined. Praise for the first chapter was particularly forthcoming from all quarters on publication, and the opening pages remain a well-known example of taut, compelling imaginative prose that hook the reader from the start. However, the narration, structure and characterisation of the novel have all drawn criticisms, and these will be touched on in this chapter.

One of the voices to have commented on the book is of course that of the author himself, and in 1998 McEwan said that he thought the three novels he had written over the previous ten years all belonged together: '[B]eginning with *The Child in Time* [1987] and really ending with *Enduring Love*: novels of a sort of crisis and transformation, rites of passage of great intensity for characters.'[1] This was indeed how *Enduring Love* was received by many reviewers – as principally another macabre McEwan story of obsession and suspense, opening with one of the most compelling beginnings in recent British fiction: a height from which it could only descend in the rest of the narrative. On publication, Merritt Moseley thought *Enduring Love* one of the best novels of 1997; Anita Brookner called it a 'brilliant novel' and 'marvellous fiction'; while Amanda Craig bemoaned its reliance on popular science – 'half-baked ideas' – and Jason Cowley thought it overdetermined and overly schematic.[2] However, fellow British novelist A. S. Byatt placed the careful structure Cowley decried in the context of the novel's thematic concerns: '[I]t juxtaposes a mad version of the plottedness of human

1 *Bold Type* (1998) Interview with Ian McEwan. Available at <http://www.randomhouse.com/boldtype/1298/mcewan/interview.html>. (Accessed 13 October 2005.)
2 See Merritt Moseley, 'Recent British Novels', *Sewanee Review*, 106 (1998): pp. 678–82; Anita Brookner, 'Desire and Pursuit', *The Spectator* (30 August 1997), pp. 28–9; Amanda Craig, 'Out of the Balloon', *New Statesman* (5 September 1997), p. 43; Jason Cowley, 'Portrait: Ian McEwan', *Prospect* (December 1998), pp. 42–5.

relations, the divine design, the instant recognition of the beloved and destiny, with a human love which is vulnerable, can be destroyed by madness and certainty.'[3]

As Byatt indicates, the book in part explores the ways in which rationalism and irrationalism can strengthen or weaken relationships. At one point early in the novel Clarissa says to Joe, 'I love you more now I've see you go completely mad. . . . The rationalist cracks at last!' (Ch. 3, p. 35). Joe replies humorously that this is 'just the beginning', but he is only right in a sense he probably doesn't mean because his mental cracking up is far from planned or intentioned. On the one hand, throughout the rest of the book Joe retreats ever further into his rationalism to combat Jed, but on the other hand his preoccupation with understanding Parry itself becomes an obsession (which the Collins dictionary defines in psychiatric terms as 'a persistent idea or impulse that continually forces its way into consciousness, often associated with anxiety and mental illness').[4] Joe finds it monstrous that Clarissa might suggest that he is obsessed with Parry (Ch. 9, p. 86), yet '[Jed was] In my mind to such an extent that I had forgotten that he was also out there, a physical entity' (Ch. 6, p. 59). Joe later refers to de Clérambault as a name 'recalling me to *my own obsessions*' (Ch. 14, p. 124, my emphasis).

In the first essay to analyse *Enduring Love* as part of a book-length study of McEwan's fiction, David Malcolm discusses how reason can only work with its own perspective on events, testing its conclusions against available evidence.[5] If reason is based on incorrect information, it can lead to terrible consequences in a world that requires action as well as contemplation. The fact that choice cannot always be based on certainty is the problem faced by the men holding down the balloon in Chapter 1. If they all hang on, they may keep the balloon from floating away, but if one of them lets go, all those who retain their grip on the ropes will be dragged skywards. To be sure of the right course of action requires knowledge of the beliefs and behaviour of others. Malcolm lists many examples of ill-founded belief and of uncertainty: Jed's erroneous conviction that Joe loves him; Mrs Logan's misguided certainty that her husband is an adulterer; Clarissa's doubt whether Joe is being stalked by Jed; the reader's uncertainty of Joe's general reliability as a narrator. This last is perhaps most important as readers have to ask whether Joe is misleading them even though there is no other sustained source of information. Malcolm, like Adam Mars-Jones below,[6] thinks the peak of this narrative aspect is the police-station enquiry after the restaurant shooting (Ch. 20, pp. 174–82) when Detective Constable Wallace patiently lists the subjects on which the witnesses disagree. Joe greets this with a 'familiar disappointment' (Ch. 20, p. 180) as he recognises that 'disinterested truth' may be both important and impossible to establish (Ch. 20, p. 181).

Malcolm thinks the reader is confronted with four epistemological possibilities. First, that Joe is simply right in his general belief that scientific knowledge will best allow him to negotiate 'the maze of human life'. Second, Joe's narration is 'an extensive piece of self-justification to conceal or fictionalise the way he has made a

3   A. S. Byatt, *On Histories and Stories*, London: Vintage, 2001, p. 83.
4   *Collins Online English Dictionary and Thesaurus* (CD-ROM), London: HarperCollins, 1992.
5   Malcolm, *Understanding Ian McEwan*, pp. 166–7.
6   Adam Mars-Jones, 'I Think I'm Right, Therefore I Am', *The Observer* (7 September 1997), p. 16.

mess of his relationships with Jed and Clarissa'. Third, 'all forms of knowledge are equal – Jed's metaphysical ecstasy, Clarissa's ill-defined feelings, Joe's traditional scientific knowledge' (this is taken up by Martin Randall's essay in Critical readings, **pp. 58–9**). Or fourth, knowledge is 'an uncertain thing, difficult to achieve, subject to revision, but is attainable', and the best way to it is through Joe's logical, fact-focused approach. Malcolm concludes that the novel supports this last position: that rationality is our best guide.[7]

There is an irony here, in that McEwan's apparent espousal of Joe's position seems to challenge the ability the novel claims to have, as an art form rooted in the imagination, to make best sense of the world. Joe himself deliberates this issue: '[In the nineteenth century the] dominant artistic form was the novel, great sprawling narratives which not only charted private fates, but made whole societies in mirror image and addressed the public issues of the day. Most educated people read contemporary novels. Storytelling was deep in the nineteenth-century soul' (Ch. 5, p. 48). Joe describes how the professionalism of science and the complexities of modernism in art diminished the emphasis on long narratives; but the art and persuasiveness of storytelling remained important, he argues, and in some cases decisive in determining whether or not theories gained acceptance. The relativity theory of physicist Albert Einstein (1879–1955) was 'too beautiful to resist' (Ch. 5, p. 49), while the British theoretical physicist Paul Dirac's theory of quantum electrodynamics was 'unattractive, inelegant [. . .]. Acceptance was withheld on grounds of ugliness' (Ch. 5, p. 50). Joe concludes that in the twentieth century, 'It was as though an army of white-coated Balzacs had stormed the university departments and labs' (Ch. 5, p. 50).[8] Which is to say that even science is mediated by language and narrative, and reason does not exist independently from the world but sits alongside empiricism, emotion and aesthetics.

This connects very directly with Clarissa's research interest in the poet John Keats discussed in Text and contexts, **p. 19**), and reminds the reader of Keats's famous dictum 'Beauty is truth, truth beauty' (Ch. 19, p. 166) from 'Ode on a Grecian Urn' (1820). So, while rationalism and knowledge are valorised in *Enduring Love*, as critics have noted,[9] McEwan is deeply interested in the stories people tell in order to make sense of the world, and also in the nature of 'truth', which may have a poetical as well as a logical quality. He is also interested in exploring how the symmetry and beauty of nature affect our relationship to science, as when Rosalind Franklin is reported as saying of the DNA molecule model that it was simply 'too beautiful not to be true' (Ch. 19, p. 165).[10] Several critics, such as Roger Clark and Andy Gordon, have noted the connections *Enduring Love* makes with Keats's love letters that I touched on in the last section (see Text and contexts, **p. 20**),[11] but a further aspect to the novel's interest in the Romantic

7 Malcolm, *Understanding Ian McEwan*, pp. 178–9.
8 Joe's thoughts here echo Jean-François Lyotard's argument in *The Postmodern Condition* (Manchester: Manchester University Press, 1984) that science legitimates itself in advanced capitalist societies through an appeal to narrative. Honoré de Balzac (1799–1850) was a prominent nineteenth-century French novelist.
9 See Malcolm, *Understanding Ian McEwan*, pp. 175–6.
10 Rosalind Franklin played a great part in the elucidation of the structure of DNA for which Francis Crick and James Watson won the Nobel Prize in 1962.
11 Roger Clark and Andy Gordon, *Ian McEwan's* Enduring Love, London: Continuum, 2003, p. 72.

poet is worth mentioning here, as the phrase from Keats's letters for which he is most famous is 'negative capability': 'that is when man is capable of being in uncertainties, mysteries, doubts, without any irritable reaching after fact and reason.'[12] Keats was here discussing literature and, particularly, what he saw as Shakespeare's ability to grant characters a remarkable autonomy, but the concept appears to contrast neatly with Joe's frequent inability to accept love's and life's emotional richness without struggling for certainties. Joe's pursuit of assurance and reassurance becomes an obsession that contributes to the deterioration of his relationship with Clarissa, the Keats scholar.

The stories that people tell in order to make sense of their lives are frequently conflicting, but even the smallest details can be remembered differently by different individuals. Detective Constable Wallace gives the clearest example of this at the police station in his list of half-a-dozen discrepancies between accounts of events in the restaurant (Ch. 20, p. 179), but, to choose another example, James Reid, the professor of logic, is called upon to resolve one misunderstanding. He explains that Joseph Lacey 'said that if it turned out there were disagreements, or conflicting stories, then he would get in touch with me' (Ch. 24, p. 229). In terms of the book's agenda, this is something of an in-joke as it provides a further example of 'logic' being the right solution to a problem of competing versions of events.

As discussed in Text and contexts, p. 23), another concern of the novel is with evolutionary theory, which is positioned as the antithesis to Jed's religious belief even though, as Clark and Gordon note, McEwan himself has observed that its explanations are sometimes questionable.[13] Joe asserts that 'Biologists and evolutionary psychologists were reshaping the social sciences . . . nature was up for re-examination' (Ch. 8, p. 69). While this provides extra work for Joe as editors clamour for articles on neo-Darwinism, evolutionary psychology and genetics, Clarissa sees it as 'rationalism gone berserk . . . the new fundamentalism' (Ch. 8, p. 70). Though Clarissa feels that some larger truths are being lost in this 'reductive' rationalism (as Jed would also argue), Joe responds by labelling Keats 'an obscurantist' who thought, like Clarissa now does, that 'science was robbing the world of wonder' (Ch. 8, p. 71). Both of them say that they are talking about love and that the other does not understand. Afterwards, Joe concludes that 'What we were really talking about this time was the absence of babies from our lives' (Ch. 8, p. 71), which flags the conversation as another occasion on which Joe does not communicate his true feelings, while he and Clarissa again do not understand each other because they speak different languages (Malcolm draws attention to Joe's unusual use of scientific language in some detail).[14] This is made worse by the fact that they are involved on parallel projects: Clarissa researching Keats's desperate love letters and Joe preoccupied with someone who 'became stricken with a love whose morbidity I was now impatient to research' (Ch. 15, p. 127). Immersed in their own obsessions and their different projects, Joe and Clarissa's perceptions of events are so diametrically opposed that we might go as far as to say that are involved in different stories.

12 Keats coined the conceptual phrase 'negative capability' in a letter written to his brothers George and Thomas on 21 December 1817 (The Letters of John Keats, ed. Gittings p. 43).
13 Clark and Gordon, Ian McEwan's Enduring Love, p. 44.
14 Malcolm, Understanding Ian McEwan, pp. 168–70.

The clearest case of deluded storytelling in the novel is of course Jed's narrative of his relationship with Joe, which Joe identifies as an example of de Clérambault's syndrome, named after the physician who wrote a study of what he himself called 'les psychoses passionelles'.[15] Cressida Connolly in her review of the novel observes that McEwan's depiction of Jed's illness is so disturbing and compelling because it in many ways closely resembles ordinary romantic attachment (the difference being that with de Clérambault's syndrome the lover is irrationally convinced that their feelings are reciprocated and indeed are a response to the feelings of others).[16] Jed's letters and pleas are those made by unrequited lovers every day, and it is in his proximity to 'ordinary behaviour' that Jed becomes most unsettling. This is precisely the conclusion that the novel reaches at the end of its first appendix when the text quotes Paul Mullen and Michelle Pathé as saying that 'the pathological extensions of love not only touch upon but overlap with normal experience', such that the most valued human experience, love, may resemble psychopathology (Appendix 1, p. 242).

In the chapter devoted to *Enduring Love* in her study of McEwan, Christina Byrnes notes that clinical psychologists 'attempt to draw the boundaries between the infatuation of falling in love, the state of being in love, and the pathological erotic fixation, in spite of the lack of response from the beloved. These last border on erotomania proper which they accept as a genuine psychosis.' Byrnes observes that McEwan's fake article in the first appendix

> concludes with a list of twenty references from British, French, American, Canadian and Scandinavian journals of psychiatry, criminology, social science and medicine, dealing with the syndrome. All these references are authentic except for the relevant paper by T. Gillett, S. R. Eminson and F. Hassanyeh, 'Primary and Secondary Erotomania: Clinical Character-istics and Follow Up', *Acta Psychiatrica Scandinavia*, vol. 82, (1990), 65–69. This is changed by McEwan to R. Wenn and A. Camia (1990) 'Homosexual Erotomania', *Acta Psychiatrica Scandinavia*, vol. 85, (1990), 78–82. The names Wenn and Camia are an anagram of Ian McEwan, and the article was written by McEwan as an attempt to write a plausible scientific article, perhaps of the kind that Joe would wish to write. McEwan has said
>
> > I devised what they call in Hollywood a back story for Wenn and Camia: that they are a couple of homosexuals, who are only inter-ested in homoerotic behaviour. If you look at their other published paper, it is called 'Homosexual Erotomania', and was published in *Acta Psychiatrica Scandinavia*, which is a real journal and the most obscure that I could find. I submitted the fictional paper for publi-cation but now I feel terribly guilty because the journal I sent it to has written back saying that it is considering it for publication.[17]

---

15 De Clérambault, 'Les Psychoses passionelles'. See p. 7, n. 10.

16 Cressida Connolly, 'Over-Fished Waters'. Available at <http://www.users.dircon.co.uk/~litrev/199709/connolly.html>. (Accessed 13 December 2004.)

17 Christina Byrnes, *The Work of Ian McEwan: A Psychodynamic Approach*. Nottingham: Paupers' Press, 2002, pp. 265–7. The final quotation is from P. H. S., 'Shrink to Fit', *The Times* (2 September 1997), p. 22.

The novel implies Joe and Jed are in some ways mirrored in each other, as when Joe remarks: 'he played with me and held back, just as he said I did' (Ch. 17, p. 142). After this, Joe tells Parry to ' "Stop bothering me with your stupid letters." Come back and talk to me was what I really meant' (Ch. 17, p. 143). Another resemblance between Joe and Jed is that they both turn to people with guns to combat each other. The handgun that Joe buys is unwittingly intimated earlier when he is searching for an explicit threat in Jed's letters: 'Please put the weapon in my hands, Jed' (Ch. 17, p. 142). Joe buys it from 'ex-hippies who had made it rich in coke' (Ch. 21, p. 190), referring to another drug, like infatuation, that alters perception. The chapter is sometimes regarded as the weakest in the book, partly because the episode appears a little preposterous, but also because it seems largely unnecessary, a slenderly connected short story inserted into the novel.[18] It is also a digression from the main plot, perhaps intended as light relief but striking many readers as a jarring expedition away from the narrative trajectory of the novel.[19] One of the effects of the chapter is to reveal some of Joe's sensibilities. He refers to the threesome's 'stinking hall' (Ch. 21, p. 192), mocks their speech, has to 'conceal a smile' at their appearance (Ch. 21, p. 194) before breaking into laughter, sneers at Johnny's description of them as 'intellectuals', and clearly objects to their lifestyle, which in its concern with ecology but not hygiene he might characterise as 'New Age' (a phenomenon he strongly dislikes). Additionally, the reader is perhaps encouraged to think that Joe sees their 'dim beliefs' (Ch. 21, p. 200) in astrology and auras, or their ill-informed opinions, as akin to Jed's delusions. Certainly, the fight between the two men, Steve and Xan, in front of Daisy, can be likened to Joe and Jed's confrontation in front of Clarissa.

Yet, McEwan's interest in *Enduring Love* concerns something more human than debates over cause and effect, which is to say the impulse towards storytelling. Roger Clark and Andy Gordon point out that for McEwan people's 'desire for things to make sense is articulated through acts of storytelling' – which are revised, updated, discredited and so forth.[20] Clark and Gordon discuss the role Jean Logan plays in the book, which they see as a further example of narrative interpretation. The rational conclusion Jean Logan comes to about her husband's adultery is based on 'evidence' found by the police: either her husband was having an affair or 'this story doesn't make sense' (Ch. 14, p. 122). This conclusion proves to be the result of a misreading but is interesting because of the light it sheds on the main narrative. Jean's conclusion is logical but is based on circumstantial evidence; and though Jean Logan is the (humanities) academic, it is Joe's (scientific) research that establishes the facts of the incident. Clark and Gordon point out that because the man Joe tracks down is a professor of logic, McEwan may again be reminding the reader that some narratives have more credibility than others. The novel here, as elsewhere, is emphasising competing ways of making sense of reality and the fact that different versions may be equally plausible but

---

18 McEwan has said that this chapter was in fact the first part of the book to be written.

19 An overview of responses, including those that see McEwan's book in terms of fragmentariness and melodrama, can be found in Clark and Gordon, *Ian McEwan's* Enduring Love, pp. 64–84. See also the discussion in Malcolm, *Understanding Ian McEwan*, p. 161.

20 Clark and Gordon, *Ian McEwan's* Enduring Love, pp. 47–8.

utterly contradictory (see the earlier discussion of Keatsian 'negative capability', **p. 34**). Though we now live in an Einsteinian world of relativity, for an individual like Joe, one account of events is still more correct, or less incorrect, than others.

When Jean Logan explains to Joe her belief that her husband was having an affair she claims, 'I'm the mad one' (Ch. 13, p. 111). Her story parallels the main narrative in several ways, not least because, like Parry, she imagines a non-existent love relationship at the scene of the balloon accident. Yet, her belief is a logical conclusion drawn from the *known* facts – it is certainly more credible than Joe's anticipation of what he thinks she is going to say: 'I was about to be accused, and I had to interrupt her' (Ch. 14, p. 122). Jean correctly deduces that there was at least one witness to the accident that the police either have not realised was there or have not cared to consider because there is no reason to think it is relevant to the accident: 'It's not convenient to answer my questions because they don't fit the story' (Ch. 13, p. 111). Joe thinks of her 'story' that it was 'a theory, a narrative that only grief, the dementia of pain, could devise' (Ch. 14, p. 123). He tells her that it's just a hypothesis and she can't believe in it, yet seconds later he has jumped to his own hypothesis about Jed Parry, that he has de Clérambault's syndrome. And Joe has no doubt that he should believe in this hypothesis.

For fellow novelist Adam Mars-Jones, *Enduring Love* is undermined by Joe's development as an unreliable narrator. When the police question Joe after the restaurant shooting, he says his sorbet was 'apple' (Ch. 20, p. 181), yet ten pages earlier he has said it was 'lime' (Ch. 19, p. 171). Mars-Jones objects not to this as error but to its enactment of Joe's single-paragraph question about self-interest opposed to objectivity: 'But exactly what interests of mine were served by my own account of the restaurant lunch?' (Ch. 20, p. 181). Mars-Jones thinks this is late in the day to make Joe out to be an unreliable narrator, crudely indulging the novel's main theme that humans are innately unreliable: '[O]ur sense data came warped by a prism of desire and belief, which tilted our memories too' (Ch. 20, p. 180).[21] Mars-Jones concludes that though the book begins superbly, it merely fizzles out at the end into a hackneyed confrontation, followed by academic paraphernalia: a case history, cod references and unnecessary appendices.[22]

Another highly respected reviewer, Sven Birkerts, compares the novel's structure – beginning with a crisis and then chronicling the aftermath – with several other novels: Russell Banks's *The Sweet Hereafter* (1992), Rosellen Brown's *Before and After* (1992) and Philip Roth's *American Pastoral* (1997); but he might have made comparison with many of McEwan's other novels, especially *The Child in Time*. Birkerts concludes that, though the novel is a tour de force, McEwan's accomplishment is less memorable for its style than its presentation of Parry's syndrome, with its unremitting intensity, and his immunity to Joe's denunciations and entreaties.[23]

Like Mars-Jones, a further critic who argues that McEwan has allowed the melodramatic conventions of genre fiction to run away with the plot is James Wood. As I will discuss in Adaptations (**pp. 123–35**), *Enduring Love* follows too

21 Mars-Jones, 'I Think I'm Right, Therefore I Am', p. 16.
22 Mars-Jones, 'I Think I'm Right, Therefore I Am', p. 16.
23 Sven Birkerts, 'Grand Delusion', *New York Times* Review, 25 January 1998, p. 7.

closely the classic trajectory of a Hollywood thriller for Wood, deflecting attention from McEwan's deeper interest in how rationalism and irrationalism construct the world. Wood argues that the novel follows a conventional formula of
set-up, confrontation and resolution. Yet McEwan certainly seems to be aware of
the conventions in play, as when he has Joe remark on why he and Clarissa do not
sink into each other's arms when Joe shoots Parry: 'The narrative compression of
storytelling, especially in the movies, beguiles us with happy endings into forget-
ting that sustained stress is corrosive of feeling' (Ch. 22, p. 213). Nevertheless,
Wood thinks that the thriller plot overwhelms the subjects McEwan actually
wants to examine: how the irrational might undermine an individual's rationalism and how Darwinian self-interest undermines love.[24]

Along similar lines, Joe observes that 'selfishness is also written on our hearts'
(Ch. 1, p. 14), but recognises that cooperation is 'the basis of our earliest hunting
successes, the force behind our evolving capacity for language, the glue of our
social cohesion' (Ch. 1, p. 14); and while Wood is quite right to suggest that one
of the central concerns of the book is the competing ways in which people make
sense of reality, McEwan seems overall to endorse Joe's rationalist approach to
problem-solving in ways that exceed those of conventional thrillers (just as he did
in his earlier Cold War thriller *The Innocent* [1990]). Most importantly, the book
repeatedly explores the significance of cultural and moral differences despite
human beings' biological and evolutionary sameness. This is acutely apparent
when Joe discusses with the Logan children whether it can be *universally* immoral
to eat horsemeat, to burp, to say you're going to kill someone, or even to do it
(Ch. 14, pp. 119–20). Joe has earlier concluded that 'a good society is one that
makes sense of being good' (Ch. 1, p. 15), but whether goodness can be defined
according to utilitarian or scientific criteria is another matter.

The moral questions that Joe discusses with the Logan children ('Wouldn't
Rachael and Leo agree, there were times when it was right to lie?', Ch. 14, p. 121)
highlight the view that *Enduring Love* is concerned with relativism throughout
from the first moment when the balloon incident is briefly imagined through
the different spatial perspectives of those who rush to save Harry Gadd. The
restaurant incident is another case of divergent perceptions of a shared event, as is
the (mis)understanding of Logan's motivation at the ballooning accident, which
Jean Logan construes in a significantly different way from everyone else. Thus, a
central concern of the plot, the incompatible perspectives of Joe, Jed and Clarissa,
is embedded throughout the narrative.

Finally, in his article on McEwan's later fiction, Jago Morrison considers the
degree to which Jed is presented as the product of Joe's own obsessions. Morrison
particularly notes Joe's impulse towards a 'violent narrativization' of Parry as he
secures justification of his treatment of Jed through medical authority:

> It is in this sense that *Enduring Love* is 'about' de Clérambault's syn-
> drome. Through the syndrome, the novel identifies the power of medical-
> scientific discourse as a guarantor of temporal and epistemological
> security. In a social sense, the appended documents are significant

---

24 James Wood, 'Why It All Adds Up', *The Guardian* (4 September 1997), p. 9.

because they cast Parry into a ratified linear-narrative framework that carries the force of juridical and disciplinary power.[25]

Thus Parry becomes a 'case' for Joe, who has been rebuffed from academic research (he has a doctorate on quantum electrodynamics [Ch. 8, p. 75]) and is now seeking another project to investigate: 'There was research to follow through now and I knew exactly where to start. [. . .] It was as if I had at last been offered that research post with my old professor' (Ch. 14, p. 124). This is reminiscent of Joe's reaction to Jean Logan's situation, making it possible to argue that Joe's relation to life is one of narrativisation bordering on obsession. Morrison sees this as present throughout the novel, from the early stages when Joe alludes to his own ability to synthesise ideas and present them in ways people can readily understand because of his 'talent for clarity' (Ch. 8, p. 75). Morrison thinks that this professional penchant for the ordering and rationalisation of the ordered becomes radically extended as Joe himself becomes neurotically preoccupied with Parry's movements and communications. It may be part of his defence mechanism, but Joe becomes as dedicated to defeating Jed as Jed is to winning him.

Overall, the criticism of *Enduring Love* to date has by no means brought out the full range of its subtleties and nuances. The aspects of narration, structure and psychological complexity have continued to dominate discussions of the novel alongside varied responses to McEwan's portrayal of love. In the following section, six essays attempt to flesh out several of the issues that have been touched on in this chapter and, in particular, the many possible approaches to Joe's narration, as well as broaching new areas for comment and analysis.

---

25 Jago Morrison, 'Narration and Unease in McEwan's Later Fiction', *Critique*, 42(3): pp. 253–70, spring 2001, p. 259.

3

Critical readings

In this section, six different readings of *Enduring Love* are offered for further discussion. Each one looks at a different angle to McEwan's novel. The critics writing here are concerned with, among many other things, issues of narrative, masculinity and 'madness' in McEwan's play on endless love. There are no easy answers to questions about the novel because so much depends on how the reader understands Joe Rose and the reliability of his narration. Joe is thus placed in a long line of fictional storytellers who hire no 'professional listener' but use the novel as a 'talking cure' (Ch. 12, p. 99), in which the reader can be likened to an analyst trying to decipher the protagonist's narration and read between the lines of the story being told.[1]

Also, at the end of the last section, it was acknowledged that one of the main themes of *Enduring Love* centres on the competing ways in which people make sense of reality (see Critical history, p. 38). In the following readings of the novel, this will surface repeatedly in the importance accorded to this dimension of the book by the essayists as well as in the fact that they take different stances on questions of narration, plausibility and sanity.

---

1 The term 'talking cure' derives from the therapeutic treatment developed by Sigmund Freud involving a patient 'on the couch' talking to a therapist, providing the careful listener with insights into the speaker's unconscious through associations, memories, revelations, slips and other linguistic or mental idiosyncrasies.

Kiernan Ryan, 'After the Fall'

Kiernan Ryan is Professor of English at Royal Holloway, University of London and a Fellow of New Hall, University of Cambridge. He is currently completing the second, updated edition of *Ian McEwan* (1994), which was the first book-length study of the author. His most recent publications include *Shakespeare* (3rd edn, 2002), *King Lear: Contemporary Critical Essays* (1993), *New Historicism and Cultural Materialism: A Reader* (1996), *Shakespeare: The Last Plays* (1999), *Shakespeare: Texts and Contexts* (2000), and the Introduction to the new Penguin edition of *King Lear* (2005).

Enduring Love's opening pages allude to the Bible, with even its initial words echoing the opening statement of the Old Testament: 'In the beginning'[1] *Enduring Love* commences by suggesting a scene from the book of Genesis, with lovers eating under a tree and the reader given a god-like perspective on events (through the eyes of a bird circling above). Into this Eden comes Jed Parry, God's messenger who has descended into darkness.[2]

Jed comes to appear as the 'evil' snake-like intruder in the prelapsarian setting of Joe and Clarissa's country picnic, before the horror of Logan's death: 'I've never seen such a terrible thing as that falling man' the first chapter concludes (Ch. 1, p. 16).[3] The book's concern with the idea of the Fall from innocence and God's grace extends to Joe and Clarissa, who become fallen lovers, cast out of their Edenic existence into deeply troubled lives. This is the guilty world of which Joe has gained knowledge through the ballooning accident and its aftermath.

In the following wide-ranging essay, Kiernan Ryan examines Joe Rose's narrative in terms of the seeds sown and revelations contained in the opening pages.

---

1   These are also the opening words of John's Gospel.
2   Satan was God's right-hand angel before he rebelled and was cast out of heaven.
3   The quotation from Milton's *Paradise Lost* follows shortly: 'Hurl'd headlong flaming from th'Ethereal Sky' (Ch. 3, p. 29).

There is the significance of Logan's fall from the balloon at the start of the narrative, but there are also, later in the first chapter, hints of another fall that drives Joe's story. In Ryan's analysis, this opening signals McEwan's novel has connections with the narrative archetypes of the folk tale and the fable but also that it may emerge as a 'cover story' in which the surface of Joe Rose's words belies the reality beneath. In Joe's narrative, love may not have turned sour with Jed Parry's appearance but might have always been, as Ryan says, 'the monster from which the hero is in flight.' For Ryan therefore, the opening to *Enduring Love* contains 'ominous intimations' of its central lovers' imminent fall from their relationship's security, and so it might also reasonably be inferred that the circumstances of Logan's fall, like that of Adam and Eve's fall from innocence in Eden, provide for McEwan an objective correlative for the emotion the reader should feel over the fate of Joe and Clarissa's love.

Kiernan Ryan, 'After the fall'

> And if one is still able to hear – but how few these days have
> ears to hear it! – in this night of torment and absurdity the cry
> *love* ring out, the cry of rapt longing, of redemption in love, he
> must turn away with a shudder of invincible horror.
>   (Nietzsche, *The Genealogy of Morals*)[4]

Almost everything that transpires in *Enduring Love* takes place in the wake of the fatal fall that expels its hero from the Eden of innocence in which his story begins. After the ballooning accident with which the novel opens, Joe Rose finds himself racked by guilt for his part in the pointless death of John Logan, who clung on to his rope when his fellow rescuers let go of theirs and consequently plunged to a horrific death. Joe also finds himself the object of Jed Parry's erotic obsession and religious fantasies as a result of their fleeting encounter after the fall and their charged exchange over Logan's corpse. Traumatised by Logan's death and stalked by the deranged Parry, Joe loses his grip on his identity and his work, on his faith in scientific rationalism and, above all, on his relationship with Clarissa, which finally collapses under the strain of his frantic fixation on Jed. He winds up utterly isolated, not only by Clarissa's incredulity, but also by the disbelief of the police, who reject his claim that the shooting in the restaurant was Jed's botched attempt to have him killed. Fearing for his life, Joe procures a gun from petty crooks and, when Jed takes Clarissa hostage, threatening to slit his own throat unless Joe forgives him for seeking his death, Joe shoots and wounds Jed, putting an end to his persecution.

The rescue of Clarissa and the defeat of Parry afford Joe no redemption, however, for his failure to save Logan. Although events have vindicated Joe's view of Parry as a dangerous psychopath, he takes little comfort from the fact that all

---

4   Friedrich Nietzsche, *'The Birth of Tragedy' and 'The Genealogy of Morals'*, trans. Francis Golffing, New York: Doubleday, 1956, pp. 226–7.

along he was right and Clarissa and the police were wrong. The last chapter, in which, thanks to Joe, Jean Logan is disabused of her belief that her husband died deceiving her, leaves Joe and Clarissa still estranged and the prospect of their reconciliation remote. From the first of the novel's two appendices, which recasts the nub of the narrative as a psychiatric case study, we infer that Joe and Clarissa were subsequently reconciled and that Parry was committed indefinitely to a secure mental hospital. But the reduction of this resolution to an extraneous afterthought, couched in the clinical prose of an academic paper, deflates its potential impact, while the second appendix, which contains a letter written by Parry in his third year of confinement, eclipses it by giving the last word to an ecstatic Jed declaring his undying love for Joe.

It is tempting to settle for the reading of *Enduring Love* that rests on such a synopsis, not least because it is underpinned at so many points by the narrative. The novel offers us a compelling tale of true love between a man and a woman surviving the threat posed to it by the demented infatuation of another man. This romantic psychological thriller, complete with crazed stalker, hit men, handguns and hostage drama, doubles as a tenacious novel of ideas, an intellectual detective story, in which reason and science finally prevail over the senselessness and lunacy that have shaken their foundations. The denouement is rendered more persuasive by the disillusionment the lovers are forced to undergo and by the crippling doubts to which the narrator's convictions must be subjected before they are validated. Any lingering suspicion of emotional or philosophical complacency the reader might harbour is deflected from the ending by the appendices. The muted mention of the couple's reunion and successful adoption of a child displaces the sentimental scene a conventional conclusion would have staged. And Jed's rapturous *cri de cœur* closes the novel on a note of defiant irrationality and invincible delusion, which makes psychotic passion our final image of enduring love and suggests that the victory of dispassionate rationality is far from secure.

As paratexts – texts at once integral to, and detachable from, Joe's narrative – the appendices also contrive to blur the line between the fictional and the factual, to obscure the point at which the novel actually ends. Both are framed as supplementary documents, appended in corroboration of Joe's diagnosis of Jed, which is thereby invested with the institutionalised authority of the medical profession. In this capacity, they conspire to reinforce Joe's narrative by underwriting his version of what happened and his trust in objectivity. But the 'Acknowledgements' of Ian McEwan that follow the appendices realign them as components of the novel's fictive world, as complex strategies of closure with narrative tasks to complete. Furthermore, the surnames of the authors of Appendix I, 'Robert Wenn' and 'Antonio Camia', turn out to be an anagram of 'Ian McEwan', and Appendix II informs us that a photocopy of Jed's letter has been 'forwarded to Dr R. Wenn at his request'. So the credibility of both appendices is compromised by McEwan's sly admission of complicity with his narrator, whose first-person account of events he has buttressed with fabricated evidence.

This playful flaunting of the artifice of endings is the culmination of the novel's concern to reflect on its own fictionality. The paradoxical effect of this sceptical self-consciousness is to offset the predictable thrust of the novel's denouement and to immunise it against critique. The devious paratextual conclusion of *Endur-*

ing Love inoculates its finale with enough pre-emptive irony to question the male fantasy it serves without confounding it. Marital, heterosexual love and parenthood triumph over the psychopathic homosexual passion of a religious maniac, thanks to one man's determination to save his own sanity and the life of the woman he loves. The plausibility of such a reading makes it vital to complicate and qualify the import of the plot, to make it palatable by making it vulnerable to mistrust.

There one might well leave *Enduring Love*, displaying an acute awareness of its unreliability, which masks its allegiance to loaded assumptions about masculinity, desire and the basis of belief. But mistrust, once aroused, is contagious, and the pains the novel takes to protect its investment in those assumptions make it hard to settle for that account of it. The application of so much ingenuity to obfuscating its commitments excites the suspicion that deeper motives underlie the design of *Enduring Love*. What if its stock-thriller storyline is a stalking horse for desires that the novel is anxious to disavow? What if the whole artfully subverted narrative is a smokescreen for a vision too dark to be overtly disclosed?

There are strong grounds for regarding *Enduring Love* as a *tour de force* of misdirection, whose mission is to distract us from the revelations it secretes. If the author's sleight of hand is most obtrusive in the artifice of the ending, it is least apparent, and so all the more beguiling, at the sensational beginning of the book. Joe's frank admission at the outset that the sequence of events and their significance are at the mercy of his reconstruction is disarming. We are disposed to trust him precisely because he stresses the arbitrariness and subjectivity of his account and because we have no reason at this point not to believe him. By 'holding back, delaying the information' (Ch. 1, p. 2) through flashbacks and digressions, Joe creates the suspense that fixes our gaze on the impending catastrophe, from which the ensuing nightmare of guilt and obsession ostensibly springs. 'The beginning is simple to mark' (Ch. 1, p. 1), the first sentence of Joe's story assures us, and our attention is immediately steered towards the disaster that has yet to be divulged. But by Chapter 2 the beginning, 'the explosion of consequences', seems much less simple to mark, because, as Joe concedes, 'There are always antecedent causes. A beginning is an artifice, and what recommends one over another is how much sense it makes of what follows' (Ch. 2, p. 17).

Joe moves swiftly on to recount the aftermath of Logan's death, to tease from 'the moments immediately after his fall' the 'subtler elements exerting powerful sway over the future' (Ch. 2, p. 18). But before he does, he dwells on a telling detail from the book's first paragraph that returns us to the question of 'antecedent causes':

> The cool touch of glass on skin and James Gadd's cry – these synchronous moments fix a transition, a divergence from the expected: from the wine we didn't taste (we drank it that night to numb ourselves) to the summons, from the delightful existence we shared and expected to continue, to the ordeal we were to endure in the time ahead.
>
> (Ch. 2, p. 18)

The narrative locks the mind's eye on the lethal spectacle of the unmoored balloon, and presses us to share Joe's belief that 'When [he] let the wine bottle fall to run across the field towards the balloon', he 'chose a branching in the paths that foreclosed a certain kind of easeful life' (Ch. 2, p. 18). But the coupling of 'the cool touch of glass on skin and James Gadd's cry' contains a clue to a different explanation of what activates *Enduring Love*.

The linking of that sound to that sensation is no coincidence, as a sharper scrutiny of the novel's opening makes plain:

> The beginning is simple to mark. We were in sunlight under a turkey oak, partly protected from a strong, gusty wind. I was kneeling on the grass with a corkscrew in my hand, and Clarissa was passing me the bottle – a 1987 Daumas Gassac. This was the moment, this was the pinprick on the time map: I was stretching out my hand, and as the cool neck and the black foil touched my palm, we heard a man's shout. We turned to look across the field and saw the danger. Next thing, I was running towards it.
>
> (Ch. 1, p. 1)

The true starting point of the story is the moment of Joe's reunion with Clarissa after a six-week separation, 'the longest Clarissa and I had spent apart in our seven years' (Ch. 1, p. 3). Their sunlit tryst beneath the turkey oak grants them only partial shelter from the wind, whose destructive might is about to be displayed. Long before the balloon has been mentioned, the violent wind is connected with the couple in a way that suggests the fragility of their restoration to each other. At the exact moment when Joe reaches for the wine they brought to seal their reunion, they hear 'a man's shout' for help and see 'the danger' that has Joe, a heartbeat later, 'sprinting away from our happiness' in response to 'a child's cry, enfeebled by the wind that roared in the tall trees' (Ch. 1, p. 1). Then, before the nature of the danger has been revealed, and before the man and the child have been identified, 'the figure of Jed Parry' materialises 'directly ahead of' Joe, who visualises himself and Parry as already in thrall to a mutual compulsion, 'our white shirts brilliant against the green, rushing towards each other like lovers' (Ch. 1, p. 2).

The implication is that the disaster and the derangement about to engulf Joe and Clarissa are the demons conjured up by their reunion, the repressed realities of their relationship 'seven years into a childless marriage of love' (Ch. 1, p. 8). In an obvious sense, as Joe recalls it, 'the encounter that would unhinge us' – meaning Jed and himself – 'was minutes away' (Ch. 1, p. 2) and he was 'running towards a catastrophe, which was itself a kind of furnace in whose heat identities and fates would buckle into new shapes' (Ch. 1, p. 3). But in another sense, the true fateful encounter, between Clarissa and Joe, has already happened, and Joe is running away from the real catastrophe. The abortive rescue bid supplies a gripping diversion from the actual source of the adversities about to afflict the couple, just as de Clérambault's syndrome will later be enlisted to rationalise the threat to their love that Jed embodies. Joe is adamant that, prior to Logan's demise and the advent of Jed Parry, 'there was nothing that threatened our free and intimate existence' (Ch. 1, p. 8). But the back-story he deploys to defer the climax of Chapter 1 tells another tale, casting doubt on 'the delightful existence we shared and expected to continue', and inviting us to impute to the fall and its sequel a quite different significance from the one Joe ascribes to them.

The pages that postpone the chapter's main event are apt to pass unremarked on a first reading, but in hindsight they are packed with ominous intimations. On his way to meet Clarissa at Heathrow, Joe picks up, along with the picnic, 'the most expensive single item I had ever bought' (Ch. 1, p. 3), which we later learn is a copy of the *Poems* of Clarissa's beloved Keats, which Joe intends to give her. As he waits at the arrivals gate, Joe observes the reunions of others – 'each beseeching an immediate return of love' and demanding 'Let me in!' (Ch. 1, p. 4) – with the dispassionate eye of an anthropologist. After watching 'more than fifty theatrical happy endings', each seeming 'slightly less well acted than the one before', he begins to wonder 'how convincing I myself could be now in greeting Clarissa' (Ch. 1, pp. 4–5). When Clarissa taps him on the shoulder a moment later, his detachment vanishes, but not before his disenchantment with such coercive charades has been underlined.

An hour later, in the Chiltern Hills, 'still elated by our reunion', Joe muses fondly on 'the months we spent falling in love' (Ch. 1, p. 5). But then he switches abruptly to another scenario: 'Or, I imagined, I was another man, my own sexual competitor, come to steal her from me' (Ch. 1, p. 5). The perception of a threat to their love that is both internal and external is imperfectly disguised by the playfulness of the thought. The fantasy nurses a premonition of Jed Parry, 'another man' who, in his role as Joe's homosexual double – and in that sense his own 'sexual competitor' – will indeed seek to rob Joe of Clarissa, but by displacing her, not him. It follows inexorably from this that 'it was while we stopped to kiss . . . that we glimpsed through the fresh foliage the helium balloon drifting dreamily across the wooded valley to our west' (Ch. 1, p. 5). For the balloon bearing the grim freight of their future takes its cue from their kiss, just as the force that will sweep the balloon away, leaving Logan dead and Joe at Parry's mercy, is unleashed by their crossing into a realm as timeless as the folk tales it evokes: 'As we walked into the wood the wind began to get up and the branches creaked like rusted machinery' (Ch. 1, p. 5).

En route to their rendezvous with calamity, the carefully planted Keats motif emerges. Clarissa is fascinated by the poet's tragically doomed love for Fanny Brawne, to whom he seems, strangely, never to have written in the days before he died of consumption in Rome. Convinced nevertheless that Keats must have written to her, because 'he never stopped thinking about her' and because 'he loved her so hard' (Ch. 1, p. 7), Clarissa has devoted her research to proving that Keats's unsent letters to Fanny do exist. She needs to believe that a man truly in love in such circumstances would be compelled to put his feelings into words, whereas Joe suspects that 'in his hopeless situation' Keats 'would not have wanted to write precisely because he loved her so much' (Ch. 1, p. 7). A direct parallel begs to be drawn, and Joe immediately draws it for us: 'Lately I'd had the idea that Clarissa's interest in these hypothetical letters had something to do with our own situation, and with her conviction that love that did not find its expression in a letter was not perfect' (Ch. 1, p. 7). In their first months together, Joe tells us, she had written him beautiful letters, 'passionately abstract in their exploration of the ways our love was different from and superior to any that had ever existed', whereas Joe could only marvel at the 'miraculous' fact that 'a beautiful woman loved and wanted to be loved by a large, clumsy, balding fellow who could hardly believe his luck' (Ch. 1, p. 7). Clarissa's romantic illusions about the uniqueness and superiority of their love are about to be shattered by the fallout from the fatal accident, and, ironically, the only letters in the book in which love finds expression are the deluded ones Jed writes to Joe.

The balloon accident itself, like Jed's besotted pursuit of Joe and all that follows from it, is a cover story. But, like all cover stories, it bears the imprint of the story it has striven to suppress. It has everything it needs to pass for a naturalistic narrative that means no more than it says; yet, on closer inspection, it mutates into a fable that says far more than it meant to. The unspoken crisis in the couple's 'childless marriage of love' converges with an appalling tragedy in which Joe's deepest fears and darkest longings are brought to life and end in death. The balloonists menaced by the wind personify human impotence in the face of nature's tyranny, but it is no accident that they turn out to be a little boy and his grandfather, who is struggling to save him. What summons Joe to risk his own life is the cry of 'A child alone and needing help' (Ch. 1, p. 13). It is a summons to both his masculine prowess and his paternal instincts, and so, when he lets go of his rope to save himself, he feels that he has failed as a man on both counts. Worse still, he stands rebuked by the terrifying death of Logan, for whom letting go was evidently inconceivable, and is left poisoned by shame and guilt as a result.

Joe's guilt and shame are compounded when Clarissa defends Logan's decision to hang on as the heroic act of a man who 'had children of his own' (Ch. 3, p. 31). Her exaltation of Logan is immediately tied by Joe to the barrenness with which Clarissa's life has been blighted by surgery, and the memory of her 'mourning for a phantom child, willed into half-being by frustrated love' (Ch. 3, pp. 31–2). Joe's instinctive preservation of himself at the expense of Logan and the boy, the surrogate incarnation of Clarissa's 'ghost child' (Ch. 3, p. 32), exacerbates his sense of emasculation. The boy, of course, survives, which makes a mockery of Logan's sacrifice. But the boy's survival cannot erase the suspicion that the roots of Joe's culpability lie deeper, in guilty relief that Clarissa's 'unconceived child' (Ch. 3, p. 32) has been symbolically dispatched along with the epitome of fatherhood, from which he secretly recoils. That Clarissa is sterile from the start is a sure sign of the novel's empathy with male anxiety about motherhood and fathering. The unmanning of the protagonist may be a high price for freedom from the toils of maternity, for 'the absence of babies' (Ch. 8, p. 71) from the couple's life, but it is a price that the novel is willing to pay.

It is willing to pay it because, from the masculine perspective of *Enduring Love*, fusion with the feminine and the yoke of paternity imply the dissolution of identity, the loss of autonomy and the prospect of mortality. Hence the curious scene in which Joe remains unabsorbed by Clarissa's lovemaking, retaining mental detachment and emotional control by engrossing himself, oddly but aptly, in a news item about men frozen to death in a freak blizzard. Joe is acutely aware of what the erotic game they are playing is really about:

> It gave her a little masochistic thrill to feel she was ignored; she wasn't noticed, she wasn't there. Annihilation! Then she took a controlling pleasure in destroying my attention, drawing me from the frantic public realm into the deep world that was entirely herself. Now I was the one to be obliterated, and along with me, everything that was not her.
>
> (Ch. 18, p. 160)

In the end, of course, Joe surrenders to the sexual imperative, confessing 'I was hers' (Ch. 18, p. 160), but the appeal of the state of abstraction he has briefly enjoyed is left in no doubt: ' "Don't you think," I had asked Clarissa later in the bathroom, "that I'm some kind of evolutionary throw forward?" ' To be disengaged from the sexual drive is to resist the extinction of the self in a reproductive process inextricable from death.

In the mangled corpse of John Logan, Joe beholds the gruesome embodiment of male mortality and the obliterated self. This is the fate inflicted on the father, the paragon of heroic paternity, in *Enduring Love*:

> The skeletal structure had collapsed internally to produce a head on a thickened stick. And seeing that, I became aware that what I had taken for calmness was *absence*. There was no one there. . . . I didn't see Logan dead until I saw his face, and what I saw I only glimpsed. Though the skin was intact, it was hardly a face at all, for the bone structure had shattered and I had the impression, before I looked away, of a radical, Picassoesque violation of perspective.
>
> (Ch. 2, p. 23)

That the corpse is as much an uncanny manifestation of Joe's unconscious fears as it is an objective fact becomes apparent as soon as he and Clarissa return home after the accident: 'I wanted to tell her I loved her, but suddenly between us there sat the form of Logan, upright and still' (Ch. 3, p. 30). Logan's mutilated form is a portent of what Joe fears love conceals. 'We've seen something terrible together,' says Clarissa. 'It won't go away, and we have to help each other. And that means we'll have to love each other even harder' (Ch. 3, p. 33). Joe agrees: 'We needed love' (Ch. 3, p. 33). Yet after the fleeting 'deliverance' of making love, 'The darkness beyond the gloom of the bedroom was infinite and cold as death' (Ch. 3, p. 34); and out of that deathly darkness comes the voice of Jed on the bedside phone, mouthing the same pieties Joe and Clarissa have just mouthed and driving a wedge between them: 'I understand what you're feeling. I feel it too. I love you' (Ch. 3, p. 37).

The character of Jed conflates the psychotic personification of enduring love with the inward threat of homosexual desire that haunts the heterosexual male mind. Jed allows the novel to transfer Joe's dread of love from Clarissa to a male victim of de Clérambault's syndrome, who can be safely demonised as an eccentric instance of erotomania. Jed's task is to provide Joe with an alibi for his illicit emotions, an external source of peril on which the blame for his estrangement from Clarissa and the disintegration of his life can be pinned. But Jed cannot perform that task without the novel betraying the real motives for his recruitment. Jed's character is born in the instant after the fall when Joe realises Logan is dead: 'I felt a warmth spreading through me, a kind of self-love, and my folded arms hugged me tight. . . . This was when I noticed Jed Parry watching me. His long bony face was framed round a pained question' (Ch. 2, p. 19). As Joe contemplates the wreckage of Logan's body moments later, Jed appears again, to stare not at Logan but at Joe. And, when Jed suggests they do something together, Joe's first surmise is startling: 'The wild thought came to me that he was proposing some form of gross indecency with a corpse' (Ch. 2, p. 25). Jed's love for Joe is triggered by Joe's response to a death in which the nature of love and his sexual identity are at stake.

As the novel develops, it cannot evade the inference that Joe's intellectual and sexual antithesis is actually his alter ego, an inverted mirror image in which he glimpses the different course things might have taken to clinch his freedom from Clarissa: 'It was as if I had fallen through a crack in my own existence, down into another life, another set of sexual preferences, another past history and future' (Ch. 7, p. 67). As a monstrous substantiation of love's insanity, Jed is an object of revulsion into which Joe 'projected all kinds of inarticulate terrors' (Ch. 8, p. 69). But as a pretext that prises Joe and Clarissa apart in a way which absolves him of guilt and that acknowledges the pull of same-sex desire while keeping it at bay, Joe needs Jed badly. His otherwise inexplicable lie to Clarissa about Jed's first phone call and his wiping of the thirty messages that would have proved to her that Jed existed, confirm his complicity with Parry. 'He's not the cause of your agitation, he's a symptom' (Ch. 9, p. 84), Clarissa tells Joe, as the suspicion dawns on her that Jed might be Joe's creation, and that it is Joe who is obsessed with Jed: 'You were so intense about him as soon as you met him. It's like you invented him' (Ch. 9, p. 86). Joe suspects in turn that

> in those realms of feeling that defy the responsibility of logic, Clarissa considered Parry my fault. He was the kind of phantom that only I could have called up, a spirit of my dislocated, incomplete character, or of what she fondly called my innocence. I had brought him upon us, and I was keeping him there, even while I disowned him.
>
> (Ch. 12, p. 102)

The novel teases us with hints that Jed might indeed be a figment of Joe's diseased imagination, a being for whose existence we have only Joe's written word. It does so, of course, in order to demonstrate all the more emphatically that Joe 'was so obviously, incontrovertibly right' after all, while Clarissa 'was simply mistaken' (Ch. 10, p. 92). It countenances the view that Jed is 'a creature of [Joe's] imagining' (Ch. 23, p. 216) expressly in order to discount it, but its psychological truth is too penetrating to be relinquished so readily.

The book's attempt to defuse its explosive subtext backfires again when Joe contends that de Clérambault's theory of pathological love

> must surely reveal, even if unwittingly, the nature of love itself. For there to be a pathology there had to be a lurking concept of health. De Clérambault's syndrome was a dark, distorting mirror that reflected and parodied a brighter world of lovers whose reckless abandon to their cause was sane.
>
> (Ch. 15, p. 128)

The scientific rationalist in Joe construes Jed's passion as a deviation from the norm of love, a gross caricature of what is felt and said and done in the 'brighter world of lovers' from which dementia has banished him. Jed's aberrant behaviour can thus be explained away as the reassuring obverse of sane and healthy love. But this ruse is confounded by the insinuation that Jed is a chilling portrait of 'the nature of love itself' disguised as a patent travesty.

No scene in the novel insinuates this more effectively than the one in which Joe, alone at home at night, hears a floorboard creak and thinks that Parry is creeping up behind him:

> My heart had made its first terrifying cold pop even before I started to turn and rise from my chair and raise my hands, ready to defend myself, or even to attack. . . . What I saw coming towards me rapidly across the room, with arms outstretched like a cartoon sleepwalker was Clarissa, and who knows by what complex intervention of higher centres I was able to convert plausibly my motions of primitive terror into a tenderly given and received embrace and to feel, as her arms locked round my neck, a pang of love that was in truth inseparable from relief.
> 'Oh Joe,' she said, 'I've missed you all day, and I love you, and I've had such a terrible evening with Luke. And Oh God, I love you.'
> And Oh God I loved her.
>
> (Ch. 5, pp. 51–2)

The delayed identification fuses Jed for an instant with Clarissa, turning her into the object of Joe's 'primitive terror', which is quickly camouflaged by the practised gestures and protestations of love. 'You love me. You love me, and there's nothing I can do but return your love' (Ch. 7, p. 63): the words are Jed's, but they could just as easily have been spoken by Clarissa or Joe to each other at any intimate moment. Jed's fervent proclamations of his love for Joe in his letters, which testify to its transfiguring bliss, display an emotive romantic rhetoric that puts his kinship with Clarissa beyond question.

At one point Joe writes of Jed: 'He crouched in a cell of his own devising' in 'love's prison of self-reference' (Ch. 17, p. 143). The same might be said of Joe himself or of Clarissa, or of the other characters that share their incarceration and expand the novel's bleak anatomy of love. Chief among these is Jean Logan, impaled on her conviction that her dead husband was unfaithful and determined to inflict on herself 'the slow agony' (Ch. 13, p. 112) of love's destruction. Then there is the couple who could have spared her that agony by coming forward sooner, Professor James Reid and his student lover, Bonny Deedes, who 'never imagined that [their] clumsy attempts at concealment would cause such distress' (Ch. 24, p. 228) and whose decision to make their liaison public is about to cause much more. The fifteen-year-old marriage of Clarissa's brother Luke has been torn apart by his adultery with an actress, and his sister is treated to 'the relentless plainsong of the divorce novitiate – the pained self-advocacy that hymns the transmutations of love into hatred or indifference' (Ch. 5, p. 46). Joe recalls, too, the time he and Clarissa had to care 'for two little girls for a week – Felicity and Grace who both wet the bed – while their parents tore each other apart in a divorce hearing' (Ch. 14, p. 118). And in the crackpot ménage of Xan, Steve and Daisy, shackled to each other in 'a complicated sexual alliance' (Ch. 21, p. 202), the novel burlesques the fraught misalliance of Joe, Jed and Clarissa.

Enduring Love pitches itself as a romantic thriller, whose sophistication is secured by its qualms about the validity of science and the duplicity of fiction. But it is from the horror story at its heart that the novel draws its subterranean power. In this narrative underworld, the reality is the reverse of the authorised version.

Here love is not the imperilled princess waiting to be saved, but the monster from which the hero is in flight. '[Parry] brought out something in you', Clarissa realises in her last letter to Joe. 'A stranger invaded our lives, and the first thing that happened was that you became a stranger to me' (Ch. 23, p. 218). In this veiled tale of terror, Joe's collusion in Logan's death, his persecution by Jed Parry and his alienation from Clarissa are the answers to his prayers, the fulfilment of his secret desires. The perfect title for this tale is hidden in the anecdote Joe tells at Clarissa's birthday dinner about the publisher who rejected *Lord of the Flies*, which William Golding first submitted under the instructive title *Strangers from Within*.

It is has often been noted that the phrase that gives *Enduring Love* its title is ambiguous. If 'enduring' is read as an adjective, the phrase can be applied ironically either to the uncertain fate of Joe and Clarissa or to the relentless devotion of a stalker in a mental institution. If 'enduring' is taken as a verb, however, the phrase wryly describes the ordeal Joe is subjected to by Jed. But both readings miss the wider irony that lurks in the title. If Jed is not a bizarre caricature of love but its spitting image, the hard core of a common affliction, the title *Enduring Love* encapsulates the predicament in which most men and women in modern Western culture still find themselves ensnared. The novel pays lip service throughout to the sacrosanctity of the emotional bond that binds Clarissa and Joe together. But covertly it contends that what we have been taught to revere as love is a creed outworn, the last illusion and nature's cruellest hoax. In the final chapter of *Enduring Love* we are told that Clarissa has been searching for a letter in which Keats is thought to have uttered a 'cry of undying love not touched by despair' (Ch. 24, p. 221). It comes as no surprise to learn that, so far at least, her search has been in vain.

Martin Randall, '"I don't want your story": open and fixed narratives in *Enduring Love*'

Martin Randall teaches at the University of Gloucestershire. His research interests include Martin Amis, the city in literature, and British writings on the Holocaust.

Among its many other facets, *Enduring Love* is a book about competing viewpoints and versions of events. It thus begins appropriately with an event that is literally seen from multiple perspectives, by many onlookers, some of whom run to converge at the balloon. The different viewpoints of the six men holding down the balloon are then a touchstone example of individual attitudes both within and affecting a larger group. According to Joe, if all the men hold firm they should be able to control the balloon, but if any one of them lets go of their rope, all those who do not release their grip within a split second will be launched into the sky. This opening is therefore interested in questions of survival and sacrifice, self-preservation and cooperation, individual and group action, but it is also interested in the different stories and points of view brought to bear on this one moment of crisis.

Like the later restaurant scene, the ballooning accident is an example of an event which means different things to different people – such as Joe, Jed, Clarissa and Jean Logan – who each have their own version of what has happened and what is important in the incident. Like the start, the end of *Enduring Love* also brings out questions of contrast and difference within apparent similarity. The end focuses on a picnic, and Joe explicitly compares the ingredients with the picnic at the start (Ch. 24, p. 220). The situation is thus superficially the same: Joe collecting Clarissa to take them both on a picnic. The difference is of course in the circumstances. Clarissa is now living in her brother's flat and the encounter with Jed Parry has created a divide between them: as was discussed in the last essay, Joe and Clarissa are now fallen lovers cast out of their innocence and separated from one another. To add to the contrasts, McEwan introduces a third picnic: that of James Reid and Bonnie Deedes, more unlikely lovers who had 'planned a picnic in the Chilterns' (Ch. 24, p. 228) which they were forced to abandon, and which Jean Logan mistakenly took as evidence of her husband's infidelity. There are thus numerous parallels and echoes throughout the book, which serve to stress the similarities and differences of human situations, perspectives, feelings and, above all, narratives.

Related to the discussion at the end of Critical history, **p. 38**), in this second critical essay Martin Randall picks up on the story Joe tells to Rachael and Leo at the close of his story. Randall's chief interest is in the kinds of narrative that *Enduring Love* includes, not just in Joe's storytelling but also in the way that McEwan has put the book together. Whether the reader's interest is in detection, evolution, psychology or love, views about these subjects are encoded in narratives: stories about the world that express individual and collective human truths in the same way that myths do in many cultures. While Randall details how the novel is indeed intrigued by and composed of competing narratives within the one text, with one author and one narrator, he also shows that one of its fundamental aims is to argue that all narratives are not equal.

Martin Randall, '"I don't want your story": Open and Fixed Narratives in *Enduring Love*'

> I can spin a decent narrative out of the stumblings, back-trackings and random successes that lie behind most scientific breakthroughs.
>
> (Ch. 8, p. 75)

It is entirely appropriate that at the 'first' ending of *Enduring Love*, Joe is about to continue telling a 'story' to Jean Logan's children, Rachael and Leo. Jean Logan has convinced herself of an imagined 'story' in which her husband was having an affair and died 'showing off' to his lover as he held onto the rope attached to the balloon. Joe has discovered that this was not true and invites the 'real' lovers, James Reid and Bonnie Deedes, to a picnic in order to show Jean that her fears are unfounded. Joe's story to the children appears to be nothing less than the 'narrative' of the beginning of the natural world. He walks with the children alongside a river and asks Rachael to 'imagine the smallest possible bit of water that can exist' (Ch. 24, p. 225). He tells her that this is minuscule but that it is 'bound together by a mysterious powerful force'. Joe continues: 'Now think of billions, trillions, of them, piled on top of each other in all directions, stretching almost to infinity. And now think of the river bed as long as a long shallow slide, like a winding muddy chute, that's a hundred miles long stretching to the sea' (Ch. 24, p. 225). Later, after Jean Logan has been told the 'real' story of her husband, Joe returns to the river and the two children. It is Rachael's prompting that concludes this 'first ending': ' "So now," Rachael said. "Tell Leo as well. Say it again slowly, that thing about the river" ' (Ch. 24, p. 231).

Enduring Love is a text defined by the construction and articulation of narratives. In this key sense it is little surprise that the novel ends – before the 'other' endings – just as another story is about to begin to be told. The novel proliferates with narratives and stories and these, McEwan stresses, are the fundamental ways in which a sense of identity and an understanding of the world is rooted. Of course, particularly in the case of Jed, the text also dramatises the dangers of narrative. Jed's unsettling and ultimately self-destructive 'story' – that of Joe's love for him and, for that matter, God's love – is seen as a misinterpretation, a 'bad' narrative relying upon skewed readings, repression and wilful misunderstandings. The centrality of these competing narratives emphasises the multiple ways in which individuals, groups and systems make sense of the world through the use of narratives. It can also be seen that each character looks to order and control their lives through the use of a particular narrative viewpoint. There are the 'grand narratives' of science, religion and art that respectively Joe, Jed and Clarissa embody. And there are the smaller, more domestic narratives that are introduced throughout the novel, such as Jean Logan's fears about her late husband's possible infidelity. In both cases, the characters hope that a particular narrative or way of ordering and shaping experience will help them to 'endure' and, subsequently, ideally, understand the world. As in the novel's multiple endings McEwan also shows how these efforts are, at best, partial and imperfect but also compelling and necessary. At worst they can be fatal misrepresentations of reality.

To return to Joe's story, it is tempting to figuratively read the 'billions' and 'trillions' of drops of water as metaphors of the countless variety of narratives available to people. *Enduring Love* embodies this potential for multiple perspectives in its various endings and also through the consistent recognition of the many points of view and ordering principles that Joe and others both encounter and use. And all through these exchanges Joe reminds himself – and perhaps the reader – that these narrative perspectives are highly contingent. Following the shooting in the restaurant, for example, the police officer tells Joe that despite his conviction as to what happened, each witness has offered a subtly different account of events. Joe realises that this is a very human weakness:

> We lived in a mist of half-shared, unreliable perception, and our sense data came warped by a prism of desire and belief, which tilted our memories too. We saw and remembered in our own favour and we persuaded ourselves along the way. Pitiless objectivity, especially about ourselves, was always a doomed social strategy. We're descended from the indignant, passionate tellers of half truths who in order to convince others, simultaneously convinced themselves.
>
> (Ch. 20, pp. 180–1)

The 'half-shared' and 'unreliable' nature of narratives is thus an inevitable result of the 'prism of desire and belief' through which individuals apprehend and understand the world. Joe sees the 'disinterested truth' (Ch. 20, p. 181) of scientific research as valuable and preferable, but even this discourse is always potentially subjected to the 'distortions' of narrative.

These 'distortions' of narrative though are accepted as essential ingredients and as necessary aspects to the ways in which the novel's characters speak of the world and achieve, or fail to achieve, some kind of self-understanding. Joe, Jed and Clarissa thus define themselves, in varying degrees, by these 'grand narratives' of science, religion and art. Each of these structuring ideologies are understood to both embrace and, especially perhaps in the case of science, resist narrative as an inevitable and necessary cognitive process. Joe recognises that even science has had to acknowledge its use of narrative in telling the 'stories' of its discoveries and theories. Indeed, the 'beauty' of a particular narrative often means that it has been accepted over a less persuasive account (Ch. 5, pp. 48–9). These 'grand narratives' can be compared and contrasted with the many private 'small' narratives that individual characters present both of events and of their own lives. Each can be seen – from the first anxious reworkings of the balloon incident between Joe and Clarissa to Jean Logan's 'fiction' of her late husband's infidelity – as unavoidably limited and dependent upon a number of highly mutable factors. Despite the apparent certainty of Joe's version of events, McEwan persistently problematises each narrative in the novel and, hence, suggests a complexity of alternative perceptions, differing beliefs and contesting principles of interpretation.

But this is not to suggest that McEwan's novel is thus a paean to the intrinsic relativism of *all* narrative in what might be construed as an emblematically postmodern gesture.[1] As David Malcolm points out, despite this apparent acceptance of stories being unavoidable and, hence, in effect, everyone's narrative being theoretically plausible, *Enduring Love* does privilege certain perspectives over others. Malcolm writes:

> Knowledge is embodied in stories, and these stories are seen to be limited in a variety of ways. Either the authors deliberately distort, as it seems Jed does, or just get things wrong through inattention and human frailty or through the particular discourse they employ. But that does not mean that McEwan is arguing all stories are equal; quite the reverse. For all the reservations the reader may have about Joe's vision of the world, and the makeup of his mind, he is righter [*sic*] than the rest and wins in the end.[2]

In other words, the novel's narrator, Joe, has a more complete 'less deceived' narrative than many of the other characters but most obviously the 'story' of Jed. In this reading of the text, despite much of Joe's questioning of narrative in scientific analysis and his evident mistrust of the various narratives and narrative structures that he encounters, his point of view is shown to be the most accurate. Indeed, given that Joe's narration *is* the novel, one can see that his rationalism is finally rewarded and Jed's 'faith' is revealed to be not only potentially dangerous but also, crucially, 'wrong' in the sense that Malcolm suggests.

Thus, McEwan explores the incomplete and ambiguous nature of narrative whilst stressing its fundamental significance for individuals. Furthermore, *Enduring Love* shows that some narratives – as embodied by Jed's home-made and neurotic religious fervour – are closed and fixed and hence are not open to change or growth. This is exemplified in the novel's endings. As has been previously discussed, Joe's beginning of the 'story' of the earliest moments in the Earth's

---

1   For a discussion of postmodernism and fiction, see Niall Lucy, *Postmodern Literary Theory: An Introduction*, Oxford: Blackwell, 1997.
2   Malcolm, *Understanding Ian McEwan*, p. 181.

history can therefore be seen as a narrative that is just about to be told. The fact that Joe is *about* to retell this story to Rachael and her brother Leo implies a tentative hope or investment in the future and the sense that this narrative is open to interruption, metaphor and elaboration. Hence, Joe is 'speaking' his narrative and by sharing it he is opening up the possibilities of its changing, moving in unusual or unplanned directions or even for it to be disputed. He self-consciously engages with the problematics of narrative and always questions the form and content of them throughout the text. Chapter 9, for example, is an attempt to tell part of the narrative from Clarissa's point of view. However successful Joe is or is not in this, one can see how he is always examining and interrogating the assumptions and meanings in any given narrative. In this he is the surrogate author figure, engaged with the process of making and also questioning each narrative strand of the novel itself.

Indeed, one can see that this sense of an 'open' narrative actively encourages further investigations and in effect further narratives of exploration. Jed's deluded and neurotic narratives – of God and of love – are abstract and closed down. These are, in effect, processes of misinterpretation and, as such, they imprison Jed in a seemingly endless narrative that cannot be negotiated, rewritten or altered. Joe is adamant that he will resist Jed's misinterpretation of events. He tells Jed: 'I don't want your story' (Ch. 5, p. 59). Later, Joe is explicit in how he sees Jed's 'wrong' story:

> He crouched in a cell of his own devising, teasing out meanings, imbuing nonexistent exchanges with their drama of hope or disappointment, always scrutinising the physical world, its random placements and chaotic noise and colours, for the correlatives of his current emotional state – and always finding satisfaction. He illuminated the world with his feelings, and the world confirmed him at every turn his feelings took.
>
> (Ch. 17, p. 143)

Thus Joe defines Jed's narrative as impenetrable and one oblivious to the external world, and, hence, it is outside of influence and possible challenge. This narrative is linked to a 'cell', and this trope of Jed's claustrophobic, introspective and apparently unchanging 'sentence' of obsession and misreading suggests the ways in which Joe, and by extension McEwan, finally view Jed. His imperviousness to the 'truth' or 'facts' – '[he] listened only to the inner voice of his private God' (Ch. 18, p. 153) – underlines the sense that Jed is incarcerated in a narrative of his own devising.

This reading recalls something of the psychoanalytical approach to narrative and its relation to the 'telling' of the self. In *Psychoanalysis and Storytelling*, for example, Peter Brooks clarifies this when he writes: '*Mens sana in fabula sana*: mental health is a coherent life story, neurosis is a faulty narrative.' One can see how such a maxim would have significance for an understanding of the ways in which McEwan utilises narrative in *Enduring Love*. Furthermore, Brooks links this with a literary subgenre: 'Such a premise closely resembles that of the detective story, which equates the incomplete, incoherent, baffling story with crime, whereas detection is the making of an intelligible, consistent, and unbroken narrative.'[3] First, the notion of a 'faulty narrative' suggests something of the intrinsic problems in Jed's story. Second, Brooks's introduction of the detective genre suggests ways in which McEwan's novel can profitably be considered. Regardless of the actual crimes that occur in the text, there is a sense that Jed's central 'crime' is that of living by an 'incomplete, incoherent, baffling' narrative. Linked to this is an interpretation of Joe as a detective *manqué*. His task is to 'solve' the 'case' by making sense of the faulty narrative, by piecing together the 'clues' that Jed leaves behind him so that he (and others) can return to their comparatively coherent narratives.

If one sees Joe as a kind of detective whose task it is to make sense of Jed's 'crime' of a faulty or closed narrative, it is perhaps tempting to suggest that the novel rather too neatly posits a binary opposition between 'good' and 'bad' narratives. As is seen in the novel's multiple endings and the ways in which narratives are raised as problematical areas of interpretation, McEwan, whilst certainly privileging the rational over the emotional, sees narrative as being a creative act of shaping and structuring events and experience into formal 'maps' of understanding. If Joe is the detective, the arch-rationalist (and atheist), reading and interpreting not only Jed's narratives of God and love, he is also under scrutiny himself. McEwan in fact unsettles any sense of a neat binary opposition by showing how *all* narratives are open to alternative readings, misreadings and amendments. The very opening line of the novel, 'The beginning is simple to mark' (Ch. 1, p. 1), acts as an ironic signifier of this trope in the novel. Beginnings, middles and ends are shown to be remarkably difficult foundations of narrative to 'mark', least of all fully to comprehend.

Scientific research itself is seen to be as reliant upon the workings of narrative as any other discourse in the novel. Early on in *Enduring Love*, for example, Joe tells the reader that he is working on an article about the 'death of anecdote and narrative in science' (Ch. 4, p. 41). He recounts the story, as reported in a turn-of-the-century science periodical, 'proving' that some animals have 'awareness of the consequences of their actions' (Ch. 4, p. 41). The story tells of a man whose friend's dog always sat in a chair near the fire. One night the dog was shooed away from its usual comfortable place. After a few minutes the dog went to the door and whined to be let out. When the dog's owner rose and came over to let it out, the dog 'darted back and took possession once more of the favoured place' (Ch. 4, p. 41). Joe sees that 'the power and attractions of narrative had clouded judgement' (Ch. 4, p. 41) and that any intentionality attributed to the dog were spurious at best. But Joe's recognition of the 'power and attractions of narrative' shows how the question of shaping the 'evidence' to suit particular desired outcomes is as much an issue for the scientist as, by implication, any individual. A little later, Joe speaks of the symbiotic relationship in the nineteenth century between the novel and science. He sees that the novel dominated the 'nineteenth-century soul' in which 'great sprawling narratives which not only charted private fates, but made whole societies in mirror image and addressed the public issues of the day' (Ch. 5, p. 48). Hence each discourse feeds off and into the other.

---

3   Peter Brooks, *Psychoanalysis and Storytelling*, Oxford: Blackwell, 1994, p. 49.

At this relatively early stage in *Enduring Love* McEwan emphasises Joe's self-conscious and personal/professional investment in the nature of narrative. Joe sees that certain narratives – because of their 'beauty' as much as anything else – come to define how certain events and phenomena are apprehended and understood. This can be seen dramatically in the many 'versions' of what happened at the balloon incident that is the 'beginning' of the novel. Joe describes himself and the other men as 'racing into this story' (Ch. 1, p. 1), a story that begins as a 'catastrophe, which itself was a kind of furnace in whose heat identities and fates would buckle into new shapes' (Ch. 1, p. 3). It is apt that Joe should use such a metaphor. The 'new shapes' that are formed by entering into this highly unpredictable narrative fulcrum – namely the balloon incident – suggest the ways in which the inevitable complications of narrative radically alter, potentially, the other narratives that come into contact with it. In other words, making sense of the 'real' requires narrative to grant the aleatory and the random inner coherence. But, in 'open' narratives at least, these are strikingly plural and mutable and hence always subject to alteration.

Joe's self-consciousness about the nature and complexity of narrative can be seen as that of McEwan. But more than this, one can see how the inevitable and necessary areas of contest within narratives of contrasting types are shown to be vital if not defining aspects of living. Throughout the novel, McEwan shows how the detective Joe is presented with various narratives whose strategies, assumptions, formal generic tropes, perspectives, prejudices, aporias and elisions he has to, so to speak, interrogate. An early example of this is when Joe phones the police to complain about Jed's behaviour. He is faced with the inevitable bureaucratic logic of the police system and he must also 'prove' that Jed poses a definite threat. Joe sees that the system is not 'refined enough to process every private narrative' (Ch. 8, p. 73). Hence, he is unable to lodge a complaint against Jed. This scene of the 'grand narrative' of bureaucracy unable, or unwilling, to accommodate the 'private narrative' of Jed's stalking of Joe is later replayed in two scenes following the attempted assassination in the restaurant. To some degree this scene replays the opening chapter in that it is a moment of high drama that is later interpreted and reinterpreted in potentially contradictory ways. Not only is the bureaucratic system shown to be inflexible in how it deals with these private narratives, but these scenes also underline the ambiguous and highly unstable essence of the 'making' of narrative. They also show how each witness represents a separate fragment that may or may not 'fit in' to the whole.

Joe's encounters with the police are pre-empted by the inclusion of how the newspapers have reported the incident. With no small degree of irony, Joe and the others in the restaurant read how the generic language of the media, a tabloid language, changes the emphasis of an event they have only recently experienced:

> One of the waiters went out for a copy and we gathered round, and found ourselves strangely exalted to read our experience assimilated to the common stock of 'restaurant outrage', 'lunchtime nightmare' and 'bloodbath'. The maitre d' pointed to a sentence which described me as 'the well-known science writer' and Jocelyn as 'the eminent scientist' and Clarissa was simply 'beauteous'.
>
> (Ch. 20, p. 174)

Joe sees that what was experienced as chaotic and sudden, an unexpected and largely confusing moment in the 'real' is thus reduced to the clichéd language of the media. Indeed, the reporters are drawn to the story because of the entirely coincidental presence of an under-secretary of state, Colin Tapp. Joe's realisation that he was the intended victim – and that Jed was behind the attempted murder – is thus a narrative (that is true) subsequently pitted against the competing narrative interpretation of the press and the police. An added irony to these readings and misreadings revolves around the fact that the would-be assassins hired by Jed mistook Tapp for Joe. It is only Jed's intervention that saves Tapp's life.

The ironic narrative strands that permeate from this single incident include Tapp's possible connections with the Middle East as a motive for the attempted killing and that Jed is described in the paper as a 'fearless have-a-go diner' (Ch. 20, p. 175). Joe considers this rewriting of what he has just witnessed: 'The coverage seemed so familiar, as well as eerily instant. It was as if the subject had been mapped out long ago, and the event we had witnessed had been staged to give point to the writing' (Ch. 20, p. 175). This can partially be read as an ironic reflection on the very notion of narrative representation. The language used to describe the event, because of its own rhetoric and connotations, constitutes it in the order of narrative rather than in the order of the real. Rereading this newspaper discourse about the event, Joe begins to feel oddly dissociated from his own experience and speculates that the representation actively 're-covers' the original in its own narrative. The event has now entered into the realm of narrative and representation and hence is 'open' to figuration, interpretation and even a 'bad' or 'wrong' reading. When Joe has to speak to the police once again, this sense of setting an event and the possible perspectives on that event into a particular discourse that will provide particular meanings is further emphasised.

Wallace, the officer who interviews Joe, becomes another interlocutor in another narrative: 'OK. Let's go from the beginning' (Ch. 20, p. 176). This is of course an ironic reference to the opening line of the novel and again it confirms that the 'beginning' is as much an arbitrary decision needed in order to get the narrative 'moving' as it is a specific temporal moment. After contacting the previous officer who dealt with Joe's first official complaint, Wallace returns and again asks, 'Can we start at the beginning?' (Ch. 20, p. 178). The interrogation that continues – the detective himself under scrutiny – unsettles Joe's witness statement. Wallace shows that Joe's 'version' differs, in small but telling ways, from the other 'versions'. Wallace pre-empts these subtly contradictory accounts by calling to Joe's attention the conversation that he, Clarissa and Jocelyn were having moments before the murder attempt. This involved a literary debate concerning whether or not Wordsworth rather cruelly mocked the younger Keats (Ch. 19, pp. 167–70). The story is, Clarissa earlier concedes, probably apocryphal, a factor that Wallace forces Joe to admit: 'Well, the only account we have is unreliable' (Ch. 20, p. 179). This then casts doubt on not only Joe's 'evidence' but also the other strands of witness testimony that have been entered into the 'official' narrative of the attack.

The plethora of conflicting narratives emphasises the difficulty, even impossibility, of reaching definitive conclusions about the 'truth' of particular events. Indeed, one can see how Joe begins to reconcile himself with this fundamental aspect of narrative and its relation to the self. In this respect his own 'open' narratives and his involvement in other further narratives means that Joe (despite accusations from Clarissa and Jed that he is such a staunch rationalist he is shut off from more emotional experiences) develops a keen sense of what amount to 'healthy narratives'. Jed, by contrast, is 'closed' by his adoption of two narratives that are quantifiably 'false': his *enduring love* of God and of Joe. As has been already alluded to, McEwan's novel is not a celebration or even a resigned acceptance of the relativity of narratives. Jed's narratives of love are faulty and although the novel at times suggests that Joe himself may be deluded, one is left in little doubt as to whose narrative one is finally encouraged to trust. But as the text's continual concern with point of view and the 'contest' of differing narratives shows – the incomplete knowledge that representation inevitably embodies – the very act of 'creating' narrative is a highly ambiguous, problematical praxis.

At the beginning of the present essay, the start to Joe's story of evolution to Jean Logan's children was seen as the start of yet more narratives. This scene reflects Joe's own acknowledgement of metaphor and plot to engage the listener, in this case a young child. Science is thus seen in the novel to rely upon narrative to underscore the value of its truth. The subsequent 'appendices' further stress the unfinished nature of narrative and also suggest other ways to interpret the 'ends' of the novel. The first appendix is a fictionalised but highly authentic 'paper' taken from the *'British Review of Psychiatry'* (Appendix I, p. 233). This narrative account is effectively a rewriting of what the reader has just read. In the recognisable register and prose style of an academic paper, McEwan introduces the history of de Clérambault's syndrome, the 'case history' of Joe's encounter with Jed followed by a clinical discussion and conclusion of the 'nosological entity' (Appendix I, p. 233) that in this particular discourse the story has become. To a degree, the 'paper' fills in some of the gaps in the narrative, providing information that Joe either wasn't aware of or didn't, for whatever reason, mention.

Jed's irrational narrative of love is thus contained and understood within the strict parameters of a medical/academic discourse. The ways in which this language transforms Jed's religious fervour and his unwavering obsession with Joe again suggests how perspective – in this case scientific – defines how a subject will be understood. The authoritative register of the paper, with its technical language and apparently 'objective' tone reconfigures what the reader has read into what amounts to another way of seeing Jed's behaviour. There is found to be, for example, 'no evidence of other schneiderian front-rank symptoms for schizophrenia' (Appendix I, p. 238). The clinical description of what has been hitherto seen as merely unstable behaviour is an effective attempt to understand a 'case' such as Jed in a language that is ultimately dispassionate, controlling and represents an attempt, based on empirical research and data, to 'understand' Jed's dilemma. Subsequent phrases such as 'cognitive impairment' (Appendix I, p. 238) and 'insight-directed therapy' (Appendix I, p. 238) are also redolent of this 'Case history'. To a large degree, Jed's irrational and potentially dangerous personality is concluded: he has been institutionalised and 'summed up'. This might be seen as a mildly ironic reference to the prevailing notion of Joe as a detective of sorts. In effect he has solved the 'case'. Joe remains convinced throughout the novel that science can and will explain Jed away and the inclusion of the paper seems to confirm this. Indeed, if *Enduring Love* can partly be read as a novel in praise of the rational, scientific mind (and its narratives) then this 'essay' vindicates both Joe's theories and McEwan's own ideological commitments.

But as has been shown, the novel's recognition of the ambiguity of narrative is problematised in a number of ways. Although the paper appears to 'end' the case, and hence it may seem to be a 'closed' narrative, it becomes evident that it is the possibility of further events, research, responses and theories that becomes available even though the 'real' has been contained within a medical discourse. For example, the necessary intertextuality and referencing that the paper relies upon suggests an epistemological lineage between the essay and a community of scientists. This is a study that refers back to earlier contributions to the subject and is itself another entry into future work on the syndrome. Hence it is not 'finished' nor even does it claim to be the 'final word'. This is an intriguing argument in the novel and in a sense it argues back against certain postmodern theories of the qualitative differences between artistic and scientific narratives.[4] Rather than seeing the scientific discourse as being fundamentally opposed to narrative – because, for example, it is 'rule-based' – the inclusion of the paper adds to the sum of knowledge about Jed but it does not finish it. Aside from the academic references to other reports, McEwan includes his 'happy ending' in the paper – 'R and M were reconciled and later successfully adopted a child' (Appendix I, p. 242). This is an ending that is not or even perhaps 'cannot' be contained within the main dramatic narrative. The 'ending' of the novel when Joe is about to tell his 'story' to the children is a beginning that hints at the 'happy ending' of the couple's reconciliation. It also suggests the ways in which the scientific discourse is inadequate in representing ordinary human happiness.

Furthermore, as C. Byrnes has pointed out, aside from the authentic papers that McEwan has referenced for his fictional essay, he includes a reference to 'WENN, R. and CAMIA, A. (1990) "Homosexual erotomania." *Acta Psychiatrica Scandinavica*, 85, 78–82' (Appendix I, p. 243). Aside from the authors' names making an anagram of 'Ian McEwan', an added irony is that the novelist actually sent the paper included in *Enduring Love* by the same 'authors' to a real journal that then considered it for legitimate publication.[5] Hence one can see further narratives being produced, indeed narratives that proliferate. The blurring between fiction and fact that McEwan's fake paper represents is another example of how strictures of differing narrative positions, for instance between history and fiction, are far more intermingled and reliant upon each other. The academic paper thus achieves a number of effects that reflect back upon the text itself. First, it confirms Joe's fears that Jed is potentially dangerous and it 'proves' through scientific research Joe's 'faith' in certain intellectual procedures. Second, the paper's narrative is by its nature intertextual and hence reliant upon prior narratives. The paper is a contribution to scientific thought and therefore it presupposes future responses, possible challenges and even contradictions to its basic thesis. Finally, McEwan's convincing fictionalisation of an academic register and his subsequent witty submission of the paper to a journal blur the distinctions between fact and fiction. Hence the narrative(s) represented in the paper are dialogic and heterogeneous.

---

4   For a discussion of such differences between artistic and scientific narratives see Lucy, *Postmodern Literary Theory*. In particular see the chapter 'Literature and the Liminal' (pp. 63–81).
5   Byrnes, *The Work of Ian McEwan*, pp. 266–8.

An immediate and dramatic contrast can be found in the final 'appendix' and the last 'ending' of the novel. This 'appendix' is a letter written by Jed to Joe that has been sent to one of the authors of the previous scientific paper. This confirms the 'closed' nature of Jed's narrative. Jed writes as if he is responding to a previous letter by Joe: 'You're right, when the sun comes up behind the trees they turn black' (Appendix II, p. 244). He continues to speak of 'the resplendence of God's glory and love' (Appendix II, p. 244) which he continues to equate with his enduring love for Joe. There is a millennial undercurrent to Jed's declarations: 'The thousandth day, my thousandth letter, and you telling me that what I'm doing is right!' (Appendix II, p. 244). Indeed, Jed now appears to be waiting for some kind of religious revelation that will bring Joe 'joyfully towards his warmth' (Appendix II, p. 245). And despite his incarceration, Jed remains committed to Joe: 'You know it already, but I need to tell you again that I adore you. I live for you. I love you' (Appendix II, p. 245). His final words – 'faith is joy' (Appendix II, p. 245) – are a bleakly ironic reminder of how incarcerated in his delusional narratives Jed is. In effect the 'appendices' show how 'faith', as defined by the deeply troubled Jed Parry, is anything but 'joy'. Because of the determinedly 'closed' narratives that Jed adopts (but never adapts) – his 'thousand letters' remain unanswered – he is condemned to a monologic rather than dialogic existence.

Nick Rennison writes that *Enduring Love* is an 'account of one man's attempt to retain narrative control of his life as it seems to be slipping into chaos and contingency'.[6] The novel dramatises this battle for 'narrative control' and, to a large degree, as has been seen, Joe achieves this through reason, rationalism and resistance. At one point Joe tells Jed, 'I don't want your story' (Ch. 6, p. 59) and this refusal of Joe to submit to Jed's 'faulty' narrative is vindicated by the end of the novel. But also McEwan is keen to show that 'narrative control' is a highly difficult thing to achieve. On the one hand, *Enduring Love* can be read as a text that dramatises the inevitable competition between narrative points of view. From the contesting views of who did or didn't let go first of the balloon at the start of the novel through to the conflicting witness statements following the assassination attempt in the restaurant, McEwan stresses how complex narratives are in the invariably incomplete ways in which they are constructed to make sense of reality. On the other hand, *Enduring Love* displays how narrative-making is an essential tool of human interaction. Narratives that are 'open', the novel argues, are preferable to 'closed' narratives in that they rely upon and encourage further narratives and further points of view. Early on in the text Joe reminds himself that 'the habit of scepticism was proof of my sanity' (Ch. 5, p. 47), and it is this more 'open' sense of enquiry into the world rather than the 'faith' of Jed's narratives of God and love that the novel endorses.

---

6   Nick Rennison, *Contemporary British Novelists*, London: Routledge, 2005, p. 110.

Rhiannon Davies, 'Enduring McEwan'

Rhiannon Davies is currently a freelance writer working in London. Previously, she worked on the fiction list at Hodder & Stoughton publishers, edited for the online newspaper silicon.com, and has written interactive marketing campaigns and web sites for online ad agencies.

Clarissa, who seems to refer habitually if fondly to Joe's 'innocence' (Ch. 12, p. 102), says of him: 'You're so rational sometimes you're like a child' (Ch. 3, p. 33). In this context, her statement implies that Joe has now come up against unpredictable and irrational forces that will threaten him.[1] 'Did she mean that rationality was a kind of innocence?' (Ch. 3, p. 33), Joe wonders, bringing to mind his own precipitation into experiences outside of his frame of reference. From one perspective, this represents a challenge to Joe's masculinity and maturity. His response to this is arguably to turn to clichés of masculine behaviour, especially those drawn from popular culture. In particular, the paradigm of masculinity the book engages is that of the man of action who saves or destroys, rescues or fights. For example, while the book begins with the attempt to save one life, it ends before the appendices with the threat to take one. The start has Joe and Jed united in trying to save Harry Gadd, but the majority of the novel features Jed, from his perspective, trying to save Joe from damnation and bring him to love – before hiring assassins to kill him. The end additionally has Jed threatening Clarissa as part of his attempt to save Joe while Joe concludes he has to shoot Jed in order to save Clarissa. In all of this is a complex shift between different traditional models of masculine behaviour that draw on codes of protection or aggression.

In this section, Rhiannon Davies examines *Enduring Love* from the point of view of its presentation of masculinity and initially explores the novel in terms of 'the gaze', as the unreconstructed male, Joe, is objectified by the unwanted attention of his admirer, Jed. She proceeds to argue that McEwan's novel con-

---

1   Parry belittles Joe's scientific articles as 'the little footstampings of a tired infant' (Ch. 16, p. 136).

cludes with the breakdown of Joe's 'strategies of masculine self-fashioning' as he tries to assert the heroic triumph of his male adventure-ideal in the display of machismo that characterises his gun-toting victory over the 'madman' threatening 'his woman'. To this end, Davies examines Joe's 'script' for his behaviour and narration, then dissects the novel's central relationships, between the lovers, the stalker and the stalked, and the storyteller and his audience. The essay is also interested in the allegorical structures that lie behind McEwan's representation of Englishness and masculinity, and Davies links this to other fantasies she perceives in the male literary psyche in the last decades of the twentieth century.

From Rhiannon Davies 'Enduring McEwan', in Daniel Lea and Berthold Schoene (eds) *Posting the Male: Masculinities in Post-War and Contemporary British Literature*, Amsterdam: Rodopi, 2003, pp. 109–20.

The stage

Throughout the novel we are made increasingly aware that all events are filtered to us through the narrative voice of Joe Rose. Joe is the raconteur, the author of events, holding an omniscient god-like point of view and thus occupying the kind of subject position Lynda Broughton has described as typical of the phallic male "I". As Broughton argues, the construction of masculinity is invariably facilitated by a singular, unifying image of the phallus:

> The phallus, literal or otherwise, thus becomes a metaphor for the self: it is the letter "I", the number one, the singular unique subject of its own discourse and the story of "I" displaces all other stories in a single, privileged act of writing – the construction of the subject.[2]

What the reader is witness to in *Enduring Love* are the projections of one man, Joe Rose, insisting on his own authority, sovereignty and influence. Joe's insistence on *his* version of events is grounded in and supported by an active self-alignment with the phallogocentric power structures of the symbolic order. However, the adopted omniscient point of view is both thwarted and exposed as an illusion whenever Joe's voice intrudes with comments such as "let me freeze the frame – there's a security in stillness" [Ch. 1, p. 12]. This cinematic technique reveals the essential fictionality of Joe's representation and alerts the reader to the fact that Joe himself produces, directs and seeks to control the images that serve to buttress his particular version of events.

---

2 Lynda Broughton, 'Portrait of the Subject as a Young Man: The Construction of Masculinity Ironized in "Male" Fiction', in Phillip Shaw and Peter Stockwell (eds) *Subjectivity and Literature from the Romantics to the Present Day*, London and New York: Pinters, 1991, pp. 135–45.

In the novel's opening scene, as the balloon surges up and fellow rescuer John Logan falls to his death, the events are recounted with a breathless excitement that is almost cartoon-like: "He fell as he had hung, a stiff little black stick. I've never seen such a terrible thing as that falling man" [Ch. 1, p. 16]. The emotional necessity of diffusing the dreadful reality of the situation is highlighted by Joe's resort to cartoon-like imagery and overtly cinematic devices. Significantly, Joe continues to distance himself from the horror before him by, right from the beginning, imagining different versions of events, different endings and outcomes which would enable him to still play the part of the hero. Thus, in his mind at least, tragedy can be held at bay by adopting a kind of choose-your-own-adventure style. Throughout the novel this tendency continues so that action always take precedence over characterization and the novel becomes a colourful collage of fragmented, yet controlled moments. Stereotypically gendered thought processes and fast-moving action anaesthetize Joe and successfully shield him from his feelings of failure and weakness which will return to haunt him later in the novel under Parry's unrelenting scrutiny. After the would-be rescuer falls to his death, Joe's strategies of emotional self-composure take over. He has survived the horrific ordeal and immediately begins to view the situation with detachment: "Like a self in a dream I was both first and third persons. I acted, and saw myself act. I had my thoughts, and I saw them drift across a screen. As in a dream, my emotional responses were non-existent or inappropriate" [Ch. 2, p. 19]. He stands quite literally like a superhero – poised and competent. His woman, Clarissa, clings to his arm – inevitably crying. Almost immediately he turns to take charge of the situation by retrieving his mobile phone and calling for assistance. Despite being in a state of shock, Joe deepens his voice and reassures the group with verbal platitudes. He then turns to Clarissa, softens his tone and artfully lowers the volume: "I was in a soap opera. Now he's talking to his woman. It was intimacy, a tight two-shot" [Ch. 2, p. 21].

It is evident that Joe is acting out a given script, taken from a film or comic book. He makes all the appropriate moves and remembers all the right things to say and successfully plays the part of the rescuing hero taking control. He actively pushes from his mind his blatant inefficiency and lack of control in the previous scene, as well as his undeniable, cowardly and selfish contribution to the tragedy. He seems resolved that trauma does not happen to him. Instead, he fashions himself after traditional images of the hard, unemotional man and the ideal superhero "pleased by the way my feet were anchored to the ground and set well apart, and the way my arms were folded across my chest" [Ch. 2, p. 19]. Joe's language here mirrors Peter Middleton's analysis of "the lost language of emotion" in *The Inward Gaze* (1992). Middleton articulates how traumatic experience poses an existential threat to the construction of a secure and stable masculine self. As Middleton explains with reference to typically masculine strategies of self-composure in the face of trauma, "the self is unable to locate its relation to expressions of feeling, so they remain alien objects of investigation, rather than means of interaction".[3] Only a resort to a pose of heroism can redeem such inarticulacy, avert the threat of emotional self-disintegration and re-fortify a

---

3   Peter Middleton, *The Inward Gaze*, Routledge: London, 1992, p. 41.

position of self-contained strength. With Joe it is exactly such an assumed pose of heroic self-management that keeps him going and his feelings of powerlessness at bay. In order to put the accident behind him, Joe shuts off his emotions and builds a wall around him to prevent any self-critical thoughts from creeping in. As he takes cover in the knowledge of his own rationality, it is to the exclusion of all other possibilities. However, despite all these precautions, it is inevitable that the ballooning accident should also trigger in Joe a growing sense of his impotence and powerlessness, which begins to trouble his relationship with Clarissa. The quickly deteriorating relations between the hero and the heroine testify to a further erosion of the strong, stable, rational and emotionally detached masculinity that Joe seems so desperate to inhabit.

The lovers

In an attempt to stave off his insecurities Joe perpetrates a reinscription of dominant gender stereotypes into his relationship with the woman he loves. Clarissa is reduced to a stereotypical woman driven by the heart, in opposition to whom Joe can recognize himself as a typical male impervious to emotional confusion and led only by the faculties of logical reason. Whereas "she wants to lie quietly in soapy hot water and reflect, he wants to set about altering his fate" [Ch. 9, p. 83]. They become locked in a conflict that shows the male yearning for perpetual progress and the female for happiness, harmony and children. Initially, a reader welcoming the influence feminist thought has undeniably had on McEwan's development might be tempted to condemn McEwan for this clichéd portrayal of masculinity and femininity, which seems not only inappropriate and out of date but also markedly out of character. However, the situation soon turns out to be far more complicated, as the reader begins to realize that all is not as Joe would like to make us believe: it is in fact Joe who is conjuring these gendered visions.

The ballooning accident brings to light Joe's hitherto latent disillusionment and frustration with himself. As if in demonstration of this fact, Clarissa returns home one night to register a look of wildness – and bewilderment – that occasionally distorts the image of the calm, organized man she loves. Little more than a scientific "go-between", an "ad-man hired to talk up other people's stuff" [Ch. 16, p. 136], Joe's journalistic work boils down to second-hand analysis or, worse still, mere regurgitation, leaving him no leeway for creative self-fulfilment. A letter from his old science department stating in black and white that the developments in science have passed him by soon confirms his worst fears. Joe is trapped within a void of physical and psychological impotence that terrifies him. John Haffenden in his excellent interview with McEwan in 1985 points out that the polarity of intellectuality and impotence in McEwan's work. A male's greatest fear, in McEwan's fiction from "Homemade"[4] to *Enduring Love*, is to find either his intelligence or his virility impeded, that is, to be unable to take control and exert a certain degree of agency. Joe Rose is threatened in both departments and, as a result, emasculation and chaos are baying at the gates. As the narrative pro-

4   In McEwan's debut *First Love, Last Rites*.

gresses, the reader begins to distrust our narrator because what he says is hardly ever supported by the reality of his circumstances. Joe is not a man driven to madness by someone else's illusions, but a man driven to madness by the revelation of his own illusions. The ballooning accident, which required one man to step forward and take control, becomes a kind of negative epiphany for Joe, disclosing once and for all his psychological and social impotency. He was not man enough to divert the tragedy. The ballooning accident throws our hitherto well-balanced and rational male into crisis and emotional chaos, disrupting the fragile self-fashioning of a man trying to establish an incontestably masculine identity for himself in the 1990s. Fellow-rescuer-turned-stalker Jed Parry compounds Joe's problem by bringing the crisis into claustrophobic focus. As Clarissa wisely remarks to Joe, "Parry is not the cause of your irritation, he is the symptom" [Ch. 9, p. 84]. It is necessary therefore to examine the third crucial relationship in the novel and the psychological battle that ensues between stalker and stalked.

The stalker

It is in fact Jed Parry's unwavering gaze which unsettles Joe and plunges him into emotional turmoil. In her much celebrated article "Visual Pleasure and Narrative Cinema", Laura Mulvey insists that in cinematic representation the female is continually constituted as image, the "looked-at" and the object of the spectacle, whereas the male is the bearer of the look, and, as such, inhabiting the position of active subject. He who holds the gaze has the power; those who exist as spectacle are powerless. Although cinema and society have changed substantially in the decades since the article was first written, in 1973 Mulvey could assert that:

> An active/passive heterosexual division of labour has similarly controlled narrative structures. According to the principles of the ruling ideology and the psychical structures that back it up, the male figure cannot bear the burden of sexual objectification. Man is reluctant to gaze at his exhibitionist like. Hence the split between spectacle and narrative supports the man's role as the active one of advancing the story, making things happen. The man controls the film fantasy and also emerges as the representative of power in a further sense as the bearer of the look of the spectator . . .[5]

Accordingly, it should not surprise us greatly that Joe cannot bear the gaze of another man. With his "freeze frame(s)" and "tight shots", Joe controls the narrative film fantasy of *Enduring Love* and repeatedly re-emphasizes *his* control over the action. Parry, by pushing in between Joe and Clarissa and thus disrupting the admiring gaze of the female heroine towards our very active male, threatens to topple the authority Joe assumes over his story. Parry's gaze reverses the traditional male/female dichotomy and puts Joe firmly in the object position of the spectacle. Joe is a middle-aged man who has never questioned his authorial

---

5   Laura Mulvey, *Visual and Other Pleasures*, London: Macmillan, 1989, p. 20.

stance as creator of his own destiny and author of his own story. In correspondence with Mulvey's assertion that, "man is reluctant to gaze at his exhibitionist like", Joe has never been objectified and was not even aware that this was a conceivable possibility. And now, closely following his negative epiphany on the hill, and for the first time in his life, Joe becomes the object of another's gaze. And, it is a gaze with which he struggles to cope. Also, this is not just the gaze of any other, but another male. The homosexual attraction that Parry feels for Joe, and the guilt that Joe feels for inspiring it, fracture his erstwhile stable sense of self.

What ensues is an uneasy introspective turn, leading Joe to do what so many men have been induced to do in the wake of feminism, that is, to examine and reassess their symbolically privileged position, which they had been accustomed to taking for granted. Interestingly, inspired by Mulvey's work, Kenneth MacKinnon has shed light on exactly this subversive return of the gaze and the impact it tends to exert on unreconstructed males who, like Joe in *Enduring Love*, suddenly find themselves in the position of spectacle. In *Uneasy Pleasures* MacKinnon writes:

> If there have long been erotic male objects, they have been left relatively undetected for so many centuries because of the cultural habit of massive disavowal. Even now they are detected, they in part disavow their own status through an emphasis on their activity and thus, it would appear, masculinity.[6]

Joe disavows the attention of Parry's gaze by any and every means possible. However, although he has solidly internalized the narrative structures and binary subject/object oppositions of patriarchy, his confusion is palpable. How can he possibly have become the object of spectacle when, by repeatedly asserting his agency and powerfulness, he is clearly still visible to himself as a subject – and as a subject only?

The battle

We must now return to the catalyst of Joe's crisis, which is the ballooning accident. Here, within touching distance of Logan's corpse, the reader is introduced to Joe's homosexual stalker, Jed Parry. At that early moment, in immediate confrontation with the shattered body of heroic man, Joe already senses Parry as a physical threat. Parry is tall, fit, tense with high-ridged cheek bones and a ponytail which "gave him the look of a pale Indian brave" [Ch. 2, p. 24]. Not only is Parry a physical threat, but Joe also senses that Parry sees through his stagemanship and right into his hesitation and nervousness, thereby instantly unsettling Joe's superheroic pose. Parry's obsessive interest in Joe dismantles the defence system that the latter has constructed for himself over the years, and Joe is convinced that Parry will expose him in some shape or form. Interestingly, it is not the physical closeness with Clarissa that forces Joe into self-examination, but an

---

6   Kenneth MacKinnon, *Uneasy Pleasures*, London: Golden Cockerel, 1997, p. 21.

obsessive relationship with another male that leaves him mentally and physically exposed.

Parry's nature repulses Joe from the start: "[Parry's] world was emotion, invention and yearning. He was the stuff of bad dreams" [Ch. 17, p. 147]. Parry's freedom to act on impulse and intuition is also completely anathema to Joe's strictly rational disposition. By rendering Joe the object of another man's obsession, McEwan reverses traditional stereotypes and, in so doing, makes Joe's dilemma not only difficult but traumatically acute. Joe easily contained and stereotyped Clarissa's "womanly" doubt and criticism, but he cannot deal with the unknown arsenal at Parry's disposal. With reference to what Thomas Byers has averred in a different context, McEwan's hero could be diagnosed as suffering from an onslaught of feminization, which not only emasculates him but moreover threatens to dissolve the very foundations of the self. Byers writes:

> The extreme form of this [male] fear of "feminization" is the homophobic's paranoia about homosexual rape ... a fear of violation of the masculine body that, in a heterosexual economy, sees itself as inviolable, as hard and sealed off rather than soft or opened, as the penetrator rather than the penetrable.[7]

Joe is terrified of Parry's deconstruction of the hard exterior he has worked so hard to put in place and cultivate. Parry turns the tables of familiarity on Joe when *he* becomes the object of an-*other* man's desire. This objectification gives Parry all of the power and places Joe in the submissive, traditionally feminine position merely able to wait for, and fear, and Parry's next attack. As Byers points out, "a male homosexual proposition puts the straight man in the traditionally feminine position of the *object*, rather than the *subject* of desire" and the male therefore "forfeits the prerogatives of patriarchy".[8] Perhaps to bring home this point, McEwan allows Parry to address Joe as a "tease", a "coquette", a master of slow torture, leading him on [Ch. 17, p. 141].

It seems imperative that in order to regain control over the narrative Joe must either contain or break the immediate threat of Parry and his emasculating gaze. Crucially, Parry is only truly threatening until he opens his mouth. Parry's mixture of accents is significant to our very English protagonist, Joe Rose, as to his immeasurable relief, it confirms his assumption that Parry is one "too hesitant and apologetic to say how things were in the world" [Ch. 2, p. 24]. Initially he poses a threat, like the "Indian brave" [Ch. 2, p. 24] to the English explorer, but then the value judgments of an English colonist are inscribed and prevail, and the threat is neutralized and "othered". Joe's question asserts itself as a command whilst Parry can only manage a "whine of powerlessness" [Ch. 2, p. 24]. Parry is from this moment relegated quite literally to the margins of discourse. Joe no longer takes him seriously. Throughout the rest of the novel Parry is constantly present, but just out of view. Joe seeks to extirpate him from his mind and encourages the reader to do likewise. It is only when the cracks in Joe's narrative cannot

7 Thomas Byers, 1995, 'Terminating the Postmodern: Masculinity and Pomophobia', *Modern Fiction Studies*, 41(1): pp. 5–33, p. 15.
8 Byers, 'Terminating the Postmodern', p. 14, Davies' emphasis.

ignored any longer that we see the damage Parry's discursive subversion has done.

Parry's gaze cannot ultimately be contained. It compels Joe to abandon his subject position in a reversal of the active/passive power constellations of traditional colonial adventure narratives. This Indian brave, by dint of his mere spiritual presence and unrelenting inquisitiveness, unsettles all the certainties that inform traditional western masculinity. Throughout *Enduring Love* Joe struggles to fight this erosion of his identity in a frantic, yet ultimately vain endeavour to salvage his former sense of control and supremacy. As Kenneth MacKinnon in *Uneasy Pleasures* explains:

> The male caught out . . . in a position deemed culturally feminine manifests his fear and loathing by energetic disavowal. Thus, the male who is looked at with desire may turn to exaggerated displays of machismo to assert his precarious sense of masculinity.[9]

And this is exactly the case for Joe, for we see a conscious effort on his part not only to overcome, but to erase his earlier inefficiency and transform himself into a swash-buckling hero who rescues his damsel in distress from a psychopathic homosexual killer.

The anti-hero

Joe's stalker, Jed Parry, is subject to no constraints of conscience, freely ignores social conventions and is "inviolable in his solipsism" [Ch. 17, p. 144]. As such, Parry is perfectly positioned to subvert all systems of control by which traditional society is bound. McEwan also gives Parry the power to contest the symbolic authority Joe Rose owns as a manipulator of the written word. As in the short story "Solid Geometry",[10] in *Enduring Love* the authority of history and scientific rationality rest with the male. However, whereas in the short story it is a literal phallus that is passed down through the generations with confidence and pride, in *Enduring Love*, Joe's privileged position within the symbolic order can no longer be taken for granted. Instead, it is questioned and then placed under assault. Through increasing scrutiny by Parry, Joe begins to doubt his own authority as an author. He begins to see himself as a "hack" and impostor, assuming an authorial stance to which he is not entitled. Parry becomes a demonic literary critic, performing a close reading of Joe's "thirty-five plus" articles [Ch. 16, p. 137] and coming to the sarcastic conclusion that "there is no problem with Joe Rose. His world is in place, everything fits, and all the problems are with Jed Parry" [Ch. 16, p. 136].

Luckily indeed, Joe discovers that Parry is in fact suffering from a well-documented neurosis: de Clérambault's syndrome. Sufferers of this mental affliction believe that the object of their obsession is in love with them, and a detailed observation of the world around them leads to the delirious detection of secret signals intended exclusively for their interpretation. Naturally, the reassurance

9   Mackinnon, *Uneasy Pleasures*, p. 27.
10 In *First Love, Last Rites*.

that Parry's condition is a proven disorder comes as a great relief to Joe by giving official sanction to his desire to write off this 'madman' once and for all. However, in spite of this diagnosis, Parry grows to inhabit the gaps and cracks within Joe's rationality, shrewdly pointing out that Joe's world depends solely on facts and intellectual arrogance. Joe Rose is shown to inhabit a postmodern atmosphere of apocalyptic hopelessness cursed by knowledge of a symbolic death-of-the-father, and of God. He seeks to maintain the illusion that he is king of his own castle; however, at the same time, he cannot stop Parry deconstructing and recontextualizing this illusion:

> I imagined you telling me in your cold way that God and His Only son were just characters, like *James Bond*, or Hamlet. Or that you yourself could make life in a laboratory flask, given a handful of chemicals and a few million years. It's not that you deny there's a God – *you want to take His place*. Pride like that can destroy you.
>
> [Ch. 16, pp. 136–7; Davies' emphasis]

To his own discomfort and consternation, Joe realizes that Parry is right. He is no James Bond or Hamlet and he cannot live up to the ideals that these universalized paragons of masculinity represent. Joe's inability to take control and prevent the ballooning tragedy is symptomatic of his increasing powerlessness. His professional life is also grinding to a halt, and he is not at all sure if he would survive a showdown with Parry. Moreover, it is becoming increasingly unlikely that he will get the girl at the end of the story. Parry's critical gaze has completely penetrated Joe's myth of superiority, sanity and control.

Parry touches a nerve when he claims: "Your mind is closed, your defences are in place. It suits you and it protects you to tell yourself that I'm a madman" [Ch. 16, pp. 135–6]. Relegated as mad and delusioned, Joe chooses to watch Parry's "antics" metaphorically from the other side of a pane of glass. Quite tellingly, however, Joe's insistence on singularity and his evasion of criticism can also be seen to replicate Homi Bhabha's analysis of the empire's need for absolute cultural rigidity. In *The Location of Culture*, Bhabha writes:

> Fixity, as the sign of cultural/historical/racial difference in the discourse of colonialism, is a paradoxical mode of representation: it connotes rigidity and an unchanging order as well as disorder, degeneracy and daemonic repetition.[11]

The reader cannot write off Parry's accusations and ultimately, neither can Joe. Despite Joe's insistence on his own singularity, sanity and rationality, disorder becomes an impending reality. Whatever Parry's mental problems, his analysis of Joe seems astonishingly sane and very accurate. Joe's control over the narrative is breaking down. The reader begins to hear things Joe is desperate to occlude and silence. The reader begins to doubt Joe's version of events.

---

11 Homi K. Bhabha, *The Location of Culture*, London: Routledge, 1994, p. 66.

The "hero"

Like many of his contemporaries, such as John Fowles, Julian Barnes, Irvine Welsh, Iain Banks and Michael Ondaatje, McEwan deliberately interferes with the authoritative stance of his protagonist, whose interaction with the other characters reveals that all is not as he would like to make us believe. After the trauma of the ballooning accident, Joe's previously mundane life is whisked out of control. It also becomes suspiciously likely that Joe *creates* the dramatic situation at the end of the novel so he can play the role of a god-like heroic figure. In Joe's words: "The task of getting us back to where we were going, was to be mine alone" [Ch. 18, p. 161]. Joe, it becomes clear, recounts the actions and events of his life to make up for its glaring shortcomings and absences. McEwan does not overtly allow Joe to dream of being Sean Connery; and yet, the hair-brained scheme at the climax of *Enduring Love* must be seen as an immediate corollary of Joe's "intent . . . to assert control over the future" [Ch. 4, p. 43]. Joe seems to be more or less unconsciously writing himself a narrative where he can play the hero.

Joe Rose seeks refuge in a fantasy that I argue is symptomatic of the British male literary psyche at the turn of the millennium. Many of McEwan's fellow authors have created fictions on the same theme: John Fowles in *Mantissa* (1982), Irvine Welsh in *Marabou Stork Nightmares* (1995) and Michael Ondaatje in *The English Patient* (1992), all feature male protagonists lying prostrate in hospital beds, existing only in a passive condition, continually subject to the control of others. They have all become the object of another's attention and are physically unable to seek out a position of agency. Suddenly deprived of strength, these male protagonists, like Cameron in Iain Banks's *Complicity* (1990) and Francis Brady in Patrick McCabe's *The Butcher Boy* (1992), retreat into their imagination to re-interpret their past by way of highly selective autobiographical memories. It is of crucial importance to Miles Green, Roy Strang, as well as Ondaatje's English patient to replay and edit their memories to remind themselves of their own starring roles in the fictions they themselves have created. Joe Rose, though not physically debilitated, fears impotence and resorts to a heroic fantasy not complete without a conspiracy theory, a shootout, a chase scene, a trip to the "other side" of civilization, a hostage-taking and, finally, the rescue of a woman detained by a madman.

On initial inspection, the novel's James Bond-like conclusion is highly unsatisfying because it seems to suggest that – despite everyone's doubts about Joe's sanity – he was right all along. However, such an overt assertion of male supremacy would be highly unusual for McEwan. To try and explain its function within *Enduring Love*, I shall turn to Kingsley Amis' commentary in *The James Bond Dossier*. Fiction such as Ian Fleming's James Bond stories are, according to Amis, "wish-fulfilments" and "collective power-fantas[ies] which are expressions of chauvinism at once smartened up and on its last legs".[12] Randall Stevenson concurs that Fleming's tales are exhibitions of contemporary consciousness

12 Kingsley Amis, *The James Bond Dossier*, London: Cape, 1965, pp. 88, 92.

reeling from the loss of empire and international status.[13] The luxurious locations, dangerous dealings and exciting events caught the imagination of a nation steeped in a severe confidence crisis. James Bond is, in effect, the modern adult equivalent of a superhero there to save the day.

Enduring Love, with its rational English protagonist, could be said to inhabit similar territory in the late 1990s and could perhaps be seen as emulating this genre. According to Jonathan Rutherford's definition, Joe's frantic activity is most certainly a prime example of the typical superheroic obfuscation of and compensation for emotional stress. As Rutherford explains, the "spectacle of the male body in action is the central signifier of the attempted recuperation of a humiliation and defeated masculine identity".[14] Joe composes his fiction with a subconscious craving for status and epistemic certainty. He begins to weave his own plot to distract himself from any intimations of his lack or loss of superiority. Joe is both Rutherford's "spectacle of masculinity attempting to assert itself over its crisis of identity" and MacKinnon's active male keen on reasserting his precarious sense of masculinity and reclaiming his position as the subject of both the action and the gaze. Hence, McEwan's conspicuous emphasis on action in *Enduring Love* is of the utmost significance. As Joe imagines for himself the most exciting and dramatic narrative in a choose-your-own-adventure style, McEwan is engaging with a much larger argument not all so dissimilar to Martin Green's in *Dreams of Adventure, Deeds of Empire*:

> The adventure tales that formed the light reading of Englishmen for two hundred years and more after Robinson Crusoe were, in fact, the energizing myth of English imperialism. They were, collectively, the story England told itself as it went to sleep at night; and, in the form of its dreams, they charged England's will with the energy to go out into the world and explore, conquer, and rule.[15]

McEwan as an English male writer has become conscious of perhaps always inevitably inscribing his own stories within and in response to a national grand narrative. By deliberately appropriating this adventure narrative, McEwan discloses not only the enduring assumptions of cultural imperialism but also the insidious inextricability of "Englishness" and "masculinity".

13 Randall Stevenson, *The British Novel since the 1930s*, London: Batsford, 1986, p. 143.
14 Jonathan Rutherford, *Men's Silences: Predicaments in Masculinity*, London: Routledge, 1992, pp. 187–8.
15 Martin Green, *Dreams of Adventure, Deeds of Empire*, New York: Basic Books, 1979, p. 3.

Paul Edwards, 'Solipsism, narrative and love in *Enduring Love*'

Paul Edwards is Professor of English and History of Art at Bath Spa University. His *Wyndham Lewis: Painter and Writer* was published by Yale University Press in 2000, and he has edited several of Lewis's books. An essay on McEwan's *The Child in Time* was published in *English* in 1995. He is currently the holder of a Leverhulme Research fellowship, researching 'Reality and Justice in Modernist Discourse'.

In his essay, Paul Edwards provides an overview of *Enduring Love*'s concern with a mix of psychology, philosophy and sociobiology (see Text and contexts, **p. 23**). From philosophy, he notes Joe's relationship to the British empiricist tradition of seventeenth- and eighteenth-century philosophers such as John Locke, David Hume and George Berkeley, who argued that *esse est percipi* (Latin for 'to be is to be perceived') is the essential feature of all sensible objects. Edwards uses this background to analyse the novel's position with regard to subjectivity and narration – the ways in which we make (sense of) our world. It is Jed's stories and beliefs that seem most obviously at odds with reality (for example, echoing the Romantic religious view that nature bears the hand of God-the-creator all around, Jed believes that Joe loves him and shows it repeatedly). However, it might also be true that Joe uses narrative to make the world to his own ends, and it is Joe who is privileged with the position of narrator in *Enduring Love*.

As Edwards notes, 'Narratives are a way of accommodating an uncomfortable reality', and both Jed and Joe are trying to find a narrative that fits the other's behaviour but that also fits their own understanding of reality. Human beings are subjective creatures, with partial knowledge and motives, trying to establish and agree upon a shared and objective reality (through religion or science, for example), but also trying to satisfy their embodied desires and preconceived beliefs (through religion or art, for example). As Edwards argues, finding the balance between the self and (significant) others, is a precarious endeavour for individuals, couples, families and lovers. Focusing, like Randall's essay, on the crucial aspect of narration, Edwards' essay also picks up on

Rhiannon Davies' observation that Joe describes Jed as 'inviolable in his solipsism' (Ch. 17, p. 144; see Critical Readings, **pp. 56–65** and **73**). From the Latin, 'solipsism' literally means the self alone, but its philosophical meaning denotes a belief that nothing exists outside of one's own mind. More generally it refers to an individual's tendency towards self-involvement, which, at an extreme, can result in mental and physical withdrawal from society and feelings of paranoia and persecution. Edwards traces Joe's own ideas about this tendency to project 'self-persuasion' onto reality, as Clarissa says Joe has done onto a maybe imaginary Jed. The novel raises the question of whether it is possible to guard against our 'solipsism' and reach truth.

Paul Edwards, 'Solipsism, narrative and love in *Enduring Love*'

Philosophical solipsism and psychological solipsism

One character in *Enduring Love* is branded a solipsist: Jed Parry. His beliefs in the reality of Joe Rose's love for him and in his own religious mission to bring Joe to God defy all the evidence of Joe's active dislike; rebuffs are only further proof of the mission of love that God has marked him out for: 'He was inviolable in his solipsism', Joe narrates (Ch. 17, p. 144). Joe evidently means that no evidence from the external world can shake Jed's delusions; his idea of reality is entirely self-generated. Joe uses the word 'solipsism' loosely, and we can easily see what he means by it. He is not suggesting that Jed has a philosophical belief in solipsism – far from it. As a philosophical theory, solipsism declares that there exists no reality outside one's own consciousness. It is a position that can flow from the idea that the sensing and mental apparatus through which we perceive the world affects how it is represented in our consciousness. The empiricist tradition in philosophy – that is, broadly, the British tradition encompassing John Locke, George Berkeley and David Hume – tried to distinguish between the respective contributions made to our perception of the world by the outside reality and by our own physical and mental apparatus of perception. For example, it could be argued that when we 'see' colour, we respond to real differences in the wavelengths of light 'out there', but that being conscious of these as colour differences is due to our perceptual apparatus 'in here'. The most daring solution to this problem of defining the boundaries of these two realms was that of Berkeley, who proposed that it could be solved by simply denying that there is any contribution from reality 'out there'; and if there is none, the existence of the external world is entirely due to its being perceived (*esse est percipi*). There is for him no residue of light waves or matter with mass and dimensions to cause our perceptual acts. This apparently bizarre solution seems to land us in philosophical solipsism: there exists no reality outside one's own consciousness. Berkeley thought that this consequence could be avoided. The founding act of 'perception' by which the world exists is performed by God, he maintains, and it is God's perception that holds the idea of an 'external' world in place for us. God guarantees that our perceptions are of a public world, the same for you and me. As far as Berkeley was concerned, all was now well; the entire 'outside world' had now been accounted for, and it was the shared world of common sense.

The purest philosophical solipsism, in a similar way, leaves everything as it found it, so it is at best nothing more than a truism: reality will disappear (for me) with the extinction of my consciousness. Since this is a view that adds nothing to what is already obvious, it can be discarded through a swipe of Ockham's razor (the philosophical move by which concepts and assumptions that aren't doing any work are removed from explanations and theories).[1] What we might call 'psychological' solipsism is another matter, however. One version would be a feeling or conviction that reality (including other people) depends on me for its existence; other people are 'fictional' characters in my own mind. Such a belief is obviously deranged. More subtly deranged is the version that afflicts Jed, where what he takes to be a shared, public world (in which Joe is in love with him) is actually a private delusion. It is worth noting at this point that the first of these two versions of 'psychological solipsism' is not so obviously deranged – not deranged at all, on the face of it – when we apply it to works of fiction. The characters in *Enduring Love* exist only as imaginary repetitions in the reader's mind of what the author has previously imagined. They really do depend upon McEwan for their existence. When Joe drives to Oxford on the M40 at close to 140 mph, it is McEwan's willed choice that he should not crash or be stopped by the police for speeding. This state of affairs is one that most novelists do not want their readers to be conscious of, and McEwan's text is full of references to a known (or knowable) public world in which the events of the novel are supposed to take place. For example, the area where Joe and Clarissa have their walk and picnic in the Chilterns near Pishill 'really' exists. Even so, the novel is in some respects a 'closed' world. It looks as if we get outside it in the appendix, but we definitely cannot go outside the text and find out a bit more about Clarissa – to check whether she really does weigh 80 pounds less than Joe, or to find out whether she really is as fixated on Keats as she seems to be.

It is easy to dismiss these matters as trivial intellectual amusements. But *Enduring Love* is about a series of episodes in its characters' lives when dealing with such problems is crucial. One of McEwan's great strengths as a novelist is his ability to show how concrete experience is implicated with frameworks of abstract ideas, and to do so in a way that enriches rather than dilutes the reader's empathetic imagination of that experience. Curiously, when we are given raw experience without reflections on it (as in the climactic scene of Joe's dramatic rescue of Clarissa), the thinning of the texture of the narrative leaves the imagined experience feeling thin too. Contrast this scene with the opening of the novel, which has been universally praised for its intense vividness. It is not just that McEwan increases narrative suspense at the opening by interpolating reflective passages that slow the pace, but that these reflections are part of the meticulous

---

1 'Ockham's razor' refers to the principle laid down by the medieval English philosopher, William of Ockham (c. 1285–1347), that explanations should be reduced to as economical a form as possible, and unnecessary assumptions and entities should be discarded from them: 'Entities should not be multiplied unnecessarily.'

re-creation of the scene through the memory of its narrator, Joe. The narrative medium thereby implicitly asserts that there is another side to the problem of separating the objective elements of events from the subjective frameworks we bring to them. These frameworks can lead to shared understanding as well as isolated delusion. Joe's (the novel's) framework for understanding and explaining the uncertainties and problems of the events in the story is not the philosophical one I have sketched here, however, but that of an extension of Darwinism into human affairs, known as sociobiology.

The distortions of subjectivity

If implicitly, through McEwan's narrative style, the novel celebrates the subjective contribution to our experience of reality, explicitly it seems to do the opposite, as it is almost a compendium of the distortions subjectivity apparently causes, and a lament over our inability to perceive objectively. As perceivers of external reality, humans are biased and selectively attentive. Reflecting on his own and others' faulty recollections of the lunchtime assassination attempt on him in a restaurant full of distracting activity, Joe comments: 'I felt a familiar disappointment. No one could agree on anything. We lived in a mist of half-shared, unreliable perception, and our sense data came warped by a prism of desire and belief, which tilted our memories too' (Ch. 20, p. 180).

Joe's axiom, 'believing is seeing' (Ch. 20, p. 181), reverses the well-known saying and encapsulates this subjective bias: we 'see' what our preconceptions make us believe we are seeing. Did the hit man shoot before the diners began their sorbets (or ice creams?) or were the desserts splashed with the victim's blood before Joe had a chance to taste his lime-flavoured (or was it apple?) treat? (See Ch. 19, p. 171 and Ch. 20, p. 181.) These are trivial instances, but along with other uncertainties they are sufficient to lead the police to reject Joe's insistence that he was himself the intended victim. I have already mentioned Joe's painstaking attempt to reconstruct from the chaos of uncoordinated actions of a whole group of people what 'really' happened in the ballooning accident. One feature of that is particularly important to the widow of the man who died, since she believes that her husband was there picnicking with a secret lover after pretending to her that he would be at a conference in London. When he ran from his car to help, were there two doors open or one, she asks Joe, but he can't remember (Ch. 13, p. 113). As readers, we perhaps look back to Joe's account at the beginning of the book (as if we could rewind the film) but find simply that the car 'was banked on the grass verge with its door, or doors, wide open' (Ch. 1, p. 2). Joe's account is filled out by what Clarissa remembers, too, however (Ch. 1, p. 2), and after his talk with Logan's widow he checks with her: 'she thought Logan's car had two doors open, perhaps even three' (Ch. 17, p. 147); the facts don't seem to be possible to fix.[2] It is important to know, since it appears crucial to deciding

---

2   It is important to remember that the novel is not an argument for complete scepticism or solipsism. However, as I shall go on to show, we do eventually discover that three doors must have been open: the driver's and those of his two hitch-hiking passengers (Bonnie Deedes in the front and her lover, the 'Euler Professor of Logic', James Reid, in the back) (Ch. 24, p. 228).

whether Logan (normally a cautious man, we learn [Ch. 14, p. 122]) was 'a good man' who 'wanted to save that kid' in the basket of the balloon, as Clarissa wants to believe (Ch. 3, pp. 31, 32), or abandoned his usual caution, as his wife believes, because he was 'showing off to a girl' by hanging on to the rope too long (Ch. 14, p. 123). Believing is seeing.

Persuasive narratives

Joe's private comment on Mrs Logan's belief signals another 'bias' militating against objectivity: 'This was a theory, a narrative that only grief, the dementia of pain, could devise' (Ch. 14, p. 123). Facts once known (if they can be) still need interpretation. Logan's death also fits two other narratives that Joe has already proposed to himself: 'He was the hero, and it was the weak [the ones who had let go of the ropes by which the balloon could be secured] who had sent him to his death. Or, we were the survivors and he was the miscalculating dolt' (Ch. 6, p. 56). The sight of Mrs Logan 'in pantomime widow's weeds' with her two children 'clinging to her knees' evokes another narrative, derived from the sentimental conventions of Victorian salon art.

Narrative, we are frequently reminded, falsifies, even when the 'facts' are clear. Again, it is Joe who makes the case, when he discusses an example of apparent canine cunning reported in correspondence in the scientific journal, *Nature*, in 1904. 'What I liked here was how the power and attractions of narrative had clouded judgement' (Ch. 4, p. 41). A behaviourist account that eliminated conscious trickery from the dog's usurpation of its master's comfortable chair would be equally adequate to the facts. Later, talking to the police about the attempted murder, Joe faces a less theoretical example. Now he himself believes that the facts speak for themselves: 'the disposition of events would do the work' (Ch. 20, p. 177), but the narrative deduced by DC Wallace is one that leads him simply to advise Joe to take a double dose of Prozac. For Jed Parry, of course, the facts also speak for themselves: they show unequivocally that Joe loves him.

The report of the apparently cunning dog leads Joe (still traumatised by the balloon incident but as yet scarcely troubled by Parry) to write an article 'as an evasion' (Ch. 5, p. 48). His argument, supported by various factual examples, is that nineteenth-century science was in thrall to the contemporary 'narrative' way of understanding that dominated through the great novels of the period. Modern science, on the other hand, is governed by a 'modernist' paradigm in which canons of formal coherence and aesthetic elegance predominate. He pursues the theory and elaborates it with dogged persistence for three hours and an (enviable) total of 2,000 words, without 'trick[ing] myself from my chair with promises of coffee' (Ch. 5, pp. 50, 48). But he eventually realises that what he has produced is also just a narrative, one that fits the selection of facts he has made, but which would not fit an equally valid set of contradictory examples. Narratives are a way of accommodating an uncomfortable reality, sometimes by falsifying it and evading it. Joe overcomes his trauma by repeated narration: 'I found myself using the same phrases, the same adjectives in the same order. It became possible to recount the events [of the balloon accident] without re-living them in the faintest degree, without even remembering them' (Ch. 3, p. 36).

There are various kinds of circularity and self-referentiality involved in this treatment of narrative, to some of which I shall return. In Joe's article a narrative about narrative has been created then discarded – to be replaced, perhaps, by a further narrative. Some overarching narrative is required (from God's perspective, 'outside the text') in order to reveal the full truth about anything. Human narratives are unreliable because they may not be motivated by a desire to get closer to reality (they may be some kind of 'evasion') and because, when they are about human beings, crucial knowledge of motivations is not available; Logan may be a hero, or he may be a dolt. One's own motivations may be equally obscure; Joe believes he is visiting Logan's widow to assure her of her husband's courage, but, he realises, he may really be visiting her 'to establish my guiltlessness, my innocence of his death' (Ch. 12, p. 107). The wildest narrative in the novel is Jed Parry's, telling how Joe has fallen in love with him and how all Joe's actions are evidence for the development of this deep and compelling relationship.

Narrative relativity

Joe gives us a Darwinian perspective on the unreliability of narratives, summarised in the phrase, 'self-persuasion' (Ch. 12, p. 104). In social interaction, the reality principle may simply not make for the survival of the individual, and it may be to our evolutionary advantage to lie, even to ourselves:

> persuading others of your own needs and interests [is] fundamental to your well-being. [. . .] Clearly you would be at your most convincing if you persuaded yourself first and did not even have to pretend to believe what you were saying. The kind of self-deluding individuals who tended to do this flourished, as did their genes. So it was we squabbled and scrapped, for our unique intelligence was always at the service of our special pleading and selective blindness to the weaknesses of our case.
> (Ch. 12, p. 104)

It is a perspective that the novel returns to, in the reflections on the unreliability of the witnesses' accounts of the shooting in the restaurant: 'Pitiless objectivity, especially about ourselves, was always a doomed social strategy' (Ch. 20, pp. 180–1).

Traditional realist novels have a way of shortcutting the potentially infinite series of framing narratives that a reader would need to traverse to reach an ultimate certainty: the device of the third-person omniscient narrator. As the word 'omniscient' implies, this narrator stands in relation to the world of a particular novel as God stands in relation to the real world, and we do not normally question this type of narrator's capacity to deliver final judgements. But, to compound the problems of secure knowledge I have outlined, *Enduring Love* has no omniscient third-person narrator. Most of it is a first-person narration by the protagonist Joe, and first-person narrators have the potential to be highly unreliable. There are also chapters comprising letters by other characters. Chapter 11 and Appendix II are letters written by Parry to Joe, and Chapter 23 is a letter to Joe from Clarissa. These letters give us direct access to these characters, so we are not entirely confined to Joe's (subjective) understanding of them. Chapter 9 is a curious hybrid, written as if by an omniscient narrator but actually by Joe, giving Clarissa's point of view 'as I later construed it' (Ch. 9, p. 79). In the context of the novel's running critique of narrative, Joe's ability to 'spin a decent narrative' (Ch. 8, p. 75) may be a dubious asset, even if he is more open to another person's point of view than DC Wallace. So in this novel there appears to be no conventional limit on the infinite regress of narratives and no access to the 'final' one that would provide certainty. The novel does gives us an apparently more 'authoritative' narrative in Appendix I, the scientific paper by Robert Wenn and Antonio Camia, 'Reprinted from the *British Review of Psychiatry*' (Appendix I, p. 233) and supported by citation of an extensive literature on de Clérambault's syndrome. Most of the references in the article's bibliography appear to be to genuine papers actually accessible in appropriate libraries, so this takes us 'outside the frame' of the fiction. The paper itself, however, is simply an alternative 'scientific' perspective on the story, supplying us with a few extra pieces of information.[3] Its claim to extra authority is a trick. There is, apparently, no finally authoritative perspective within *Enduring Love*.

These theoretical considerations, all raised in the narrative itself (except the status of the scientific literature), might in themselves encourage a 'postmodern' reading of the novel in which each of its three main characters are solipsists and there is no fixed perspective available from which to adjudicate among them. Each of their versions of what is going on accounts for the 'facts'. But actually such a totally relativist reading, with each isolated 'solipsist' equally justified, would be mistaken, though we can imagine an alternative incarnation of the novel where it would not be. In this 'alternative', Jed's narrative (in which Joe is in love with him); or Clarissa's suspected version (in which Jed simply seeks a little understanding and support, while Joe, under stress himself, builds up a paranoid fantasy of persecution, using as evidence letters he has actually written himself); or Joe's (in which he is the victim of a deluded stalker but is on his own because his lover Clarissa's intuition takes no account of reason or evidence) would all be equally valid. The same physical events as take place in the novel that we have could still occur, yet these three contrasting interpretations of them could still be imagined as equally viable.

Had McEwan chosen to write this alternative conception of the novel, and had done so with sufficient skill and ingenuity to leave us as readers in this state of uncertainty, he might have produced a more aesthetically impressive novel than he did (it is easy for an unwritten novel to achieve perfection). But he did not. In the novel we have, it must be emphasised, Joe is basically right about what is happening. Despite all the difficulties of knowledge and despite the pressure of others' scepticism, Joe, helped by the scientific knowledge he acquires about de

---

3   The surnames of the authors, Wenn and Camia, form an anagram of Ian McEwan, so the effect of having come outside the frame of the novel itself is partly an illusion; we remain in the fictional world, or on its borders. Note that beyond the final page of the second appendix there is an 'acknowledgements' page, written by McEwan in his own person. Here, it seems, we are at last outside the novel. Some early reviewers of the novel assumed that 'Wenn and Camia's' paper was genuine, and that McEwan had fictionalised a real case study. See Laura Miller, 'Ian McEwan Fools British Shrinks'. Available at <http://www.salon.com/books/log/1999/09/21/mcewan>. (Accessed 23 February 2005.)

Clérambault's syndrome, and using it to interpret Jed's likely behaviour (Ch. 17, p. 142), is able to predict that behaviour and intervene to prevent it. Jed, on the other hand, is genuinely completely deluded – insane, even. Clarissa's suspicions are quite misplaced. And it might be felt that the pumped-up thriller elements of the story's climax – Clarissa held hostage and rescued by Joe with a fortuitously disabling shot from his illicitly acquired Browning 9-millimetre handgun – are simply a narrative distraction from the slight anticlimax of Joe's having been right all along.

A world made in common

But nothing is as cheap as relativism, not even, perhaps, the narrative devices of cheap thrillers and, philosophically, McEwan was evidently more concerned to tackle the more difficult and more worthwhile question of how it can be that there is actually a correct (or objective) version of this story even though so much of what 'happens' is not just concrete fact but is saturated with the subjective dimensions of belief and emotion. Given that so much of our experience is private to ourselves, how do we manage to have a world in common? In other words, instead of making the easy (and uninteresting) point that we are all, like Jed Parry, living versions of reality that are 'true for us', the novel asks why we are (at least most of us, most of the time), not like Parry. It also tries to understand what, morally, it means to have a world in common.

That common world is the correlate of a shared biology. Joe comments on the 'universal', 'genetically inscribed' emotion of joy as it is expressed by the multi-cultural collection of welcomers at the airport, each person greeting their newly arrived loved one in an almost identical fashion (Ch. 1, p. 4). We have a species-specific repertoire of emotions and responses that are pre-cultural, as Joe again notes, accounting for his own almost unconscious response to the hidden presence of Parry in the London library: 'Wasn't [fear] an elemental emotion, along with disgust, surprise, anger and elation, in Ekman's celebrated cross-cultural study?' (Ch. 4, p. 43.)[4] It kicks in again shortly afterwards as a shot of noradrenalin to the heart, when the person creeping up behind him turns out to be Clarissa (Ch. 5, p. 51) (there are other moments, as we shall see, when the novel, slightly ominously, associates Clarissa with Parry). Such physiological reactions are pre-cultural, but our shared world of culture is built on these foundations. Culture is the shared subjective superstructure by which the immediate world of physical actions and responses (as well as things we make, such as signs) 'mean' something extra, or convey messages to us.[5] Language is an example: without a knowledge of a language, to a hearer its sounds will remain simply a set of voiced

---

4   The reference is to Paul Ekman's work in extending and modifying Darwin's study of the expression of emotion. For example, P. Ekman, 'Expression and the Nature of Emotion', in K. Scherer and P. Ekman (eds) *Approaches to Emotion*, Hillsdale, NJ: Erlbaum, 1984, pp. 319–44. Joe gives a fuller Darwinian perspective on our shared psychology in Chapter 8, pp. 69–70.
5   The 'meaning' referred to here is what H. P. Grice called 'non-natural meaning'. Natural 'meaning' is exemplified by such observations as 'the sun setting means that it will soon be dark'; on the other hand, 'the red light at the road junction means you must stop' is an example of cultural, 'non-natural meaning'. See H. P. Grice, 'Meaning' (1948, 1957) in *Studies in the Way of Words*, Cambridge, Mass.: Harvard University Press, 1989, pp. 213–23.

noises; with knowledge (culture) they becomes words, sentences and meanings. This is one way that we differ from the dog, who, even if it learns to respond consistently with a repertoire of behaviours for a range of voiced noises does not, we assume, understand the noises as parts of a language system. Language, as well as other language-based superstructures, extends reality to a degree that transfigures it from what it would otherwise be. A basic physical skill such as catching a small moving object in flight is shared by dogs and humans, for example, but only humans play cricket, in which accomplishing this feat when one is 'fielding', counts as getting an opponent 'out'. Notoriously, cricket is a quite incomprehensible and tedious game for anyone who happens to be watching without knowing any of the rules; to one who knows its conventions and rules, however, it can be absorbing. A pure physical capacity, common to the species, is being built on here, as in most games involving physical skill (games such as chess or bridge are built on something else that may nevertheless be just as basic).

But it is not only in games that our actions take on an additional meaning. A key feature of de Clérambault's syndrome is an aberrant attribution of meaning to physical actions. If Joe moves the curtains, it means simply that the sun is in his eyes or it's getting dark, but for Jed Parry these movements are coded messages that 'mean' love (Ch. 8, p. 72). Joe's brushing the privet hedge with his hand means nothing at all, but for Jed the touch creates 'a pattern that spelled a simple message' of overwhelming love (Ch. 11, p. 96). In these cultural superstructures, then, is another danger of solipsism, of failure to connect. Jed is an extreme case, in that his misinterpretations can never be corrected (even the fact that Joe shoots him proves Joe's love for him, as it prevents Jed from committing suicide (Appendix I, p. 238), but anyone can make mistakes. When Joe goes through Clarissa's desk and reads her letters it means that he has paranoid suspicions of her faithfulness because of her lack of understanding of his predicament. But for her (as for Parry) it must 'mean' something more:

> You even left the drawer open so I'd know when I came in. It's a statement, a message, from you to me, it's a signal. The trouble is, I don't know what it means. Perhaps I'm being very stupid. So spell it out for me now, Joe. What is it you're trying to tell me?
>
> (Ch. 15, p. 132)[6]

Love as biology, love as culture

Enduring Love is concerned above all with one human phenomenon that comprises both a natural foundation and a cultural overlay. As the title suggests, it is

---

6   A reader may be tempted by the popular conception of the unconscious into thinking that 'subconsciously', Joe really does want to send a message (even that, subconsciously, he returns Jed's love). *Enduring Love* does not seem to subscribe to the idea of this kind of unconscious, however. It uses, rather, the sociobiological notion of 'self-persuasion' (discussed on **p. 82**). It is used to explain the covert processes (hidden meanings) of Joe's actions in reading Clarissa's correspondence in Ch. 12, pp. 104–5.

love. Jed's love for Joe is not itself the central issue but is a distorting mirror in which we can trace the lineaments of 'normal' love: specifically the love of Clarissa and Joe. Jed's 'love' serves this function on a conceptual level (which is the level at which most of the present analysis has taken place): it 'was a dark, distorting mirror that reflected and parodied a brighter world of lovers' and hence might 'reveal . . . the nature of love itself' (Ch. 15, p. 128). On a narrative level it is the trigger for a crisis that forces Joe and Clarissa to examine their love and move on to a new stage: 'In other words, what could I learn about Parry that would restore me to Clarissa?' (Ch. 15, p. 128.) The novel, through Joe, proposes that love is one of the basic, biological, human universals, but Joe appears to be uneasy about saying what else it might be beyond that: 'all that sincerity would permit me were the facts, and they seemed miraculous enough to me: a beautiful woman loved and wanted to be loved by a large, clumsy, balding fellow who could hardly believe his luck' (Ch. 1, p. 7). But facts do not speak for themselves, and in Western (and all other) societies, love is profoundly 'cultural' – indeed, the purest and highest love is that which completely transcends its biological foundations and perhaps even turns against them. Love is not just physical desire. Nevertheless the novel is not concerned with criticising Joe for his banal, fact-based description of what he does, after all, recognise as 'miraculous'. Gifts and sharing are components of love, and Joe performs well in this department, buying Clarissa a first edition of Keats's poems, as well as packing her a gourmet picnic to share on her return from America at the beginning of the book.[7] Clarissa, on the other hand, is well versed in the cultural overlays that make love what it is and argues against Joe's relentless reduction of it in their conversations to the concepts of evolutionary psychology: the baby that awakens its mother's love survives. Unlike Joe, however, Clarissa may be good at receiving the homage due to a loved object (the book, physical pampering, the birthday lunch and a valuable brooch from her godfather), but is not much of a giver.

One of the cultural overlays that have made 'love' what it is in the West is the 'love letter', and here Clarissa has an expertise that amounts to an obsession. Having in the early days of her relationship with Joe attempted to write letters that would express (as against Joe's plodding recognition of the 'facts') the uniqueness of their love (Ch. 1, p. 7), seven years later she is (officially as part of her academic research) travelling the world on the trail of a lost, unsent last love letter she is convinced the dying John Keats must have written to Fanny Brawne. For her, Joe believes, 'love that did not find its expression in a letter was not perfect' (Ch. 1, p. 7). He jokingly refers to Keats as a rival lover for Clarissa (Ch. 1, p. 8). In one of the ironies of the novel that insidiously link Clarissa to the insane Parry, the only 'perfect' love letters here are those written to Joe by Parry.[8] The second of these, a 'birthday letter' written three years into his

---

7   The copy of Keats's *Poems* is likely to have cost around £10,000.
8   The 'Dear Joe' beginning Chapter 23 (p. 216) is likely to cause momentary confusion in the reader's mind, and may at first be taken for another letter from Parry. 'I'm sorry about our row' would be an appropriately mild response from him to being shot in the elbow. The letter is actually from the ostensibly repentant Clarissa but is full of veiled, resentful reproaches. She announces that she is separating from Joe and moving to her brother's vacant flat. An earlier note from her was signed 'Love, Clarissa' (Ch. 20, p. 183); this is merely signed 'Clarissa'. Joe's judgement of the letter's 'wounded, self-righteous tone' (Ch. 24, p. 222) is surely correct.

incarceration when he must know he has little chance of meeting his love again, shows him exalted by love beyond the physical hell of his grubby lifelong confinement: 'I've never felt so free. I'm soaring, I'm so happy, Joe!' (Appendix II, p. 245). Once she has separated from Joe, Clarissa maintains her obsessive quest for the perfect Keatsian love letter. She plans to fly to Japan, not to find the letter, but to read another scholar's notes – further and further from the authoritative document. They are actually no more than notes from a reading of correspondence in the British Library (a mile or so away from her new flat in Camden). The correspondence is by a 'distant relation', not of Keats, but of his friend Joseph Severn, and she already knows what the notes say (Ch. 24, p. 221). A reader from outside the academic world may well surmise that such a research trip is customary in that privileged world (elsewhere a fax or airmailed photocopy would suffice), but it is not. Something is not quite right with Clarissa.

One of the extensions of love into the public world is the institution of marriage. It is a step that Clarissa and Joe have not taken, and their relationship remains undefined and a matter of their own, private understanding. Joe twice simply identifies Clarissa as 'my friend' (Ch. 2, p. 26, Ch. 13, p. 113), while Wenn and Camia give her the culturally chilling title of Joe's 'common-law wife' (Appendix I, p. 237). This is not a designation with any force in the legal framework that regulates marriage in England. Confiding in the reader at the outset, however, Joe thinks in terms of marriage: 'We were seven years into a childless marriage of love' (Ch. 1, p. 8). It is as if the private emotion of love itself can validate this version of 'marriage'. In its religious sense, marriage is a sacrament sanctifying the procreation of children, but they have no children, for Clarissa is infertile as a result of medical treatment that went wrong. It is a desolating affliction for her (Ch. 3, p. 31). How, then, can Joe and Clarissa be sure of their love? At first glance it seems that their still-flourishing sex life is a guarantee (Ch. 3, pp. 33–4), and when, in the depths of their alienation from each other, facing each other in bed, Joe feels a repetition of a familiar wordless, slow arousal, it seems that this is indeed sufficient (Ch. 17, pp. 144–5). But this arousal and its hoped-for effects exist solely in Joe's world, not Clarissa's, for she is about to announce that she thinks they are 'finished' as a couple; they are still in 'very different mental universes' (Ch. 9, p. 82).

Love is potentially a private madness (as it is for Parry), and not even the Euler Professor of Logic at Oxford is immune. Against all reason and logic he is about to abandon his career and reputation because he is smitten by the 'blonde, blue-eyed peachiness' of a self-centred girl thirty years his junior (Ch. 24, pp. 227, 228). Clarissa's 'adulterous' brother is about to get divorced because of 'love', and Joe imagines him reciting to her 'the relentless plainsong of the divorce novitiate – the pained self-advocacy that hymns the transmutations of love into hatred or indifference' (Ch. 5, p. 46). Something prior to morality is at stake here: it is a terrible human instability that leaves people the victims of their own errant subjectivity.[9]

---

9   Note that the issue of morality and moral relativism is discussed by Joe and Mrs Logan's children in
    Ch. 14, pp. 119–20.

God and science

At the outset of this essay I pointed out that philosophers had 'used' God as a guarantee of validity for our external perceptions. It has to be a particular kind of God that we can trust for that purpose, however, one who himself is communally recognised as authoritative through shared texts, rituals and practices that conform to canons of rationality. This was pre-eminently the case with God in Berkeley's time, and his God answers well to the sardonic description given by Ernest Gellner of the God of Descartes – who performs a similar function of guaranteeing our knowledge of the world – as 'an exceedingly bourgeois deity' who only issues guarantees for subjective states that are 'orderly, clear, distinct, systematic – in brief, *rationally* compelling'.[10] How different from the God of Jed Parry, whose guarantee is extended to cover any wild inner conviction. This God is a Romantic descendant of the Protestant God, a God for the isolated individual, who finds Him through his or her own intuitions. Joe gives an accurate account of Parry's God as revealed through his letters:

> Often, God was a term interchangeable with self. God's love for mankind shaded into Parry's love for me. God was undeniably 'within' rather than in his heaven, and believing in him was therefore a licence to respond to the calls of feeling or intuition. . . . There were no constraints of theological nicety or religious observance, no social sanction or congregational calling to account, none of the moral framework that made religions viable, however failed their cosmologies. Parry listened only to the inner voice of his private God.
>
> (Ch. 18, pp. 152–3)

Parry declares that he wishes to set Joe 'free from his little cage of reason' (ironically seeing him as the one confined in solipsism) (Ch. 16, p. 133), and this cannot but remind us of Clarissa's attitude to Joe's rationality. At first condescendingly indulgent of it ('You're such a dope. You're so rational sometimes you're like a child' [Ch. 3, p. 33]), she later characterises it as a form of madness, 'rationalism gone berserk', when it presumes to analyse and account for 'love' (Ch. 8, p. 70). Clarissa is *almost* (this qualification is important) a Jed Parry who has dispensed with his reliance on a 'God' to validate her convictions, believing that the quality of the convictions is its own guarantee. For her (at least according to Joe's account, which seems to be supported by her later letter), Joe's systematic scientific investigation of de Clérambault's syndrome and his analysis of Parry's words and actions are 'unhinged' and 'mad' (Ch. 18, p. 150). Evidently she regards him (as does Parry) as a 'solipsist', inside his own head and not connecting with the outside world: 'You say he's outside, but when I go out there's no one. No one, Joe' (Ch. 17, p. 148). When Joe speaks factually and truthfully about Parry she accuses him of 'not speaking from the heart' (Ch. 12, p. 103). As Joe, apparently accurately, states, 'Clarissa thought that her emotions were the

10 Ernest Gellner, *Reason and Culture: The Historic Role of Rationality and Rationalism*, Oxford: Blackwell, 1992, p. 12.

appropriate guide, that she could feel her way to the truth' (Ch. 18, p. 150), and in this she is identical to Parry. The difference is that, finally, she is capable of changing her mind.

In the stand-off between on the one hand Darwinian science and on the other religious belief and its humanist remnants, the novel would seem, then, to come down on the side of the former. Not only does the plot reinforce this (Joe the scientist and rationalist is proved right about Parry; Clarissa's intuitions are shown to be wrong), but science is allowed to explain religion away. Even Joe had caught himself momentarily almost restrained by the remnants of a faith in God in his moment of 'self-persuasion' when he wandered into Clarissa's room to look at her correspondence (Ch. 12, p. 105), but the novel seems to endorse his pre-dominant view that such ineffective remnants are in fact all that are left of God. Typically, in one of his articles (one that particularly enrages Parry), Joe explains how the methods and techniques of science have made it possible to trace the 'invention' and development of 'God' and to disentangle the elements that went into the invention of Christ in the writings of St Paul and whoever wrote the Gospel of St Mark (Ch. 16, p. 134). God is just another product of narratives, not the guarantee of their ultimate truth. Likewise, the Darwinian rationale for religion, as an individual and communal version of 'self-persuasion' that confers selective advantage in evolution, is rehearsed in one of Joe's inner monologues (Ch. 18, p. 159). When Joe praises science (along with metaphysics) as 'such courageous enterprises, such startling inventions [. . .] human artefacts set right against the grain of human nature' (Ch. 20, p. 181), he is voicing an important truth.[11]

A marriage of true minds

Joe's rationalism and scientism may be the best guides in the emergency he faces, but this does not mean that they are in all respects adequate. When Clarissa and Joe argue about the two paradigms of (roughly) Romantic feeling and scientific analysis, Clarissa's resistance to what she sees as Darwinian science's reduction of larger wholes to their gritty origins in evolutionary function establishes a valid point, or at least enters an important caveat. For although humans are grounded in biology, we have seen that they are able to extend their world through culture in a way that transfigures mere function, something this novel shows as essential but also hazardous. Looked at from the perspective of biological function, Clarissa is simply redundant, despite the few token 'carer' functions she fulfils, for she is incapable of reproducing, and she apparently has no family beyond her brother. Yet there are human institutions by which these merely biological lacks are supplemented. Ironically (given the novel's scepticism about religion), one of these is the system of virtual kinship validated by the church. Clarissa has no surviving parents, but she has a godfather who is very generous to her (Ch. 19, p. 162). She has no children, but there is a room in the flat that she calls 'the

---

11 Note that this characterisation of science acknowledges that it is another cultural overlay beyond, but apparently contradicting, biological evolutionary function.

children's room' (Ch. 17, p. 149), which is used by her 'extended' family of seven godchildren. Both Joe and Clarissa care for them occasionally, like parents. Finally, it is a further cultural and institutional extension of the biological family that, beyond the confines of Joe's narrative, contributes to our realisation that they have 'moved on' and re-established some kind of constructive relationship after the crisis the novel recounts. Wenn and Camia report that after their separation they 'were reconciled and later successfully adopted a child', even though few other relationships survive the stress of persecution by a de Clérambault's sufferer (Appendix I, p. 242). We do not know if they marry, but must assume that their experience of adoptive parenthood is fulfilling (or 'successful', in the clinical vocabulary of the case study).

In retrospect, it seems to Joe that the rigidity of the battle-lines they drew up between science and Romanticism were a cover for something else: 'What we were really talking about this time was the absence of babies from our life' (Ch. 8, p. 71). At first glance, since it is Clarissa whose life has been apparently desolated by the lack of a child, it would seem that there is a covert sexist message in the book that women's function is motherhood and that without this role they become irrational and obsessed. But the novel by no means confines this 'need' to women, and it seems that the novel is actually more interested in fatherhood than in motherhood. Clarissa believes that Joe 'would have made a wonderful father' (Ch. 14, p. 118), and he certainly takes to the role. In a kind of rehearsal for his later role as 'virtual' or cultural father, in the final chapter of the book he briefly acts as surrogate father to Jean Logan's now fatherless children at the third (and only successful) picnic in the book. He captivates the young Rachael's imagination by describing the river before them in scientific terms as a long shallow chute down which an almost infinite number of molecules slide to the sea (Ch. 24, p. 225). It is a description that belies the view of John Keats that 'science was robbing the world of wonder' (Ch. 8, p. 71) and appropriately thereby reconciles the different perspectives of Joe and Clarissa.

The novel does not recount that reconciliation in full or delineate their future 'successful' relationship, but we do not need to rely on Wenn and Camia's aside to know that it occurs; the narrative method of the novel itself offers proof. Just as in the account of the ballooning accident Joe incorporates Clarissa's memories in order to establish as truthful a representation as possible, so the composite Chapter 9 could only have been written by Joe after the whole crisis has passed ('as I later construed it') (Ch. 9, p. 79). It is exemplary in its re-creation, through discussion, cooperation and imagination, of a reality that appeared at the time irreconcilably bifurcated. In a world where simple biology is overlaid by culture, the establishment of a shared reality – the avoidance of solipsism – must be a social, joint endeavour. But it is a precarious achievement whose security can never be guaranteed. All sorts of accidents can blow us off course, and it takes teamwork to keep us grounded. Despite our efforts at cooperation it is always possible to float away, 'soaring' (Appendix II, p. 245) into solipsistic delusion.

Sean Matthews, 'Seven types of unreliability'

Sean Matthews is the Director of the D. H. Lawrence Research Centre at the University of Nottingham, where he teaches modern and contemporary literature. Current projects include a study of Raymond Williams for Routledge, an account of 1980s and 1990s fiction to be published by Edinburgh University Press, and an introduction to contemporary writing for Continuum.

In the ballooning accident that opens the book, McEwan presents one example of the kinds of cooperative behaviour analysed by game theory in which a shared goal can be achieved by everyone taking the same selfless course of action but in which each participant also has to calculate the likely behaviour of the others and make a judgement on their own best decision as an individual (the theory is mentioned explicitly later: 'the evolutionary perspective, drawn from game theory' [Ch. 22, p. 206]).[1] In this instance, one unnamed person's decision to save themselves has resulted in Logan's death, Joe believes.

The psychological blow of their collective failure is acute for Joe as he struggles to decide whether or not that person was him. Following this line of inquiry, the reader can consider the extent to which Joe's narrative is an attempt to excuse, forgive or account for himself. Joe's narration in *Enduring Love* is not in competition with another – he does not need to cooperate or consult in telling his story – and the critic must at some point ask questions about the degree to which Joe's account of events is reliable.

Issues of narration have been analysed at various points throughout this book and, having explored reasons for scepticism in Randall's essay (see Critical readings, **pp. 56–65**) and matters of solipsism in Edwards' (see Critical readings, **pp. 78–80**), this next essay by Sean Matthews takes the debate in another

---

1   Game theory is a branch of applied mathematics that studies how people try to maximise their returns in different (economic, social, psychological) situations or 'games'. See the section entitled 'Cultural contexts' in Text and contexts, **pp. 21–7** for a fuller discussion of game theory and the 'Prisoner's Dilemma'.

important direction by considering questions of trustworthiness and sanity. In particular, Matthews dissects the narration by offering a taxonomy of unreliability in which Joe Rose's knowledge, self-knowledge, veracity and self-delusion all come under scrutiny and into focus. Joe emerges as more of a controlling, possibly even obsessive narrator than he is usually considered to be. Taking particular note of Adam Mars-Jones's criticism of McEwan's novel, discussed in the last chapter (see Critical history, **p. 37**), Matthews illustrates the ways in which McEwan has constructed a deceptively complex narrator who, far from revealing a case of authorial unreliability, might himself be disturbed to the extent that he is the chief source of his unusual problems: one for whom the most telling appeal is not against Jed Parry, but against himself: '*Don't leave me here with my mind*' (Appendix I, p. 242).

Matthews' title alludes to a famous book of criticism from 1930 by William Empson entitled *Seven Types of Ambiguity*, which sets out to elucidate a theory of metaphor in poetry that identifies seven kinds of ambiguity through close attention to irony, suggestion, allusion, image, argumentation and so forth. Matthews here attempts something not entirely dissimilar by closely observing the twists and turns of Joe's narration in *Enduring Love*. The question as to whether Joe is a reliable or unreliable narrator thus becomes enriched by Matthews' attention to detail, revealing that the answer to this question is a lot less black and white than at first appears, and the matter of (un)reliability is itself deeply ambiguous.

Matthews also departs from the usual convention of referring to the central couple in the novel as 'Joe' and 'Clarissa' and suggests that this critical habit skews readings of the novel because forenames are usually reserved for the characters with whom the writer is thought to have sympathy. The surnames 'Rose' and 'Mellon', with their associations of love and fruit (bringing Adam and Eve to mind), are thus used in the essay alongside that of the character with whom Joe fights: 'Parry'.

Sean Matthews, 'Seven types of unreliability'

> The only account we have is completely unreliable.
>
> (Ch. 20, p. 179)[2]

In Roger Michell's recent film adaptation of *Enduring Love*, discussed in Adaptations (see **pp. 126–35**), chapter, we follow Joe Rose (Daniel Craig) as his comfortable and pleasant world is disrupted and steadily destroyed by the intrusions of the troubled, obsessive figure of Jed Parry (Rhys Ifans). It is primarily on Rose's face that the camera lingers, revealing in close-up the increasingly anxious, uncomprehending and angry emotions to which the character is subject as he gradually loses the things in life he most values. He is a lecturer and 'media don', and his classes and his relation with his television producer begin to unravel as he

---

2   In its development, this paper has benefited from the comments of Dominic Head, Sarah Churchwell, Emily Horton, Julika Griem, John McRae and Peter Childs.

struggles to cope with Parry's intrusions. His girlfriend Claire Mellon (Samantha Morton) starts to fear him, and he moves out of their shared apartment to stay temporarily with an old friend (Bill Nighy). Throughout these tribulations, however, our point of view and our sympathy remain squarely with Rose. We know that Parry has no reason to pursue him and that Rose is a decent man under extraordinary pressure. When Rose finally traces Parry to his squat, he finds the walls covered with a sinister collage of images, impressions and articles about Rose and his work, even a shrine – all of which offer further evidence of Parry's obsessive behaviour. Rose seizes a handy baseball bat and smashes all this before confronting Parry, who is lurking in a corner. We are given to believe, however, that Rose resists the urge to do violence to Parry. Parry, alone, begins to beat his head against the wall.

Later, we follow Rose speeding through the city following a call from Mellon telling him that Parry is with her. We enter with Rose and find Mellon on the sofa with an apparently badly beaten Parry. Mellon, having long since concluded that it is Rose who is unhinged, demands an explanation. For the briefest of moments, in the spirit of films such as *Angel Heart*, *Total Recall*, *The Usual Suspects* or *Memento*, we are allowed to wonder if our proximity to Rose has, in fact, amounted to unwitting complicity. Perhaps a narrative position so absorbed with representing Rose's terrible trial, with permitting us such sympathy with his experience of this unjust and bizarre persecution, has actually been a tool of deceit. What if Rose has constructed a solipsistic narrative, suppressing or obscuring those elements of the story which demonstrate his own responsibility for the course of events, his relationship with Parry? Is there to be a classic twist to the tale, a further turn of the screw?

Our hesitation only endures a fraction of a second. Parry's next action confirms his psychosis, and the film rolls to the same resolution as the novel, with Rose's character redeemed and reinforced. A good man, chastened, he gets his life (and his girl) back at the end, and even acts as the sleuth in a sub-plot, solving a mystery involving John Logan, the man killed in the ballooning accident. The final shot reveals the sinister Parry confined to a mental hospital.

McEwan's status as an associate producer on the film implies that it is something of an 'authorised version'. The adaptation is certainly closely faithful to the original narrative – the balloon accident in particular is stunningly realised – and the very few, minor changes to the original plot of the novel serve only to give further emphasis to this understanding. Readers and critics of the novel have largely replicated this interpretation of the tale, as the contributions to this volume make clear.[3] Parry irrupts, irrationally, madly, into Rose's life, and in so doing demonstrates the fragility of the social and personal order which we take for granted. In many ways Parry's behaviour, his 'love', is indeed a 'dark and distorting mirror' (Ch. 15, p. 128), which shows us how similar our normal passions and affections are to psychosis and mental illness. Our sympathy for Rose, who begins to doubt his own sanity in this world turned upside down, and who has the honesty to acknowledge that Parry's love for him is but an extreme

---

3   See Peter Childs (ed.) *The Fiction of Ian McEwan: A Readers' Guide to Essential Criticism*, Basingstoke: Palgrave Macmillan, 2006, pp. 104–17, for evidence of the overall consistency of this critical consensus.

form of his own love for Mellon, is a measure of our recognition of the dangers which might face us all. This sympathy is demonstrated perhaps most obviously in the way in which readers – including professional critics and students – commonly refer to the characters: following the narrator's example, Joe Rose and Clarissa Mellon (the 'Claire' of the film) are consistently 'Joe' and 'Clarissa', but Jed Parry is only ever Parry. This use of Parry's surname is telling. We are intimate, on 'first-name terms' with Joe and Clarissa, while Parry's status as the outsider is continually emphasised by the more formal designation. There is a fascinating variety of critical perspectives, such as those explored in this volume, on the novel's framing of issues around the relations of science and literature, reason and emotion; on the tensions between masculine and feminine ways of seeing the world; on the moral implications of Joe Rose's behaviour; on the effectiveness of *Enduring Love*'s generic interweaving of psychological thriller, postmodern metafiction, love story, psychiatric case study and novel of ideas. There is no doubt, however, but that these questions are generated by a powerful, reliable account of one man's experience of an extraordinary and impossible situation.

There is, however, a different, more troubling reading of *Enduring Love*, a reading which, in terms of the film, expands upon the moment of doubt about Rose's actions which I discussed in the opening paragraphs. In terms of the novel, this reading takes its cue from a number of inconsistencies and problems – from several different types of *unreliability* – within Rose's narrative, and gains substance from a much more sceptical approach to the diagnostic flourish with which Parry is defeated and dispatched to the asylum. It is a reading, in many ways, 'against the grain', a reading full of suspicion and doubt, a reading which withholds sympathy from Rose, which wonders about the *representation* of these events, and which, with Mellon (and, for that matter, the police), makes the point that Rose's 'being right is not a simple matter' (Ch. 23, p. 216). It is a reading which, in probing the reliability of Rose's narrative, leads on to questions about the ways in which he sees and explains the world which radically destabilise the apparent closure and coherence – the 'happy ending' – of the story.

Adam Mars-Jones, reviewing the novel, points out that Rose tells an ostentatious lie to the police following the shooting in the restaurant.[4] Mars-Jones argues that this lie, about the dessert Rose has ordered (Ch. 19, p. 171, Ch. 20, p. 181), is evidence of an artistic failure. 'McEwan is anything but a crude writer,' writes Mars-Jones,

> even when he chooses extreme subject matter, and such a sharp-elbowed nudge to the reader is out of character. To introduce at this late stage an unreliable narrator is perverse: it recapitulates on the level of gimmick, the novel's central theme, that unreliability is an ineradicable part of what we are.[5]

The device of the unreliable narrator – like the amnesiac, psychotic or deceitful characters of those films mentioned earlier – is a familiar one in fiction, particularly

---

4   Mars-Jones, 'I Think I'm Right, Therefore I Am', p. 16.
5   Mars-Jones, 'I Think I'm Right, Therefore I Am', p. 16.

in recent years. Mars-Jones, however, draws attention to the matter only in order to insist that, on the whole, Rose *is* reliable, and that it is the *author's* preoccupation with a general theme of unreliability that has led him astray. One function of a book review, needless to say, is to discuss the extent to which a novel succeeds as a work of art, but it is intriguing that, at the limits of Rose's narrative, where his credibility begins to break down, it is the author, McEwan, whom Mars-Jones holds responsible, rather than his narrator – a pattern which is generally repeated, as we shall see, when readers voice doubts about the book, most notably in reactions to the article by Wenn and Camia which forms the first appendix. In most readers' minds, Rose is above suspicion, if not moral or intellectual criticism, despite the doubts of Mellon and the police, which he dutifully records. Responses to the novel thus consistently follow the line reproduced in the film adaptation: Parry's madness is ultimately self-evident; the doubts about Rose are shown to be erroneous – after all, Parry *is* incarcerated. David Malcolm, in his study of McEwan's work, states that in *Enduring Love* a 'substantially reliable first-person narrator gives an account of events [. . .] The reader is surely meant to feel at ease about Joe's account, and to believe and trust him.'[6] Similarly, despite their conviction that the novel is centrally concerned with stories and storytelling, with the problems inherent in knowing anything, Roger Clark and Andy Gordon, in an extended reading of the novel, never question the integrity of Rose's narrative.[7] As Malcolm concludes, 'Joe's view of the world is ultimately endorsed and he is shown to be right.'[8]

Mars-Jones is wrong, however, to complain that Rose's unreliability is introduced 'at a late stage'. He also sidesteps a significant formal issue when he suggests that the 'central theme' of the novel, 'that unreliability is an ineradicable part of what we are', can somehow be assessed independently of its narrator. These judgments categorically exclude precisely the analysis of unreliability that *Enduring Love* demands. Rose is a narrator explicitly concerned with the unreliability of narrative, continually fretting at the difficulties he has in telling his own story. There is, thus, overwhelming evidence not only of the inherent unreliability of narrative form (McEwan's 'central theme'), but of the specific unreliability of *this* narrative and *this* narrator, an issue which has been largely ignored or excused in accounts of *Enduring Love*. It will be helpful, therefore, to define more closely the different types of unreliability which characterise the narrative in order better to understand the implications for our understanding – and the distinction is crucial – both of Joe Rose's story and of Ian McEwan's novel.

Only a few pages before the dessert deceit, Rose tells a lie in his first interview with the police. He claims to have informed Mellon of Parry's initial telephone call 'the next day' (Ch. 18, p. 156), when in fact he made a point at the time of explaining his failure to have done so (Ch. 5, p. 53), and Mellon herself has reminded him of his delay (Ch. 9, p. 87). The two lies to the police, which we might term acts of *deliberate unreliability*, may seem petty irregularities, but they are not Rose's only falsehoods or inconsistencies. Rose remarks to himself, while recalling his excuses for rifling through Mellon's desk, 'how dishonestly we can

6 Malcolm, *Understanding Ian McEwan*, p. 170.
7 Clark and Gordon, *Ian McEwan's Enduring Love*.
8 Malcolm, *Understanding Ian McEwan*, p. 170.

hold things together for ourselves' (Ch. 12, p. 107), one of his many asides to the reader concerning the veracity of his narration. There are a number of instances when he withholds information from the reader and from those around him, information which, when it is revealed, casts his earlier comments and reflections in an odd light and aggravates our unease about the reliability of our narrator. Not constituting actual lying, this type of ambiguity should perhaps be characterised as *discrepant unreliability*, since it is impossible to ascertain any specific intention or motivation. For example, Rose's negative comments about Parry's habit of ending his sentences with a rising inflection (Ch. 2, p. 24) are undercut by the fact that his own first words to Parry – before ever Parry speaks – employ the same verbal tic: 'I meant it as a suggestion, but it came out as a request, something I needed from him' (Ch. 2, p. 21). Similarly, when he rummages through Mellon's desk and reads her letters, he reproaches himself fiercely, 'Now I really did have something to conceal from her' (Ch. 12, p. 106), but the next day (some thirty pages later), when she goes into her study and realises immediately what has happened, her bewilderment reveals that Rose had actually made no attempt at concealment: 'You even left the drawer open so I'd know when I came in. It's a statement, a message, from you to me, a signal' (Ch. 15, p. 132). Combined with the particularly confused chronology of this section of the book, the reference to signals reminds us that we are faced with a narrator who is also a primary agent in the action.[9] Collecting Mellon before the final picnic, Rose notices her new dress and espadrilles and comments, 'I experienced a sudden ache – part desolation, part panic – to observe the speed with which this mate, this familiar, was transforming herself into a separate person' (Ch. 24, p. 221). It is Mellon, however, who then remarks, 'I like the new jacket', drawing our attention to the fact that Rose himself has begun the process of transformation. The accumulation of such moments, such signals, even troubles Rose. As Mellon reads Parry's first letter, he wonders, 'What was I so anxious about if I had nothing to hide?' (Ch. 12, p. 100). Recalling his lies to the police about the shooting, he asks himself, 'Just what interests of mine were served by my own account of the restaurant lunch?' (Ch. 14, p. 181).

These types of unreliability are, perhaps, not particularly grievous matters. It is even possible to argue that Rose explains them through the loose, exculpatory framework of 'evolutionary psychology' with which he is concerned throughout the story.[10] However, they also combine with other elements of the narrative to form a wider, more troubling pattern. There is a further type of unreliability in Rose's story which is less obvious, because it is explicit, but which is equally significant: a category we might call *candid unreliability*. This refers to the many occasions when Rose fails to notice, remember or understand events around him, a fact to which he consistently draws attention. Astonishingly, most of the key events in the story are marked either by Rose's inability to recall, above all to visualise, what has happened or by his admission that he has not actually

---

9 Chapters 12–15 are the novel's most complicated in this regard, with a number of flashbacks and prolepses. Surprisingly, our narrator does not draw our attention to his extensive use of these sophisticated devices.

10 The significance of 'evolutionary psychology' in the story is discussed in Text and contexts, pp. 21–7).

witnessed the event at all. At one level, as Mars-Jones indicates, this is a reinforcement of the novel's preoccupation with the inherent problems of narrative and memory, but such a reading ignores the implications of such a powerful and insistent motif for our understanding of Rose's character. Rose's quest to discover who was first to let go of the rope during the balloon accident is the ostensible motive behind much of his action (Ch. 6, p. 55, Ch. 12, p. 107, Ch. 14, p. 122), but he never identifies the precise course of events (Ch. 1, p. 14), despite the geometrical precision of his account (see below). He also, crucially, cannot recall how many of Logan's car doors were open at the scene of the accident (Ch. 1, p. 2, Ch. 13, p. 113, Ch. 15, p. 128). He is unsure as to whether he has really seen Parry, or rather Parry's distinctive shoes, in the London library, remarking that the 'unreliability of such intuition I was prepared to concede' (Ch. 5, p. 47, Ch. 6, p. 57). His lie about the dessert does not distract the police from the fact that his recollection of the order of events leading up to the shooting in the restaurant does not agree with that of others present; he tells us that he has found himself 'inserting into my recollection of the scene an image of the man who sat eating alone, facing away from us. I didn't see him at the time but I was unable to exclude him from later reconstructions' (Ch. 19, p. 167). Neatly, we should note, this statement avoids the issue of whether Parry was there or not. 'What a sorry picture memory offers', Rose reflects, 'barely a shadow, barely in the realm of sight' (Ch. 20, p. 182). It is not even clear *when* Rose pulls the trigger of his own gun during the shooting at the climax of the novel (Ch. 22, p. 213).

There are a multitude of similar occurrences of less direct importance to the plot but serving to confirm a psychological pattern concerned with not quite seeing things, with things being just out of sight (or 'barely in the realm of sight'), literally and metaphorically. Faced with Logan's body, Rose's prose ties itself in knots as he tries at once to see and not see the effects of the fall; 'I didn't care to look [. . .] I kept Logan at the periphery of vision [. . .] Not until I was twenty yards away did I permit myself to see him [. . .] I didn't see Logan dead until I saw his face, and what I saw I only glimpsed' (Ch. 2, pp. 22, 23). Reflecting on his experience in the London library, he wonders whether it was 'illusion caused by visual persistence, or a neurally tripped delay of perception' (Ch. 4, p. 44). He struggles to bring to mind the name of the Victorian picture he associates with Jean Logan (Ch. 6, p. 56). The meaning of the image of the curtain which finally leads him to a diagnosis of de Clérambault syndrome remains frustratingly inexplicable for some time (Ch. 10, pp. 89–90). In one extraordinary paragraph, Rose informs us what he 'would have seen' had he not been facing the other way during Mellon's birthday lunch (Ch. 19, p. 169). This insistent motif extends into all the levels and areas of Rose's narrative. He is even preoccupied with what other characters can and cannot see, repeatedly drawing attention, for instance, to Parry's visual habits, to where he looks during their conversations (Ch. 7, p. 62, Ch. 22, p. 211). Intriguingly, the narrative is also studded with incidental references to failures of sight and perception, from the anecdote about the initial shortcomings of the Hubble Telescope (Ch. 4, p. 39), to the inability of the DNA team to see what was 'staring them in the face' (Ch. 19, p. 165). The significance of this motif, as I discuss further below, is reinforced by the terms of Wenn and Camia's psychiatric case study. The paper contests an earlier diagnosis of Parry as suffering from schizophrenia, and confirms Rose's case for de Clérambault's syndrome. They note in evidence Parry's lack of 'front-rank symptoms for schizophrenia', specifically his 'above average visuo-spatial abilities' (Appendix I, p. 238). This comment draws Rose's dismal visuo-spatial abilities into a different frame of reference, in which they might be interpreted in relation to the schizophrenia and psychosis he reserves for Parry, but it also suggests a belated, if ironic, validation of at least one element of Parry's view of the world.

The combination of *deliberate, discrepant* and *candid unreliability* becomes still more significant when we consider the extent and nature of Rose's self-consciousness about the construction of his narrative. The 'metafictional' elements of the text have been widely discussed. Malcolm, in particular, examines how the text self-consciously draws attention to its status as a narrative, how Rose reiterates his subjection to the demands of form, structure and organisation in telling his story.[11] Rose even boasts of his professional facility as a narrator; 'People say I have a talent for clarity. I can spin a decent narrative out of the stumblings, back-trackings and random successes that lie behind most scientific breakthroughs' (Ch. 8, p. 75). The balloon accident is narrated in a number of different ways, with Rose maintaining a commentary on the different versions: 'a post-mortem, a re-living, a de-briefing, the rehearsal of grief, and the exorcism of terror' (Ch. 3, p. 28); 'as comedy' and, 'in the married style' (Ch. 3, pp. 30–1). An article on which Rose is working allows him to reflect on the negative impact of narrative form on the structure of scientific knowledge: 'the power and attraction of narrative clouded judgment' (Ch. 4, p. 41). Flourishing his credentials as a sophisticated narrator, he remarks in passing the impact of modernism, its celebration of 'formal structural qualities, inner coherence and self-reference' (Ch. 5, p. 49) – qualities which, as we see below, are present to a heightened, even exaggerated, degree in his own narrative. We should note, moreover, that Rose's partner is a lecturer in English literature, and the tale as a whole is studded with references to canonical authors and literary texts: Rose is demonstrably a man of broad literary culture. His implication in the problems of narration even becomes a source of physically painful anxiety. Thinking about the visit to Jean Logan, his mind drifts to 'late-Victorian, narrative style' painting and, suddenly, he shares a cry of anguish: 'Narrative – my gut tightened at the word' (Ch. 6, p. 56).

Although there has been telling discussion of these issues around narrative form, there has been little attention to the unusually strict formal and structural patterning of Rose's own narrative, to his precise, formal responses to the dilemmas inherent in storytelling.[12] The rational, scientific characteristics of the narrator have been subject to extensive analysis, but there are peculiarities to Rose's style and narratorial personality which have gone unremarked, peculiarities which suggest two further, related types of unreliability. First, there is what we might call *controlling unreliability*, which refers to fundamental characteristics of Rose's organisation of the story, the extent to which he manipulates both events and the narrative to his own ends. Second, there is a category best described as *uncanny unreliability*, which refers to elements of the narrative

---

11 Malcolm, *Understanding Ian McEwan*, p. 179.
12 Morrison, 'Narration and Unease in Ian McEwan's Later Fiction', pp. 253–69. See the essay by Randall, Critical readings, pp. 56–65.

which 'break frame', constituting forces within the story which disrupt or undermine its own plausibility. Such forces place an additional burden of interpretation on the reader, who must decide how far credibility can be stretched, whether these elements are sufficient cause to wreck entirely our trust in the narrator.

Rose habitually organises and manipulates the environment around him. We see repeated evidence of this trait. At the Logans' house, for instance, he tells us that before sitting down he 'straightened the cushions' (Ch. 13, p. 109). His fastidious organisation of his own study and research materials, so sharply contrasted to Mellon's (Ch. 10, p. 92, Ch. 12, p. 104), is reproduced in the precision of descriptions and attention to detail which so consistently characterises this novel. *Controlling unreliability* reproduces this behaviour at the level of the imparting of information about the course of the action and of active orchestration of events themselves. He tells us repeatedly that he considers himself to be 'on his own' (Ch. 17, p. 149, Ch. 18, p. 161), and of his delight and excitement when he is able to act, either in commencing 'research' into de Clérambault's syndrome (Ch. 14, p. 124), or in obtaining a gun (Ch. 20, p. 188). We are not, however, always told precisely what Rose's actions entail. He informs us that, 'Ten days after the shooting I drove to Watlington to keep my appointment with Joseph Lacey. The following day I spent the morning in my study making arrangements on the phone' (Ch. 24, p. 220), but we do not know what the appointment concerns. In fact, Rose manipulates the other characters in such a way as to achieve an elegantly patterned conclusion, the closing picnic that constitutes the final chapter and brings resolution to the different strands of the narrative. Rose and Mellon are reunited, the disrupted picnic that began the novel redeemed and transcended. The mysterious Professor of Logic, James Reid, and his student lover Bonnie Deedes are triumphantly paraded, with flourish and unnecessary drama, before Jean Logan, who not unsurprisingly breaks down faced with the strain of such a perverse and superfluous encounter so soon after her husband's death. Rose's delight in his tidy finale, and any initial readerly satisfaction at such a comforting denouement, should be dispersed not only by second thoughts about the exploitation of Jean Logan, but also by an increasingly pressing concern for Rose's motives and modes of organising the narrative.

The different ways in which Rose overtly controls the story – both what happens and the way it is told – are closely connected with the further category concerned with elements of style and form, *uncanny unreliability*. *Enduring Love* is particularly marked by the prominence in the narrative of geometric motifs and images which generate patterns in and from the material of the story. The opening ballooning accident is illustrated by analogy to the balls in a game of snooker:

> the convergence of six figures in a flat green space has a comforting geometry from the buzzard's perspective, the knowable, limited plane of the snooker table. The initial conditions, the force and the direction of the force, define all consequent pathways, all the angles of collision and return, and the glow of the overhead light bathes the field, the baize and all its moving bodies, in reassuring clarity. I think that while we were still converging, we were in a state of mathematical grace.
>
> (Ch. 1, pp. 2–3)

Rose compares his choice of 'beginning' for the story to 'a pinprick [. . .] as notional as a point in Euclidean geometry' (Ch. 2, p. 17), and subsequently refers to his inability to recollect entirely the course of events as 'a failed extension into mental space as difficult to describe as one's first encounter with the calculus' (Ch. 15, p. 128). His antipathy to the Detective Inspector Linley focuses on 'his curious globular face' (Ch. 18, p. 156), a face which concentrates Rose's anger in terms of its shape: 'It wasn't the pallor that was repellent, it was the puffy inhuman geometry of its roundness. A near-perfect circle centred on his button nose and encompassed the white dome of his baldness and the curve of his fattened chin. And this circle was inscribed on the surface of a barely misshapen sphere' (Ch. 18, p. 157). In the restaurant, 'the ice bucket sat in a rhombus of sunlight on a white table-cloth, the tall restaurant windows showed off rectangles of blue sky between the buildings' (Ch. 19, p. 162). The gift from Jocelyn Kale to his niece, Rose notes, is a brooch representing the double helix of DNA (Ch. 19, p. 163). In Oxford, 'The trees lining the tranquil street made a tunnel of green light broken by brilliant points of sunshine' (Ch. 24, p. 223). Rose's narrative is consistent and precise in its delineation of angles, perspectives, patterns. Emotional states are repeatedly defined in relation to space and geometry. Recollection of the shooting is 'warped by a prism of desire and belief' (Ch. 20, p. 180). Rose feels 'a flat and narrow sense of grievance' (Ch. 22, p. 214), and at another point dreads 'personal talk in such an enclosed space' (Ch. 24, p. 222). Rose even reports Mellon's critical comments on the way his emotional life seems constituted of 'inner double-entry book-keeping and calculations' (Ch. 12, p. 103).

There is, needless to say, nothing particularly unusual, or uncanny, about this stylistic tendency taken on its own terms. However, the attention to geometric patterning extends beyond Rose's style and character to the shape of narrative itself. His repeated emphasis on the complexities of beginning and ending in narrative is matched with an equally strong concern for its 'centre'; the 'middle of the story' is plotted uncannily precisely. Rose tells us that Jean Logan, 'was having to lead me by the hand towards the self-evident centre of her torment' (Ch. 13, p. 114). On page 122, he announces, 'At last, we were at the centre of the story.' *Enduring Love* has precisely 244 pages. Even more oddly, or uncannily, the story strains to contain the number of characters, or references to people, whose first names begin with J. With the exception of Clarissa Mellon, all the principal characters' names begin with J: Jed, Joe, Jean, John, Jocelyn, Joseph, James. Moreover, the first letters of the *surnames* of these 'J' characters combine to cover almost the whole alphabet (James Bond/J. C. Bucknell, Jimmy Carter/Jesus Christ, J. E. D. Esquirolle, James Gadd, Joseph Haydn, John Keats/Jocelyn Kale, Jean Logan/John Logan/Joseph Lacey/J. W. Lovett Doust; Johan Miescher/John Milton, John Nolan, Jed Parry, Joe Rose/James Reid, Joseph Severn, Johnny B. Well) – there is even a teasing jaunt through the missing letters in a scene in which Rose leafs through his address book, 'the scrub desert of the final reaches, the U, V, X, Y and Z that aridly encompass the oasis of last chances' (Ch. 20, p. 185). These two examples of *uncanny unreliability* might readily be dismissed as authorial jokes, *jeux d'esprit* in the manner of an Oulipo exercise, though to take this line – as with Mars-Jones's position – is to deflect attention from narrator to author, to break the frame of the narrative at precisely the moment where the narrative frame is most in question.[13] Moreover, these 'uncanny' elements of the narrative become more difficult to ignore when considered in relation to the extraordinary overdetermination of motifs of paternity and parenting in the novel, and of the teasing complexities of the Wenn and Camia article.

McEwan has commented on the way in which fathers have not been 'kindly presented' in his fiction, and a number of reviewers remarked how *Enduring Love* is unusual in his œuvre for its focus on a childless couple.[14] It is not, however, childlessness which is the centrally structuring aspect of Rose's narrative, but orphanhood or, more precisely, fatherlessness. The only significant father in the text – John Logan – is killed in the opening scene, though technically he is dead before Rose begins his story, and it is his death – the death of a father – which is the prime origin or cause of the whole narrative. The only other father is Colin Tapp's, whose presence at the adjacent table gives the grounds for Rose's belief that *coincidence* has led to Tapp being shot mistakenly (Ch. 19, p. 173). Rose's parents are mentioned once, cursorily, with no detail (Ch. 14, p. 118). Clarissa Mellon is an orphan (Ch. 9, p. 83). Jean Logan is the widowed mother of Leo and Rachael after John Logan's death. Jed Parry's father died when he was eight years old (Appendix I, p. 236). The boy in the balloon is out with his grandfather (Ch. 1, p. 12), his father is never introduced. The pattern is not limited merely to characters. Wordsworth's famous refusal of a paternal relation to Keats is discussed (Ch. 19, p. 168). The painting to which Rose refers is Yeames's *And When Did You Last See Your Father?*, even though he is thinking of a different painting (Ch. 6, p. 56).[15] Rose's eye is drawn repeatedly, compulsively, to fathers and children: at the airport (Ch. 1, p. 4); at the museum (Ch. 8, p. 76); at the next table during the birthday lunch (Ch. 19, p. 163). In his meeting with Jean Logan, 'Father and children were the words that undid her' (Ch. 13, p. 111). Jean Logan, Rose notes, guesses that James Reid must be Bonnie Deedes' father, rather than lover (Ch. 24, p. 226). Rose speculates as to whether his own behaviour during the accident might have been different had he been the father of the boy in the balloon (Ch. 1, p. 15) and later consoles himself that he would have made 'a wonderful father' (Ch. 14, p. 118). He even daydreams about being a surrogate in the role at the Logan house (Ch. 14, p. 125). In Wenn and Camia's article, there is also speculation about Rose potentially appearing in that role in relation to Parry (Appendix I, p. 238). Still more curiously, Rose and Mellon, who cannot have children, nonetheless keep a room they call the 'children's bedroom' in their house (Ch. 17, p. 149). The temporary adoption of Mellon's nephews and nieces is ultimately exchanged for the permanent adoption of a child according to the case study (Appendix I, p. 242). Most bizarrely of all, in this narrative overflowing

---

13 'Oulipo' stands for the Ouvroir de Littérature Potentielle or Workshop of Potential Literature. This is a group of writers and mathematicians including Raymond Queneau, Georges Perec and Italo Calvino. Among the literary games invented by the group is the S+7 method, for example, where each noun in a poem is replaced by the noun located seven places away in a selected dictionary.

14 Ian McEwan, 'Mother Tongue', in Zachary Leader (ed.) *On Modern British Fiction*, Oxford: Oxford University Press, 2002, p. 41. Mars-Jones: 'At one time, it would have seemed inconceivable for Ian McEwan to write a novel with a childless couple at its heart, so central did parenthood seem to his idea of human completeness' ('I Think I'm Right, Therefore I Am', p. 16).

15 See <http://historyonthenet.com/Civil_War/when_did_you_last_see_your_father.htm> for a discussion of the painting. (Accessed 15 October 2005.)

with references to parenting and paternity, there is even a fatherly element to Rose's sexual relations with Mellon, who likes, he tells us, to be kissed 'as though she were a child at bedtime' (Ch. 3, p. 33). There can be little dispute with Wenn and Camia's succinct comment that, 'The case confirms the reports of some commentators [. . .] on the relevance of absent or missing fathers' (Appendix I, p. 240). The critical question for the reader, therefore, is to determine that 'relevance', to assess the significance or implications of Rose's obsessive, uncanny attention to these 'absent or missing fathers'.[16]

This brings us back, once more, to the appendix. 'Wenn' and 'Camia' form an anagram of 'Ian McEwan'. This may offer us licence to treat the article, and indeed this whole category of *uncanny unreliability*, as evidence of authorial manipulation, perhaps even as *authorial unreliability*, a knowing, ironic reminder of our complicity with McEwan in the fact of this fiction. The problem with a shift of responsibility for these elements of the text from narrator to author, however, is that it is ultimately arbitrary: by what criteria do we decide which bits are McEwan's little jokes and which are important elements of Rose's character? We abdicate our readerly right to assess a character if we hold the author to blame for the most problematic aspects of his narrator. Moreover, as I argued earlier, to condemn or dismiss those parts of a book with which we are uncomfortable as artistic failure, subsumed under *authorial unreliability*, as in Mars-Jones's review, is to refuse to address the significance of unreliable narration at precisely the moment it is most challenging, most awkward for our sympathy with Rose, most testing of our own function as readers. If, on the other hand, we proceed with our 'suspicious' reading of the text, leaving the author out of our frame of reference, the Wenn and Camia article leads us to a final, crucial form of difficulty within *Enduring Love*, an area perhaps best described as one of *psychotic unreliability*.

At one level, *psychotic unreliability* refers us to concerns about the narrator's own sanity. Rose worries about his psychological state, acknowledges others' doubts about his grip on reality and recognises that the only way to prove his own soundness of mind will be through the exposure or demonstration of Parry's madness. At a more complex level, a level which takes account of the cumulative, overlapping pattern of these differing types of unreliability, I would argue that addressing *psychotic unreliability* involves us in a reconsideration not only of Rose's way of seeing the world and telling the story, but also of the nature of reason and madness themselves.

Enduring Love is saturated with references to madness. Rose's story, after all, hinges on his diagnosis of Parry, and the eventual incarceration of Parry as clinically insane legally ratifies his perspective. The novel refers to madness in its full range of colloquial and clinical meanings. In the famous opening, for instance, we are told, 'What idiocy, to be racing into this story and its labyrinths' (Ch. 1, p. 1), the word 'idiocy' directing us to an older, now pejorative term for the insane, a hint buried in etymology of the central problem of the story. Apart from his analysis of Parry, Rose often doubts his own sanity, though usually as playful or self-deprecating rather than serious comments. He wonders if his anxieties about Parry indicate that his 'mental state was very frail' (Ch. 5, p. 47); he bids farewell

---

16 See Critical history, p. 121, note 6.

to Clarissa one morning with the admission, 'I felt like a mental patient at the end of visiting hours. *Don't leave me here with my mind*, I thought. *Get them to let me out*' (Ch. 6, p. 58). Following one encounter with Parry he heads home, 'feeling slightly mad' (Ch. 7, p. 68). As the story proceeds, 'Clarissa thought I was mad, the police thought I was a fool, and one thing was clear: the task of getting us back to where we were was going to be mine and mine alone' (Ch. 18, p. 161). Under questioning from the police, it is perhaps no surprise that Rose is asked as to whether he has psychological problems, 'Any history of psychiatric illness, Mr Rose?' (Ch. 18, p. 156). Needless to say, he curtly denies the inference. At the centre of Rose's self-conception and self-presentation is his idea of himself as a man of reason, science and rationality, besieged by the irrational, the insane, in the person of Parry. Mellon, he thinks, loves him because 'it's always been a fear that she'll live with someone who goes crazy. That's why she chose rational Joe' (Ch. 9, p. 83). Rose's recurrent stress on the importance of a rational approach to the world functions to sharpen the contrast between his sanity and Parry's madness. Madness is the antithesis of reason, and it is defined and ultimately defeated by the rational man.

Nonetheless, if we consider more closely Rose's relation to Parry, we find a pattern of evidence that further complicates the conventional assumption which contrasts Rose's rationalism and sanity with Parry's madness. First, there is Parry's name, a word with connotations of rejoinder and rebuttal, signalling immediately one aspect of his relation to Rose.[17] Such connotations are made still more explicit during an early conversation: 'Parry crossed his arms and adopted a worldly, man-to-man tone. I thought perhaps I was being parodied' (Ch. 7, p. 63). Rose's failure to resurrect his research career is, by the time he receives the letter from the professor, merely 'a parallel development' (Ch. 12, p. 106). There are a number of parallels between the two men. They are both orphans. As we noted above, despite his irritation at Parry's 'rising cadence' (Ch. 2, p. 24), Rose employs the same speech tic himself (Ch. 2, p. 21). Rose describes Parry's appearance during the conversation after the accident as 'a little melodrama of the reasonable man perplexed' (Ch. 2, p. 26), a phrase echoed in his own adoption of 'the gruff and reasoned tone of a responsible citizen' (Ch. 8, p. 73), when first dealing with the police. On being shown Parry's letter, Mellon comments on the similarity of the handwriting to Rose's own (Ch. 12, p. 100). They share a desire for order, for meaning: 'There had to be a design in this' (Ch. 11, p. 97), Parry writes of his inheritance. Convinced of his own interpretation of the restaurant shooting, Rose angrily dismisses the evidence which he feels has misled everyone else: 'Statisticians call this kind of thing random clustering, as a useful way of denying it significance' (Ch. 20, p. 174). There is an unsettling ambiguity to the phrase Rose uses when reporting Parry's repeated telephone calls, which he has maintained he does not answer: 'Every hour or so I went into the living room to

17 The *Oxford English Dictionary* offers, for the noun, 'An act of opposing or averting something unwelcome or threatening; a check, a counter; a rejoinder; an act of warding off or turning aside a blow or weapon, esp. with a countermove; a verbal exchange, esp. of a combative nature; a dispute, an argument.' For the verb, most pertinent for this context, 'To stop, ward off, or turn aside (a weapon, blow, etc.), esp. with a countermove; to parry something unwelcome, threatening, or awkward; to give an adroit or evasive reply.'

check, and he was always there, staring at the entrance, like a dog tied up outside a shop. On only one occasion was he talking on the phone to me' (Ch. 8, p. 77). Telephone calls are a significant motif. It is a telephone call from Rose to Parry that Parry returns early in their relationship, a call which he interprets as evidence of Rose's initiative towards him (Ch. 5, p. 47, Ch. 6, p. 59). Indeed, once Rose has settled on a diagnosis of de Clérambault's syndrome, he positively seeks out Parry and is irritated to be unable to find him (Ch. 17, p. 143, Ch. 20, p. 182). Parry mentions signals he believes Rose has been making (Ch. 8, p. 78, Ch. 11, p. 96), and Rose openly employs just such signals later in the story (Ch. 17, p. 143). They are both preoccupied with the interpretation of signs, clues and signals. 'My responsibility was to be finely tuned, prepared for the first sign' (Ch. 11, p. 97), remarks Parry. Rose fumbles with his curtain, 'foolishly expecting to find a clue' (Ch. 8, p. 78), as he struggles to interpret Parry's behaviour. Rose notes, before the climactic scene, Parry watching him from the window: 'He looked down and we exchanged a glance, inverting our usual perspective' (Ch. 22, p. 209).

This effect of doubling, with Parry as parody, parallel or doppelgänger, is reinforced by a further set of motifs concerned with mirroring and split person-alities. At one level, these are facetious asides and incidental comments, but taken together – along with the other types of unreliability we are considering – they reinforce a pattern. Rose repeatedly views himself, and narrates his actions, from the third person, and even speculates as to the neurological (rather than psycho-logical) bases of this habit: 'I was another man, my own sexual competitor, come to steal her from me' (Ch. 1, p. 5); 'like a self in a dream I was both first and third persons. I saw myself act' (Ch. 2, p. 19); 'I had fallen through a crack in my own existence, down into another life' (Ch. 7, p. 67). 'I saw myself configured in their eyes' (Ch. 14, p. 119), he remarks, and boasts in one passage of his attaining, while having sex with Mellon, 'full and complete experience in two places at once' (Ch. 18, p. 160).[18] Rose even reports Mellon's contention that '[Parry] was the kind of phantom that only I could have called up, a spirit of my dislocated, incomplete character [. . .] I was disturbed, she said' (Ch. 12, p. 102). A suggestive leitmotif of 'cracks' punctuates the text (Ch. 3, p. 37, Ch. 7, pp. 62, 67, Ch. 11, p. 93, Ch. 18, p. 153).

It would be an extreme, even perverse, reading of *Enduring Love* which con-cludes that Rose rather than Parry is mad. David Malcolm dismisses such a read-ing, arguing it could only reduce the novel to 'an extensive piece of lying': after all, Parry *is* a threat, and he *is* locked up at the end.[19] However, it is equally perverse to ignore the overwhelming evidence of Rose's unreliability, to ignore the remarkable range of ways in which his rational self-confidence and narrative control are brought into question, or to dissolve this problem by invoking the figure of a facetious, trickster author. Our privilege as readers is a critical perspec-tive not only on the narrator's character but also on the limits of that narrator's way of seeing and explaining the world. We might, indeed, take our cue from

---

18 The anecdote of this sexual episode is a curious echo of the boastful, psychopathic narrator of Vladimir Nabokov's *Despair* (Harmondsworth: Penguin, 1981), pp. 32–3, who is not only obsessed with doubles and doubling, but also proud of his experiments in what he calls 'dissociation'.

19 Malcolm, *Understanding Ian McEwan*, p. 179.

Rose himself, who presents the police with a dossier culled from Parry's correspondence with an aggressive injunction to look beyond the surface of the text to the threats which lie beneath: 'They're not right out in front. You'll need to read them carefully' (Ch. 18, p. 156). As he ruefully admits when faced with yet another of Parry's letters, 'It needed the skill of a literary critic like Clarissa to read between the lines of protesting love' (Ch. 18, p. 151). In thus drawing attention to the need for careful reading, to the problems of reading, Rose accentuates quite what is at stake in *our* reading of his story. Rose's reading of Parry is ultimately verified by the appropriate authorities, thus apparently endorsing Rose's perspective and condemning that of Parry. Our reading of *Enduring Love*, therefore, must somehow take account of both his rightness *and* his unreliability. If Rose is not insane, what is the significance of his unreliability? In reading or misreading Rose's narrative, we confront nothing less than our distinctions between sanity and madness.

It is surprising that, as a popular historian of science with an extensive, serious body of research behind him, and a pressing personal interest in the history and definition of madness, Rose makes no mention of Michel Foucault, whose most famous and influential work, *Madness and Civilisation*, is a seminal account of the emergence of our contemporary categories of sanity and insanity.[20] Foucault would be a figure whom Rose could scarcely not have encountered, either directly or in the work of others, although we might readily place his writing in that category of things which Rose can't quite see, which are 'barely in the realm of sight' (Ch. 20, p. 182). Rose's own narrative reproduces Foucauldian turns of phrase and tricks of argument: 'For there to be a pathology', he notes, 'there had to be a lurking concept of health' (Ch. 15, p. 128), employing Foucault's trademark interpretative strategy of inversion. During the passage of the novel when he directly researches mental illness, he uses terms such as 'discourse' (Ch. 17, p. 140), and 'overdetermined' (Ch. 17, p. 147), which are commonly associated with Foucault's theoretical idiom. It is ultimately immaterial whether Rose knows Foucault's work or not, but the absence of such a point of reference, in a narrative which is so confident of its diagnostic force and which is yet, in the multitude of ways we have explored, so unreliable in its marshalling of the evidence, is important. Both Foucault and Rose tell stories about sanity and madness, but it is only Foucault who, in his attention to the *relation* between the two, offers a critical perspective that might help us to interpret Rose's unreliability.

Foucault's study explores the interdependence of madness and sanity, of reason and unreason. He traces the mechanisms by which legal and medical authority combined, over the course of several centuries, first to define, or pathologise, and then to control (through the incarceration and treatment of the mad), insanity. He argues that, since Descartes coined his famous maxim 'I think, therefore I am', philosophers and scientists have striven to define sanity and reason not only positively, through attention to their attributes, but also, and perhaps more compellingly, negatively, through the definition of their opposites: insanity and madness. Our capacity for rational thought, our reason, is what separates us from that which is not us, the 'Other', the beasts and the mad. Our normality

---

20 Michel Foucault, *Madness and Civilisation*, trans. Richard Howard, London: Routledge, 1989.

depends upon the boundaries we draw against the abnormal and the subnormal. It is, then, through rational, empirical knowledge that we come to know, and to define, madness. 'The language of psychiatry', concludes Foucault, 'is a monologue of reason about madness'.[21] The logic of the case is inexorable: the mad are unable to speak for themselves; they have no voice because their words and actions, which would otherwise be *by definition* incomprehensible, can only be interpreted by reason and sanity.

Enduring Love is also a monologue of reason about madness. Parry is wholly controlled by Rose's narrative, which contains his speech and writing, and through the Wenn and Camia article. Parry's behaviour is diagnosed, though not without apparently dissenting voices (Wenn and Camia mention these in passing) as conforming to de Clérambault's Syndrome. In one sense, Rose 'reads' Parry right, in predicting how he will act and in finally thwarting catastrophe. However, read otherwise, the narrative comes dangerously close to disaster, exposing the limits of Rose's rational, scientific self-confidence, the limits of reason itself. As Rose grimly acknowledges, 'I was getting things right in the worst possible way' (Ch. 23, p. 215). Rose is unable to speak to, or with, Parry, and he is helpless to prevent the narrative's acceleration towards violence and tragedy. It is in this context that his unreliability should be understood. Following Foucault, we might say that Rose's confident diagnosis, his rational reading of the situation, *produces* Parry. Rose is unable to countenance the idea that he is in 'a relationship' with Parry, just as surely as reason is premised upon the exclusion of irrationality. Rose's unreliability represents at profound psychological, formal and stylistic levels the internal disturbance and contradiction generated by reason's drive to distinguish itself from madness: what Rose most fears, which is embodied in Parry, is also that aspect of himself he is least able to recognise or repress.

In this reading of *Enduring Love*, the extraordinary patterning and craft of the text, its saturation with troubling leitmotifs, its playful excesses, its hints and suggestions and contradictions, become a still more complex achievement, rather than merely Malcolm's 'extensive piece of lying'. It is an unsettling meditation on madness and civilisation, which implicates the act of reading itself in the fatal, urgent dialectic of reason and insanity. Our reading of Rose's monologue is an exploration of the boundary reason has set up against madness, a deconstruction of the conventions by which identity is formed. The quotation from Dostoevsky with which Foucault begins his work might stand as a fitting final comment on the complex meanings of this troubling novel: 'It is not by confining one's neighbour that one is convinced of one's own sanity.'

---

21 Foucault, *Madness and Civilisation*, p. xiii.

Peter Childs, '"Believing is seeing": The eye of the beholder'

Peter Childs is Dean of Research and Professor of Modern English Literature at the University of Gloucestershire where he teaches twentieth-century and post-colonial literature. He has published widely in the areas of modern writing, British culture and critical theory. Recent books include *Contemporary Novelists: British Fiction Since 1970* and *The Routledge Dictionary of Literary Terms*.

In Critical history, I noted that Joe and Clarissa, despite both being involved on personal quests driven by their research, might be considered to be in different stories because their perceptions of events are so far apart (see **p. 34**). As a final essay in this series, I want to look more closely at some of the similarities between Joe, Clarissa and Jed as well as the ways in which the three main protagonists are wrapped up in different narratives. This can be examined from a point of view that concentrates on the veracity and subjectivity of Joe's narration, as has been seen in several of the previous readings, but it can also be considered in terms of the ostensible differences between the characters that seem to be revealed by that narration. *Enduring Love*'s phrase to express this difference between people's understanding is 'believing is seeing': a reversal of the conventional phrase that in its revised form draws attention to the role in perception of faith, conviction, prejudice and perspective.

Peter Childs, '"Believing is Seeing": The Eye of the Beholder'

> The lunatic, the lover and the poet
> Are of imagination all compact.
> > William Shakespeare, *A Midsummer Night's Dream*,
> > Act IV, Sc. 1,

Love and relationships

Joe says he believed that he and Clarissa would remain together because it 'had always seemed to me that our love was just the kind to endure' (Ch. 18, p. 158). This is a view echoed in Clarissa's later phrase, 'I always thought our love was the kind that was meant to go on and on' (Ch. 23, p. 219). Though the estranged couple's later reconciliation is referred to in the first appendix, by the end of the narrative their shared faith in mutual love has been severely tested and it is the love of the interloper Jed Parry that bears comparison with an endurance test. This is in keeping with the diagnosis of Jed's condition: '[T]his is indeed a most lasting form of love ... The victims of de Clérambault patients may endure harassment, stress, physical and sexual assault and even death' (Appendix 1, p. 242).

The main characters in *Enduring Love* hold to three different versions of what love is: for Jed it is a human derivative of God's love; for Joe it is an evolutionary survival mechanism; and for Clarissa it is an emotional force that bonds people together. After the ballooning accident, it is therefore Clarissa who understands that what she and Joe need to support their relationship is intimacy and physical closeness. Joe subsequently agrees that this is true but can only muse to himself: 'Of course. Why didn't I think of this? Why didn't I think *like* this? We needed love. . . . Clarissa had effected a shift to the essential' (Ch. 3, p. 33). The consequence of Jed's intrusion in their lives is to highlight such differences and potential difficulties in Joe and Clarissa's love: they are opposites who attract but who also do not understand each other's worldview, and this is something that at a time of crisis is capable of isolating both of them within the relationship.

From Joe's perspective, Jed's attachment to him is to be read in terms of his own isolation from simple human contact, resulting in an over-exaggeration of a chance encounter, transferring the life-or-death intensity of the ballooning disaster into a spiritual intensity charging through his meeting with Joe. As James Reid later pithily asserts, 'These things bind you together you know' (Ch. 24, p. 229), and though tighter bonds ought to be the effect that the accident has on Joe and Clarissa, Logan's death in fact drives a wedge between them as effectively as Jed does. Joe and Clarissa have been together for seven years and are reunited at the beginning of the narrative after six weeks apart, the longest period they have been separated. Their relationship is thus susceptible in two familiar ways, from the possible temptations of novelty after seven years together and from doubts over how strongly they will feel about each other after their period spent apart. Which is to say that the question whether Joe and Clarissa's love will endure is intimated at the start of the narrative before the ballooning accident, as Kiernan Ryan has already noted (see Critical readings, p. 49).

Love as a universal and persistent human feeling of attachment is clearly fundamental to McEwan's novel. In a digression towards the start of his narrative, when he recounts his trip to the airport to meet Clarissa, Joe observes 'human sameness' in the way people greet those they care for: 'fathers or grandparents, cajoling, beseeching an immediate return of love. Hann-ah? Tom-ee? Let me in!' (Ch. 1,

p. 4).[1] This is precisely the plea that Jed will deliver to Joe, but there is no familial, sexual, experiential or emotional reason for Joe to give a response to his call. Yet Jed believes his love for Joe is an accompaniment to his faith in God's love. He also believes it is similar to divine love in that it is freely given, irrespective of reciprocation, as Joe discovers: '[H]is love was like God's, patient and all-embracing' (Ch. 17, p. 141). A little later, Joe similarly concludes from Jed's letters that 'God's love for mankind shaded into Parry's love for me' (Ch. 18, p. 152).

Joe also understands that Parry's love resembles the love that he and Clarissa (wish to) share: 'De Clérambault's syndrome was a dark, distorting mirror that reflected and parodied a brighter world of lovers whose reckless abandon to their cause was sane' (Ch. 15, p. 128). Clarissa and Jed are thus separated by Joe into dark and bright alternative realities marked by similarities as well as contrasts. Joe is seen by both of them as someone cut off from his feelings, or at least as an individual for whom 'logic was the engine of feeling' (Ch. 22, p. 213). At the time Joe himself uses this phrase, he realises that such a world based on this principle would be 'inhuman' (Ch. 22, p. 213), yet it is in these terms that others perceive him. Jed says he wants 'To bring [Joe] to God, through love. You'll fight this like mad because you're a long way from your own feelings?' (Ch. 7, p. 66). While Joe thinks 'I hadn't tricked my own feelings like this since I was an adolescent' (Ch. 10, p. 90) only when he indulges a fantasy of being poor, Clarissa believes that Joe constantly rationalises his emotional life and will not share his inner life with her because he relies too heavily on his own resources of reason and logic. Joe indeed realises this but sees no way of bridging the gap between their different ways of viewing the world: 'Clarissa thought that her emotions were the appropriate guide, that she could feel her way to the truth, when what she needed was information, foresight and careful calculation. It was therefore natural, though disastrous for us both, that she should think I was mad' (Ch. 18, p. 150). The difference between their perspectives on the world is succinctly highlighted near the end of the novel when Joe talks about the colonisation of Mars and Clarissa replies 'What's the point? It's beautiful here and we're still unhappy' (Ch. 24, p. 222). For Clarissa, science is important as a means to minimise suffering, to enhance subjective beauty and to promote human happiness, whereas for Joe objective facts provide a basis for action.

His rational materialism drives Joe away from Clarissa and into a world of 'careful calculation', as she later explains: 'You did the research, you made the logical inferences and you got a lot of things right, but in the process you forgot to take me along with you, you forgot how to confide' (Ch. 23, p. 217). This is at least comparable to what Jed feels from his very different perspective: that Joe fills his head with science and misses out on the 'real things like love and faith' (Ch. 16, p. 137). Joe himself acknowledges that he is unable to believe in dialogue over action when he says that 'Twenty years ago I might have hired a professional listener, but somewhere along the way I had lost faith in the talking cure' (Ch. 12, p. 99). Yet, Joe does realise the importance of what he is losing at the moment he

---

1   Robert Wright observes that 'today's Darwinian anthropologists, in scanning the world's peoples, focus less on surface differences among cultures than on deep unities' (*The Moral Animal*, p. 7).

comprehends the enormity of Jean Logan's loss of her husband: 'Jean's grief reduced my own situation to uncomplicated elements, to a periodic table of simple good sense: when it's gone you'll know what a gift love was. You'll suffer like this. So go back and fight to keep it. Everything else, Parry included, is irrelevant' (Ch. 13, p. 112).

Of his relationship with Jed, forged in the emotional intensity of their shared moment standing 'with a dead body sitting between us' (Ch. 1, p. 24), Joe reluctantly concludes that 'It took an act of will to dismiss the sense that I owed this man, that I was being unreasonable in holding something back' (Ch. 7, p. 67). As has been noted, Clarissa also says that she feels Joe is holding something back, and Jed's arrival in their lives is akin to that of a rival lover. In line with this, Joe finds in his conversations with Parry that he is 'talking to a stranger in terms more appropriate to an affair, or a marriage on the rocks' (Ch. 7, p. 67). To an extent, Jed thus usurps Clarissa in Joe's emotional life, as Joe speaks to him about *their* relationship more than he seems to talk to Clarissa about theirs, which by this stage is indeed 'on the rocks' because from at least the moment of the ballooning accident Joe's 'emotional responses were non-existent or inappropriate' (Ch. 1, p. 19).

Joe's narration does at times imply he has a difficulty with empathy, and his observations on the emotions of others can seem callous. For example, when Jean Logan hears that she has falsely accused her dead husband of adultery, she is deeply upset because he can never forgive her and James Reid is apologetic for not coming forward sooner. Joe's comment on this is that the 'breathless scrambling for forgiveness seemed to me almost mad' (Ch. 24, p. 230). From the reader's perspective as analyst in Joe's 'talking cure', it is evident that a breathless scramble for forgiveness has in fact motivated Joe himself throughout the narrative: his own anxiety that he was the first to let go of the balloon mooring rope or is at least culpable for John Logan's death, has driven him to seek expiation and justification from others as well as in his own mind: 'Had we killed him really, or simply refused to die with him? But if we had been with him, stayed with him, no one would have died' (Ch. 6, pp. 55–6). Which is to say that in his insistence that reason triumph over intuition and passion, Joe remains insufficiently sensitive to the emotions driving human beings, including himself. Clarissa puts forward this view in her letter to Joe after the shooting:

> That evening after the accident – it was quite clear from the things you were saying then that you were very troubled by the thought that it might have been you who let go of the rope first. It was obvious you needed to confront that idea, dismiss it, make your peace with it – whatever.
>
> (Ch. 23, p. 217)

For Clarissa, this was the moment at which she and Joe needed desperately to talk: to understand what had happened and to relieve Joe of the shame he seemed to be experiencing at the possibility of his guilt. She says to him in her letter at the end of the narrative when they are reduced to communicating in the way that Jed has communicated with Joe: 'your feelings after the accident were real enough. Isn't it possible that Parry presented you with an escape from your guilt? You seemed to be carrying your agitation over into this new situation, running from your anxieties with your hands over your ears' (Ch. 23, p. 217). This viewpoint connects with Joe's description early in the story of his sense of unease being transferred from guilt to fear or anger over Parry's first telephone call:

> If it was guilt, where exactly did it begin? At the ropes under the balloon, letting go, afterwards by the body, on the phone last night? The unease was on my skin and beyond. It was like the sensation of not having washed. But when I paused from my typing and thought the events through, guilt wasn't it at all.
>
> (Ch. 4, p. 39)

At this point in the narrative Joe denies his sense of guilt, unsure what it is he is feeling, and yet the disquiet stays with him, nagging away – as we are told when he visits Jean Logan to establish his own innocence and guiltlessness (Ch. 12, p. 107).

Joe's unease about the past is mingled with, if not transferred onto, his apprehension over Jed, and what he should do: 'The unnamed sensation returned, this time in the form of a prickling along my nape and a rawness in my gut which resolved itself, for the third time that day, into an unreliable urge to crap' (Ch. 4, p. 40). Joe thus finds himself caught between two feelings: guilt about the past and 'apprehension' about the future (Ch. 4, p. 43). To avoid focusing on these anxieties he concentrates on his writing ('Working was an evasion' [Ch. 5, p. 48]) but his own deep concerns surface again and again as his research seems to mirror his own situation: 'the last words I had written before losing control of my thoughts had been "*intentionality, intention, tries to assert control over the future.*" These words referred to a dog when I wrote them, but re-reading them now I began to fret' (Ch. 4, p. 43).

According to Clarissa, Joe runs from his guilty feeling into attempts to rationalise and control his situation. In his more abstract fashion, Joe himself realises that human truth is not disinterested and 'There could be no private redemption in objectivity' (Ch. 20, p. 181). For him, this is because, as Joe understands about Clarissa's brother Luke ('the pained self-advocacy that hymns the transmutations of love into hatred or indifference' [Ch. 5, p. 46]), evolution has built a subjective perspective into humans' views of events to protect them:

> We're descended from the indignant, passionate tellers of half-truths who in order to convince others, simultaneously convinced themselves. Over generations success has winnowed us out, and with success came our defect, carved deep in the genes like ruts in a cart track – when it didn't suit us we couldn't agree on what was in front of us. Believing is seeing.
>
> (Ch. 20, p. 181; the final sentence also appears
> earlier on Ch. 14, p. 122)

As Paul Edwards noted earlier (see Critical readings, pp. 77–90), Joe here reverses the usual formula for belief through perception to assert that what people see is conditioned by what they believe in their 'mist of half-shared, unreliable perception' (Ch. 20, p. 180). While this complements Joe's comment about the restaurant shooting – 'I did not believe what I was seeing' (Ch. 19, p. 172) – it is a subject that he has also touched on earlier when discussing evolutionary psychology's understanding of self-persuasion. Joe explains that, for a social animal, persuading others of one's own needs is best achieved by convincing oneself first: 'The kind of self-deluding individuals who tended to do this flourished, as did their genes' (Ch. 12, p. 104). He argues therefore that human intelligence is always based on 'special pleading and selective blindness' (Ch. 12, p. 104), and this inevitably throws light on Joe himself for the reader.

This reminder that first-person narration will always be unreliable plants seeds of doubt in the reader's mind over the veracity of Joe's story which have been explored already by Sean Matthews (see Critical readings, **pp. 92–5**), but it also signals that Joe has a blind spot concerning his own motives for devoting so much energy to investigating Jed. His framing of events, for example, includes the conjecture that Clarissa is having an affair: 'My rationalizations crystallized around a partial concept of justice: I had a right to know what was distorting Clarissa's responses to Parry. What was stopping her from being on my side? Some hot little bearded fuck-goat of a postgraduate' (Ch. 12, p. 105; he has earlier described Clarissa as also 'in love with another man' – Keats, Ch. 1, p. 8). Because he cannot see events from Clarissa's perspective, though of course he presumes to do this in Chapter 9, Joe imagines that she is having an affair and not that she wishes him to be more honest and open with her about his feelings of guilt over the balloon accident. The couple's inability to see things through each other's eyes is further exposed by Jed Parry's appearance in their lives, the effect of which is described by Joe in terms that again place him in relationship to Clarissa in a way that parallels his association with Jed: 'To her I was manic, perversely obsessed, and worst of all, the thieving invader of her private space. As far as I was concerned she was disloyal, unsupportive in this time of crisis, and irrationally suspicious' (Ch. 17, p. 139). In terms of sexual attraction, opposites may attract, but therein lies the danger for the endurance of their love as each of them faces the 'ancient, irresolvable dilemma: us, or me' (Ch. 1, p. 15), which applies as much to Joe and Clarissa's relationship as it does to the balloon incident at the novel's start, when Joe allows himself to imagine he and Jed 'rushing towards each other like lovers, innocent of the grief this entanglement would bring' (Ch. 1, p. 2).

Guilty feelings

Through Joe, McEwan unravels the novel with reference both to religion and science, two of the novel's competing narratives. In an interview with Dwight Garner for *Salon* magazine, McEwan explained that scientific research had formed a sizeable part of his preparation for writing the novel. He explained his interest thus:

> [T]here is a subject matter which would have been completely ruled out of court 15 years ago as a matter of scientific inquiry, and now it's central. It's called human nature. That interface between biology and social sciences, between biology and psychology, is increasingly clear. And . . . anthropology . . . is now exploring not how exotically different

we are from each other, but how exotically similar we are. Which seems to me a really fascinating problem . . .[2]

As I noted earlier, this interest shows itself in Joe's observations about human sameness, such as when he thinks he finds at the airport proof of 'Darwin's contention that the many expressions of emotion in humans are universal, genetically inscribed' (Ch. 1, p. 4). Such emotional detachment has made the ballooning accident very difficult for Joe to come to terms with. Using religious imagery, Joe recognises that the 'element of ritual' in their repeatedly ranging over the incident when they arrive home indicates it is 'an exorcism of terror' (Ch. 3, p. 28) for him and Clarissa, but he also understands that 'blaming others could not protect us for long from thoughts of all the things we should have done to avert Logan's death' (Ch. 3, p. 29). Unfortunately for Joe these are private rather than shared thoughts and the couple do not talk about the one thing that Clarissa at the end of the novel tells Joe they should have: his sense of guilt. Joe acknowledges this to the reader but not to Clarissa: 'I felt the sickness of guilt, something I couldn't yet bear to talk about' (Ch. 3, p. 29).

This introversion contrasts with Clarissa's own cathartic inclination to express her feelings about the attempt to save Harry Gadd, though this reminds her of her inability to have a baby and of a friend's lost child. Joe notes that he had never seen 'such disabling grief' as Clarissa can express at such losses (Ch. 3, p. 31), but he remains unable to articulate many of his emotions, as when he remembers: 'I wanted to tell her I loved her, but suddenly between us there sat the form of Logan' (Ch. 3, p. 30). Later, when he senses Parry near him in the London library he says 'I was afraid of my fear, because I did not yet know the cause. I was scared of what it would do to me and what it would make me do' (Ch. 4, p. 44). Joe emerges as someone who knows a scientific theory of what it is to be human very well, but is unable to stop the theory getting in the way of feeling and interacting. Even when he does something for 'luck' he finds himself reflecting that on such hopeful acts 'whole religions were founded' (Ch. 4, pp. 44–5). Joe's view that his reactions are the product of evolution (Ch. 5, p. 51) seems to overlay his life such that, instead of experiencing his feelings, he perceives them as examples of the forces driving human behaviour. Later, as he contemplates Parry, he conjectures that there is 'a skin, a soft shell round the meat of my anger, limiting it and so making it appear all the more theatrical' (Ch. 10, p. 89). Thus Joe processes and contemplates his emotions more thoroughly than he feels them. For him, this can be a source of comfort as it enables him to put his own fears into a wider context of the animal world: 'What I thought might calm me was the reminder that, for all our concerns, we were still part of this natural dependency' (Ch. 22, p. 207), but he also realises that human life now has very little to do with the cycles of nature: 'We were no longer in the Great Chain. It was our own complexity that had expelled us from the Garden' (Ch. 22, p. 207). Joe's difference from Clarissa is brought out well when he shows her one of Parry's letters:

2   Dwight Garner, Interview with Ian McEwan.

It wasn't that she believed Parry, I told myself, it was that his letter was so steamily self-convinced, such an unfaked narrative of emotion ... that it was bound to elicit certain appropriate automatic responses. Even a trashy movie can make you cry. There were deep emotional reactions that ducked the censure of the higher reasoning processes and forced us to enact, however vestigially, our roles – me, the indignant secret lover revealed; Clarissa the woman cruelly betrayed. But when I tried to say something like this, she looked at me and shook her head slightly from side to side in wonderment at my stupidity.

(Ch. 12, p. 101)

Given what the reader gleans about Clarissa's view of Joe later in the book, part of her response to Joe here is based on her perception that he is refusing to deal with his guilty feelings over the accident. As we have seen, Joe appears to be aware of these feelings but does not know how to share them. Instead of discussing them with Clarissa, he channels his disquiet into introspection and into confrontations with others: 'I hadn't come to tell Mrs Logan of her husband's courage, I had come to explain, to establish my guiltlessness, my innocence of his death' (Ch. 12, p. 107). The reader learns this, but Joe again does not talk about his anxieties with anyone around him. His feelings of guilt also predate the ballooning accident and surface in a recurring nightmare he once had in his twenties and thirties and which is now recalled by Logan's fall: 'terror, guilt and helplessness were the components' (Ch. 2, p. 18).

After the meeting with Jean Logan, Joe returns to the scene of the balloon accident. He retraces his steps, seeing them now as his 'stations of the cross' (Ch. 15, p. 127) before he climbs the hill once more near 'Christmas Common' (Ch. 24, p. 228).[3] He imagines many of the people that he has come to consider involved in the accident (the Logans, Logan's putative lover, Clarissa, Parry and even de Clérambault) have arrived to accuse him, but he is not sure of what. Guilt surrounds him but he is unable to discuss it directly with anyone. Joe evidently feels guilt as far as Jean Logan is concerned because he cannot fully banish the thought that he may have been the first one to let go of the mooring ropes. But this is also linked with his feelings about Clarissa. When Clarissa says to Joe that she thinks they are 'finished', Joe decides he is in a 'state of denial' where he feels nothing, but his thoughts make a surprising leap: '[M]y cold-blooded thoughts hopped, frog-like, to Jean Logan with whom Clarissa now shared a neural address, a category in my mind of women who believed themselves to be wronged and who expected something from me' (Ch. 17, p. 146). Instead of explaining to Clarissa how he is feeling, he jumps into action and calls Toby Greene to try to solve the mystery of the picnic in John Logan's car. Again Joe internalises an external confrontation and thinks in terms of guilt (wrong-doing), genetics (neural address) and groups (categories) instead of talking with the person in front of him, Clarissa. Joe says he 'couldn't motivate himself to reply' to Clarissa and his thoughts float away to Jed Parry. They both agree that Joe has a

---

3   The Stations of the Cross is a series of fourteen scenes that represent events in the Passion of Christ and its immediate aftermath.

'problem', but while he thinks it is the practical matter of Parry's threats, Clarissa is 'talking about [his] mind' (Ch. 17, p. 148).

So, as Joe becomes increasingly preoccupied with Parry he understands that Clarissa thinks he may be delusional – a thought that drives them further apart as their misunderstandings multiply. Joe's response to this is to consider himself alone rather than to imagine he can enlist her support: 'It needed the skill of a literary critic like Clarissa to read between the lines of protesting love, but I knew that she would not help me' (Ch. 18, p. 151). Over the course of the story the reader has been told that Joe appears to Clarissa as 'agitated and obsessed . . . manic, and driven' (Ch. 23, p. 217) – the kinds of trait that Joe has ascribed to Jed Parry.

The elements of Judaeo-Christian religion that presage Jed Parry's arrival in Joe's life are clear in the suggestions of Eden and 'the event I am about to describe, the fall' (Ch. 1, p. 2). From a scientific perspective of cause, effect and creation, Joe presents the incident in terms of a singularity, an event like the Big Bang which sets events on a particular course:

> I'm lingering in the prior moment because it was a time when other outcomes were still possible. . . . The initial conditions, the force and the direction of the force, define all the consequent pathways. . . . I think that while we were still converging, before we made contact, we were in a state of mathematical grace.
>
> (Ch. 1, pp. 2–3)

That last phrase is a key one because 'grace' means, among other things, both 'elegance and beauty of movement, form, expression, or proportion' and 'the condition of being favoured or sanctified by God.'[4] 'Grace' is a term that can have meaning in terms of aesthetics, geometry and Christianity. For Joe (as opposed to Clarissa or Jed) it is a word that suggests equilibrium, at the moment before the emergence of a new world:

> It was an enormous balloon filled with helium, that elemental gas forged from hydrogen in the nuclear furnace of the stars, first step along the way in the generation of multiplicity and variety of matter in the universe, including ourselves and all our thoughts. We were running towards a catastrophe, which itself was a kind of furnace in whose heat identities and fates would buckle into new shapes.
>
> (Ch. 1, p. 3)

The novel's conclusion also points up the differences of opinion and perspective that have been the human emotional equivalent throughout the narrative to relativity and parallax (apparent changes in what is observed resulting from a change in the position of the observer). After the shooting at the flat, Clarissa sends Joe a letter in which she criticises his behaviour, arguing that he has concealed his feelings from her and inserted a wedge between them. Joe's

---

4   *Collins Online English Dictionary and Thesaurus* (CD-ROM).

response is that 'Clarissa's letter simply drove us further apart. . . . [T]he years harden us into what we are, and her letter appeared to me simply unreasonable. I disliked its wounded, self-righteous tone, its clammy emotional logic, its knowingness that hid behind a highly selective memory' (Ch. 24, p. 222). As Joe has earlier observed, a selective memory is a human defence mechanism that foregrounds those aspects of experience which are most important or beneficial to the individual, reminding the reader that Joe's account will also have been partial and necessarily presented from a self-centred perspective. For Joe, self-interest is less a failing than a consequential fact of evolution that operates in complex ways – but this *thought* alone will do little to assuage his guilty *feelings* over his treatment of Clarissa, John and Jean Logan, or even Jed.

Self and others

When Joe thinks he finally proves his story of Jed Parry's unprovoked harassment to have been true, he also realises that 'I was getting things right in the worst possible way' (Ch. 22, p. 215). Clarissa is appalled that he has procured and fired a handgun, and though Joe still believes he has acted in a logical way, 'there isn't only ever one system of logic. For example, the police, as always, saw things differently' (Ch. 22, p. 214). In line with this, Joe has earlier concluded that 'Clarissa thought I was mad, the police thought I was a fool' (Ch. 18, p. 161). Such judgements drive Joe deeper into himself and into relying on his own reserves. The one time at which the police would be obliged to act, when Jed has Clarissa held in the apartment, he elects not to contact them as he believes he will only get through to a 'weary bureaucrat' (Ch. 22, p. 208).

This self-reliance extends to Joe's narration, which is claustrophobic in its reliance on his mediation – telling *his* story. Jed and Clarissa are only directly represented in the text by their letters. This is one of the sources of Clarissa's name, derived from the heroine of Samuel Richardson's 1748 novel-in-letters *Clarissa: Or, The History of a Young Lady* (which has a parallel to Jed's harassment of Joe in Lovelace's single-minded pursuit of the eponymous Clarissa). Unlike Joe's direct address to the reader in the book, Clarissa is associated throughout the novel with letters. She is working on Keats's 'last letters' (Ch. 24, p. 221) and is concerned with tracking down the poet's possible unsent final letters to Fanny Brawne, a young woman with whom he had fallen passionately in love and to whom he had become engaged in 1819, the year before he contracted the tuberculosis from which he died.

According to Joe, Clarissa believes that love needs to be expressed, especially in letters:

> In the months after we met, and before we bought the apartment, she had written me some beauties, passionately abstract in their exploration of the ways our love was different from and superior to any that had ever existed. Perhaps that's the essence of a love letter, to celebrate the unique.
>
> (Ch. 1, p. 7)

While the earlier comment may prefigure the letters that Jed will send to Joe, Joe's last observation about love letters here exposes the shortcomings of his rational approach to life and love because 'the unique' is what he finds difficult to celebrate and explain, seeing each individual thing as an example of the general. Consequently, in his replies to Clarissa's letters, 'all that sincerity would permit me were the facts' (Ch. 1, p. 7).

Exceeding in number those passages presented directly from Clarissa's perspective, Jed has three parts of the book given over to his letters: Chapters 11 and 16, and the last appendix. Though Joe never makes the connection, the emotions expressed in the letters in these chapters presumably bear a resemblance to those described in the impassioned letters that Clarissa wrote to Joe at the start of their relationship, as when Jed opens the first by saying 'I feel happiness running through me like an electrical current' (Ch. 11, p. 93). Though Joe of course recounts some of his conversations with him, these letters constitute Jed's only direct voice in the book. We learn from the first letter that both of Jed's parents are dead and that he now lives alone in the large house he has inherited in Hampstead (the district of London where Keats met Fanny Brawne), which is large enough to include a mini-cinema and a snooker room. He is the most educated of his family, has a sister in Australia with whom he has lost contact and some cousins. He has taught English as a foreign language but left this job when he thought the other teachers talked about him behind his back because of his religious beliefs. In this first letter, Jed conceives of his relationship with Joe and Clarissa as a love triangle in which Clarissa is the one who needs to be told that she is no longer loved.

Jed's second letter is the one in which he berates Joe for his scientific articles, which deny the truth of God's reality: 'You pretend to know who or what He is – a literary character, you say, like something out of a novel' (Ch. 16, p. 134). For Jed, the only enduring love is God's, which is channelled through him and which is the source of all human love. He accuses Joe of reducing God's world to chemistry, and of therefore lacking joy, in which he resembles Clarissa. His perspective also resembles that of the police when he summarises Joe's attitude towards him as 'Help! There's a man outside offering me love and the love of God!' (Ch. 16, p. 136). Jed's final letter, in Appendix II, says it is 'The thousandth day, my thousandth letter' (Appendix II, p. 244), suggesting that Jed has, on average, written to Joe every day over the course of the nearly three years since they met. The letter is 'collected' from Jed and there is no reason to believe it was ever sent, reminding the reader of Keats's final unsent letters to Fanny Brawne, proclaiming undying love.

The last words of this final letter are the last words of the novel before Jed's name and have a particular resonance: 'faith is joy'. On the one hand they assert again that Joe's scientific perspective denies him the happiness that Jed finds in God and Clarissa finds in her belief in romantic love. On the other hand they reassert Jed's exuberance in his belief in the word of God through a familiar expression of Christian celebration based on sections of the testaments (most particularly, James 1:2–4, which describes true faith as 'Joy and endurance in the midst of trials').

One of the most significant aspects of Jed's letters is the way they highlight that what Joe sees as 'random clustering' (Ch. 20, p. 174) or a 'meaningless coincidence' (Ch. 20, p. 180), Jed sees as a divinely ordained, fateful conjunction. As Mullen and Pathé are quoted as saying in the article by Wenn and Camia that likens ordinary Keatsian romantic love to the 'lunacy' of de Clérambault's syndrome: 'it is not always easy to accept that one of our most valued experiences may merge into psychopathology' (Appendix I, p. 242).

Clarissa's sections of narration are not uniform, and her only true first-person account is in her letter in Chapter 23. She is also given a perspective in Chapter 9, which is Joe's attempt at rendering her viewpoint. This chapter is anomalous in that it is unique in the novel, but as a device it is also rare in fiction. Joe narrates the chapter from Clarissa's point of view as he 'later construed it' (Ch. 9, p. 79), taking the position of a third-person narrator of events focalised through her perspective. This could be seen as another attempt by Joe to achieve objectivity: this time by making himself into a 'character' in a scene centred on someone else. Yet, it is important to remember that this is not Clarissa's point of view: it is Joe's version of it. So, when we read 'it has always been a fear that she'll live with someone who goes crazy. That's why she chose rational Joe' (Ch. 9, p. 83), this is Joe's understanding of Clarissa. Much of the rest of the chapter works against this reading of Clarissa's attraction to Joe and is a very pragmatic view of love – one that Clarissa seems unlikely to share. At several points, the chapter reports Clarissa's feelings, but these are all imagined by Joe and so are conjectural, seen from Joe's perspective. The reader also must wonder why 'It would make more sense of Clarissa's return to tell it from her point of view' (Ch. 9, p. 79), when nothing else is narrated from her perspective. To address this issue, it is worth reiterating here that the chapter is not so much from Clarissa's point of view as from Joe's reconstruction of it, such that, when the text reads 'But Clarissa does not hear reason' (Ch. 9, p. 87), these are Joe's words – his language – and not hers. From the position of the reader as analyst listening to Joe's talking cure, the chapter is arguably best read as either a further example of Joe trying to deal with his guilt (a rationalisation of it) or as another attempt to show how Clarissa was unable to empathise with him presented as a chapter in which he empathises with her.

The second chapter given from Clarissa's point of view and containing her letter after the shooting at their apartment, is indeed presented without Joe's intervention, except inasmuch as Joe, or McEwan, selects it for inclusion. The chapter appears after twenty-two chapters narrated by Joe (except for the chapters devoted to Jed's letters), and the importance of this could be too easily overstated were it not for the fact that *Enduring Love* is very much a novel about perspective. For McEwan, here lies the significance of these interpolations into Joe's monologue, but for Joe Clarissa's letter presumably appears as further evidence of the difficulties of their relationship. Joe does not himself comment on these epistolary interjections, Clarissa's or Jed's, but this final letter before the appendices is preceded by the comment 'Perhaps we really were finished' (Ch. 22, p. 215). This leads on to a consideration of Joe as arguably a disingenuous narrator, as several critics have debated in the course of this study.

Yet McEwan's comments on the novel suggest that from the point of view of authorial intention, Joe's perspective is the right one (that Jed's threat proves to be real is one of the ways in which McEwan signals his support for Joe's rationalism despite the phantasies (unconscious desires) running beneath it). However, after this violent confrontation in which Joe shoots Jed, *Enduring Love*, suitably for a book that relies so heavily on tripartite structures, concludes with three endings. Each of these endpoints brings to the fore the belief system of one of the central characters. As has been noted, the final one, the second appendix, ends with Jed's restated conviction that 'faith is joy' (Appendix II, p. 245): faith in God, in himself and in Joe. The penultimate ending, the first appendix, offers a deeply contrasting scientific case history, in which Jed's behaviour is fixed into a clinical syndrome, the discovery of which has earlier allowed some catharsis and enabled Joe to explain adequately for himself what has happened, and why. Joe's normality and indeed his faith in science are endorsed by the documented history of de Clérambault's syndrome, turning his individual experience into that of someone else's pathology, thus not only helping to depersonalise Joe's individual experience but to authorise his understanding of its meaning (Jed becomes 'my de Clérambault', Ch. 22, p. 207).

Clarissa's perspective may seem unrepresented by the novel's endings, unless the chapter before the appendices expresses it in some way. If Clarissa's belief system, emphasised not only by her comments on love and emotion to Joe but also by her interest in Keats, is taken to exist somewhere between the brute physicality of Joe's materialism and the metaphysical certainties of Jed's faith, then the endorsement of love and human relationships in Chapter 24 seems closest to her set of values. Here, completing the terrible cycle of events that began with Joe and Clarissa's picnic under the oak on Page 1, Joe's narration ends with a picnic at which Logan is proven innocent of the accusation of adultery and in which children feature prominently. Indeed, a child's question concludes the narrative. Rachael asks Joe to tell Leo 'the thing about the river' (Ch. 24, p. 231). What Joe has told Rachael is that the 'smallest possible bit of water that can exist [is] Two atoms of hydrogen, one of oxygen, bound together by a mysterious powerful force' (Ch. 24, p. 225). Millions of these particles then make up the river, he says. Drawing on the traditional image of the river of life and likening the millions of particles in the river to the millions of people in the world, the analogy here is evidently with the couple, bound together by the 'mysterious' force of love and, alongside them, their child.[5] This at least is the benign reading, but of course McEwan allows the interpretation that takes Joe's story to allude to the force that has bound Jed to Joe and Clarissa – which also is a kind of love. The ending of *Enduring Love* before its appendices presents a child-friendly scientific anecdote, but the explanation Joe offers is a metaphor and a small story, something concerned with language and literature. What Rachael asks Joe to tell Leo thus suggests a common ground for fiction and science in their joint reliance on narrative, which recalls Joe's earlier deliberations on this subject (Ch. 5, pp. 48–9). This final scene is also a gesture towards sharing and inclusion, as Rachael asks Joe to explain his story to Leo too, which may remind the reader that Clarissa has

5   This story also brings to mind Professor Kale's work on the Human Genome Project, whose goal is to map the double-stranded molecule of DNA, represented by the gold brooch he gives his goddaughter: 'Two gold bands were entwined in a double helix. Crossing between them were tiny silver rungs in groups of three representing the base pairs', (Ch. 19, p. 163). The story Professor Kale tells of Phobus Levine's scepticism about DNA inevitably reminds the reader of Jed Parry: 'He dismissed it, and then, in that peculiar human way, it became a matter of faith with him, deep faith' (Ch. 19, p. 165).

accused Joe of keeping his thoughts to himself and not sharing with her the burden of Jed Parry's attentions.

As with much of *Enduring Love*, the final passage before the appendices is in fact in dialogue with other sections of the novel, as I've indicated. To take another example, there is Jed's earlier response to Joe's scientific articles, in which, if God is (a metaphor for) love, Clarissa's voice can also be heard:

> You write that we know enough about chemistry these days to speculate how life began on earth. Little mineral pools warmed by the sun, chemical bonding, protein chains, amino acids, etc. The primal soup. We've flushed God out of this particular story, you said, and now he's driven to his last redoubt, among the molecules and particles of the quantum physicist. But it doesn't work, Joe. Describing how the soup is made isn't the same as knowing why it's made, or who the chef is. It's a puny rant against an infinite power.
>
> (Ch. 16, p. 135)

Conclusion

It might be said that the ending of the novel can easily be read as suggesting that what Joe and Clarissa most need to bring the two of them together is a child. The influence of their joint visit to the Logans may have been to bring them closer together, like the effect of the mysterious force that Joe talks about in his story to the children. To a greater extent than Joe, the children's father John Logan is innocent of his partner's suspicions. Joe's sense of guilt throughout the narrative is now arguably passed on to others: James Reid, Bonnie Deedes and, especially, Jean Logan. It is they who now regret their behaviour and feel in need of forgiveness from others.

Joe and Clarissa will go on to adopt a child, filling a void in their lives that they have often felt. They have kept a room in their half-million-pound Maida Vale apartment, 'part nursery, part teenage-den' (Ch. 3, p. 31), for others' children and it is to this 'children's room' (Ch. 17, p. 149) that Clarissa retreats when she and Joe fall out. Also, Clarissa's study at home is hardly used and becomes 'a tracking station for godchildren' (Ch. 12, p. 104). Children are largely missing from the narrative, despite references to 'the various children in [Joe's and Clarissa's] lives' (Ch. 24, p. 224), apart from the attempt to rescue Harry Gadd at the start and the two visits to the Logans – but they are an absent presence throughout. For example, Joe pointedly describes his and Clarissa's 'marriage of love' as 'childless' on his first discussion of their circumstances (Ch. 1, p. 8). And while Joe shoulders an acute sense of guilt ('I had helped kill John Logan . . . I felt the nausea of guilt return', Ch. 3, p. 32), Clarissa carries a heavy burden of loss after a surgical procedure in her early twenties has prevented her from having children:

> Slowly, she buried the sadness, and built her life again, and ensured that children remained a part of it. Nephews, nieces, godchildren, the children of neighbours and old friends all adored her. . . . Friends considered

Clarissa to be successful and happy, and most of the time they were right. But occasionally something happened to stir the old sense of loss.

(Ch. 3, p. 31)

Joe believes the balloon accident has brought out Clarissa's buried feelings: 'in John Logan she saw a man prepared to die to prevent the kind of loss she felt herself to have sustained. . . . His kind of love pierced Clarissa's defences. . . . [S]he was asking her own past, her ghost child, to forgive her' (Ch. 3, p. 32). In line with this, 'childhood was central' to the stories that Clarissa and Joe tell each other (Ch. 3, p. 34). On this occasion after the accident Clarissa talks of a missing girl, suggestive of her sense of loss, and Joe talks of childhood nerves, suggestive of his anxious state of mind (Ch. 3, p. 35), but they do not talk directly of their current situation. Also, when Joe imagines going to see Jean Logan and her children he brings to mind an image from 'a half forgotten painting in the late Victorian narrative-style, in the idiom of "And when did you last see your father?" Narrative – my heart tightened at the word' (Ch. 6, p. 56).[6] On the one hand this signals Joe's deep and hopeless desire not to perceive the world in the terms of 'narrative', as opposed to the scientific language of facts. On the other hand it signals a preoccupation of the narrative he is himself constructing: that of absent fathers.

A concern with fatherhood and the role of surrogate fathers (as Joe will become when he and Clarissa adopt) is an important aspect to the story, from James Gadd's fatherly care of his grandson and Clarissa's benevolent godfather Professor Kale, through Wordsworth's harsh reaction to Keats and Hoppe-Seyler's treatment of Miescher (Ch. 19, p. 167), to Jed's search for a father figure in Joe (mirrored in Bonnie Deedes' love for the much older James Reid). In addition to this there is Jed's concern with God the Father 'and His Only Son' (Ch. 16, p. 136), and several instances of paternal loss beyond that of the Logan children: Clarissa's brother Luke is leaving his wife and twin daughters (Ch. 5, p. 52), Clarissa's father died of Alzheimer's when she was twelve (Ch. 9, p. 83) and Jed's father died when he was eight (Ch. 11, p. 95). Joe never talks about his own desire for children but does remark at one point that 'Clarissa sometimes told me that I would have made a wonderful father' (Ch. 14, p. 118). To bring the discussion full circle, it is worth remembering that Joe's only paragraph of reminiscence about his background is in terms of his childhood relationship with adults (Ch. 14, pp. 118–19), accentuating once more that the strongest bond of love often involves three people, in the family unit of a couple and their child.[7]

---

6   *And When Did You Last See Your Father?* is a nineteenth-century painting by W. F. Yeames, which depicts a Royalist family in the English Civil War captured by the enemy. At the centre of the picture is a boy who is being questioned about the whereabouts of his father by a panel of Parliamentarians. Behind the boy his sister is in tears and at the rear of the picture are two women, one of whom presumably the children's mother.

7   With regard to the primacy of the number 3, a Christian view of the Trinity would here highlight the Father, Son and Holy Ghost, but also the unique relationship of the first humans Adam and Eve watched over by God the Father in the Garden of Eden.

4

Adaptations

Enduring Love begins with a scene of spiralling horror – a balloon accident – which, on rereading, allows us to appreciate how precisely it has been staged, how tautly calibrated: the technique is almost filmic, deploying a swooping crane shot, zooms and freeze frames.[1]

Several of McEwan's fictional works were made into movies in the 1990s. The first to be filmed was *The Comfort of Strangers* (directed by Paul Schrader, 1990), with a screenplay by Harold Pinter. There then followed *The Cement Garden* (written and directed by Andrew Birkin, 1993), the most successful adaptation to date, and *The Innocent* (screenplay by McEwan, directed by John Schlesinger, 1993). Finally, *First Love, Last Rites* (directed by Jesse Peretz, 1998) reinvented McEwan's short story for a new generation over twenty years after its publication.

The next adaptation, in 2004, was of *Enduring Love*, a novel whose story was compared to a Hollywood film on first publication when the critic and reviewer James Wood argued that McEwan had allowed the melodramatic conventions of genre fiction to run away with his plot. For Wood, the narrative follows too closely the classic trajectory of a Hollywood thriller, obscuring McEwan's deeper interest in the competing ways in which rationalism and irrationalism construct the world:

> The plot almost exactly matches the ideal scheme commanded by Syd Field, in his how-to manual, *Screenplay: The Foundations of Screenwriting* (1984). The Hollywood formula, according to Field, is tripartite: set-up; confrontation; resolution. Field suggests that the classic thriller involves a subject who is the victim of a danger which is revealed to us in the set-up; in the second act, the victim has to confront this danger; and in the third act, the victim must go from being a victim to an aggressor – he must react to, and conquer, danger.

1   Anthony Quinn, 'Lighter Shade of Dread', *The Daily Telegraph*, Arts & Books section, 30 August 1997, p. 5.

... It is a pity that McEwan felt a need to serrate his plot to this blade-like acuteness. For a thicker story, which is McEwan's real interest, gets cut away in the process, and is rather mocked by the narrative excitements. McEwan wants to examine how the irrational might undermine a man's rationalism; and how two people who supposedly love and know each other – Joe and Clarissa – can interpret the same experience quite differently, and quite selfishly.[2]

While Wood is probably quite right to suggest that one of the central concerns of the book is the competing ways in which people make sense of reality, McEwan seems overall to endorse Joe's rationalist approach to problem-solving. The 2004 film by contrast presents Joe less as a rationalist than an introspective and abstract thinker with an academic, but not necessarily scientific, cast of mind.

The film script was an adaptation by Joe Penhall, an award-winning playwright. It is a script that follows the thriller template outlined by Field but that, like McEwan's novel, also incorporates other familiar narrative types into its telling: the chronicle of psychological breakdown, the story of marital crisis, and the love-and-betrayal plot that turns full circle, symbolically starting and ending in the same place with, at the end, the emotionally weary characters unsure of their future. Directed by Roger Michell, the film premiered at the London Film Festival on 26 October 2004. McEwan approved the changes made to the book's narrative for the film and is credited as an associate producer. Penhall says 'Ian's novel is very discursive and philosophical. He uses interior monologues and letters. We had to find ways of dramatizing the book without distracting from the central relationship that had to remain believable for the audience.'[3] The film thus lacks the intimacy of the book's first-person narration, but there are very few times when Joe is off screen, and events are mostly seen from his perspective even though certain issues, such as that of his relationship with Jed, are no longer open to query. The film's narrative suspense nonetheless rests on several questions: how far will Jed go in his pursuit of Joe and how will Joe respond? Will Joe retain his sanity? Was Logan having an affair? And will Joe and Clarissa's relationship survive?

On first viewing, the film inevitably strikes the viewer who has read the book in terms of the elements it has excised. There is no Keats, no gun, no restaurant scene, no police (except Jed says they gave him Joe's phone number) and no science (except one character is called a 'gene machine' when it is announced he has become a grandfather). Joe is now a sociology lecturer who has a new book on the general theme of the science of love; Clarissa has become Claire, a sculptor; and Jed appears more of an impoverished and unemployed tramp than an affluent and idle misfit who does not need to work. The scene with the hippie gunsellers has gone, and there is the addition of two married friends, Rachel and Robin. Penhall comments that 'the "best friend" conceit is standard cinema fare but . . . we needed someone for Joe to confide in and to offer a counterpoint to his views of love and family as being some kind of evolutionary accident'.[4]

2   James Wood, 'Why It All Adds Up', *The Guardian* Review, 4 September 1997, p. 9.
3   Ian Johns, 'Lost in Translation', *The Times*, Weekend Review Section, 23 October 2004, p. 18.
4   Johns, 'Lost in Translation', p. 18.

A synopsis of the film

Though no specific date markers are given, the time of the film is broadly speaking the present: for example, Joe uses the Internet for his research on Jed in the film, which would have been unlikely at the time the novel was written. The opening picnic scene with Joe and Claire still takes place in the Chilterns in Oxfordshire. In broad-brush terms, considering the difference in medium, the episode that follows immediately with the flyaway hot-air balloon is quite close to that found in the first chapter of the book but lacks its descriptive intensity, its complex imagery, flashbacks and digressions. At the scene of the accident, in addition to the grandfather in charge of the boy in the basket, there are Joe, Jed Parry, John Logan and an unnamed farmer who join together to try and stop the balloon racing away. When Logan plummets to the ground, Joe and Jed walk over to the slumped man in an adjacent field. Jed asks a resistant and reluctant Joe to pray, but when Jed falls to his knees and entreats him Joe acquiesces. The other men and Claire then join them by Logan's body.

In short sequences interleaved with much of the visual presentation of the accident and its aftermath, the film takes the small mention in the book of the dinner party with friends (Tony and Anna Bruce, Ch. 3, p. 36) and makes it into a more important scene, introducing a couple called Robin and Rachel, who have twins but none of the relationship problems that face Joe and Claire. For the second half of the balloon incident, the film thus brings together the visual presentation of the accident with its subsequent narration by Joe and Claire, interspersing showing with telling. As the dinner-table scene ends, the camera moves to an elevated vantage point and observes the candlelit table from above, a bird's-eye or balloonist's view it repeats in a spiralling, vertiginous movement over Joe's sleeping body that night. Joe then awakens as if from a nightmare to examine the rope burns on his hand.

When the narrative then moves to Joe at the university, he is lecturing to a class of students about love as perhaps an 'illusion', or a 'trick' played by nature to persuade humans to reproduce. Subsequently, when he works at home in his North London apartment, he repeatedly sketches images of the balloon and searches out balloon shapes and toys. Only at this point does he receive the first phone call from Jed, who is in a children's playground opposite the flat. Joe and Jed meet in the park play area and Jed insists that they need to talk despite Joe's reticence. Jed asserts that Joe knows what he wants to talk about, but Joe meets this with incomprehension. When Joe leaves and returns to the apartment, he sees from a window that Jed not only fails to help but completely ignores a woman who accidentally drops a bagful of oranges in front of him. This is the first suggestion that Jed is in some way socially dysfunctional.[5]

Joe and Claire dine out with Claire's brother Frank (Luke in the book, Ch. 5, p. 52) who has left his wife for their Polish au pair. When they leave the restaurant, Claire and Joe joke together about fidelity and temptation, marriage and

---

5   As mentioned in Text and contexts, p. 26, humans are social animals who often instinctively seek to help others as the best way to ensure that others help them, but this is something Parry lacks, illustrating his difference.

children. Occasionally in these early scenes, Jed can be fleetingly glimpsed in the background as Joe leads his day-to-day life, but it is only when the film cuts to Joe browsing in a bookshop that Jed appears in front of him again, taking a snapshot and then asking Joe to sign a copy of his book: *Simpatico: The Art and Science of Love and Understanding*. At this stage Joe still thinks that Jed's name is Jez and asks to be left alone. Jed declares his love for him but Joe remains baffled by this attention, enquiring if he has offended Jed or whether this confrontation is about the balloon accident and Joe's possible guilty part in it – especially as Jed has said: 'Don't let me down like you let down that other bloke.' On this occasion, it is Jed who walks away as Joe struggles to understand what their meeting means.

The next scene shows Claire sculpting a bust of Robin, who, it transpires, not only has a grown-up daughter in addition to his and Rachel's new twins but has become a grandfather. When Joe enters they all chat amiably, but after Robin leaves, Joe claims that he feels marginalised because Claire is not sculpting him. 'I want you to be my lover not my subject,' Claire replies. To her question 'What's wrong?', Joe describes his meeting with Jed, who he now thinks is perhaps 'a fan' for whom he should feel sorry. Joe explains how he is still agonising over Logan's death and Claire comforts him with kisses, saying 'I love you'.

The camera cuts to Joe crossing the Millennium Bridge to have lunch with a television producer at Tate Modern. As they eat, Joe explains that he feels he should 'do something' with his life because he has never made anything with his hands (like Claire has) or helped anyone (especially Logan). Suddenly Joe spots Jed sitting at an adjacent table and they argue once more. After swearing repeatedly in anger, Joe explodes in rage and Jed leaves the restaurant. Joe is visibly shaken such that the producer (like the reader in the book) is unsure which of the two people is disturbed, especially as Joe refuses to talk about the incident.

After a contretemps with Claire at her workplace, a foundry, during which she repeatedly offers to speak to Jed and Joe asserts that he doesn't want her to, Joe drives along the M40 to Oxford. He heads to the office of the local newspaper and scours past editions for details of the balloon accident. The scene cuts to the home of the dead man's widow (Jean Logan), where Joe explains his belief that if somebody had not let go of the rope first they might have saved her husband. She replies: 'I wish you hadn't told me that.' As in the book, her interest lies in whether one or two doors were open on her husband's car. She produces the picnic ingredients found in the vehicle and states categorically that her husband, who she says didn't take risks and was afraid of heights, must have been showing off to a woman and therefore having an affair.

Joe returns to the field and imagines seeing Logan rushing from his car with a young woman emerging from the passenger seat, and then the same scene with Jed instead of the woman. Three short scenes follow: Claire takes a drink to Joe at his desk and observes the balloon shrine he is building on the wall above; Joe leaves work and sees Jed watching him; and Joe has a birthday dinner cooked for him by Claire (replacing Clarissa's birthday in the novel, Ch. 18, p. 150). At the dinner, which Claire has gone to great trouble to prepare, Joe is initially responsive but soon extremely distant and utterly incommunicative. He begins to talk to himself under his breath, at which point Claire hurriedly clears the table. She swears to herself before her anger gives way to a look of deeply pained frustration. In the next scene, Joe is swimming in an indoor pool. Jed appears outside and, through the glass wall that separates them, shows Joe a newspaper article about Claire (which Robin was reading to Claire earlier as she sculpted). Next, the two of them sit and talk in a café as the film continues to translate the novel's story-told-in-letters into meetings between Joe and Jed. In this scene, though there is no mention of de Clérambault's in the film (the name only appears fleetingly on an Internet page when Joe is looking for information later), Jed makes reference to Joe's secret communication with him via the curtains in his flat. Joe accuses Jed of believing there is a special relationship between them simply because of the intense experience they went through and there is a suggestion that for Jed, he and Joe need to make their relationship work because of their failure to save Logan: 'We can't let go again. Hold on.' Jed presents Claire as the only barrier to their future together and produces the crumpled birthday card that she had given to Joe, which he claims had been thrown away.

Over drinks in Joe and Claire's apartment, three couples talk about love: Joe and Claire wrangle as Joe explains his theory about the biological roots of love; Robin and Rachel seem relaxed and at ease with one another; and Claire's brother Frank eulogises over the magnetism of the non-English-speaking Natasha beside him, for whom he has left his wife. Joe also reveals that, at the picnic that opens the film, he had intended to propose to Claire. When everyone has left, Claire upbraids Joe about the strident expression of his odd theories: 'Do you realise how mad you sound. To people like me'. This echoes Joe's accusation that Jed is mad in the previous scene.

Back at the university, Joe is distracted and then agitated when lecturing. Suddenly he realises that Jed is at the back of the room. Jed starts singing the Beach Boys' song 'God Only Knows'. The scene moves outside, where Joe rails against Jed. Jed shouts back, accusing Joe of 'starting this', declaring his love volubly, and asking if Joe is trying to destroy him.

Echoing an earlier scene, the camera films Joe and Claire in bed from above. It is different this time inasmuch as Joe is sitting up, evidently perturbed. Rising from the bed in the middle of the night, looking out at the rain in the dark and then playing with the curtains, Joe is evidently struck by an idea. He does some investigation on the Internet and discovers the strange, suggestive story about the woman who believed herself loved by George V (Ch. 14, pp. 123–4 in the novel). Drunkenly he tries to explain to Claire what he has discovered about Jed's illness. As he moves the curtains back and forth to illustrate the story, he suddenly notices Jed outside watching him in the rain. Claire is clearly exhausted, emotionally drained and out of patience with his explanations.

The next day, in a scene that substitutes for Joe's rifling through Clarissa's belongings in the novel, Joe begins snooping in Claire's studio. He discovers several drawings and finally a sculpture of himself. Turning, he finds Claire has entered the room. He asks her about the sculpture and she merely replies 'It's my work', before adding, 'It's over.' Joe rants at her and accuses her of thinking that marriage and children in a country house would solve their problems. He forces a ring on her and storms out of the flat into the rain. Unable to locate Jed he phones Mrs Logan to find out his address.

Joe walks to Jed's bedsit, which is in a rundown block of flats. The flat, whose door is open, is filthy and extremely cluttered. Perhaps most importantly, Joe discovers, alongside numerous photographs of himself, a balloon shrine similar to his own. Joe is further enraged when he sees a newspaper picture of Claire which has been defaced. He picks up a baseball bat and begins to smash the things in front of him. When he realises that Jed is in the flat he rushes into another room to confront him. Jed protests his love once more and claims the two of them are similar: 'I'm lonely. You know what that's like.' Joe rushes out while Jed remains in the room in anguish beating his head against a wall.

After leaving the bar where he has been drinking, Joe goes to visit Robin and Rachel. They explain that Claire has been in contact and suggests he collects his possessions from the flat. The following morning at Robin and Rachel's house Joe arises from the living room sofa in a shaft of sunlight. Claire phones to say that Jed is at the flat.

Joe races home to find a bruised Jed has told Claire that Joe has beaten him violently. When Claire is unsure whom to believe, Joe rushes to the bedroom to pack and leave. Jed pursues him but when Joe does not respond he picks up a knife and stabs Claire. Joe reacts by seeming to accept and welcome Jed for the first time. When Jed kisses him, Joe turns the knife on him. Jed falls to the ground and Joe rushes to phone the emergency services and tend to Claire, who is lying in a pool of blood that recalls the red balloon from the start.

The film cuts back to the field in which it began. Joe and Mrs Logan stand waiting. A car pulls up where Joe had imagined Logan stopping on the day of the balloon accident. Out step a professor and his student, Penny, who explain their story to Mrs Logan much as it appears in the novel. She says she can forgive them but, as in the book, asks who is going to forgive her. The film ends with Joe explaining to Mrs Logan's daughter what happened at the balloon accident and that it doesn't matter who let go of the ropes first before joining Claire on the spot they started the film. The screen closes to black after a series of distancing dissolves that move away from the couple.

A few moments into the credits a coda is introduced to match the book's second appendix. The camera pans across a hospital to settle on Jed writing what appears to be a letter by the window. He seems healthy and happy, and before the film fades to black again he moves his head and looks directly into the camera. This is the only time that the film breaks its narrative frame.

Novel into film

To an almost oppressive degree, recurrent images and heavy symbolism (such as hands, the use of the colour red, and the recurrent appearance of balloons) are employed throughout the film, especially whenever Jed appears. Along with the use of music, these create the ominous sense of expectation that in the book is conveyed by Joe's intense narrative. In a more direct way than McEwan's novel, the film's primary narrative style appears to be straightforward juxtaposition: contrasting and comparing different sorts of relationship and several kinds of love, such as the vulnerable couple whose love is threatened, the stable loving couple with children, the new couple of separated husband and au pair, the widowed woman with her fantasy of her husband's affair, the middle-aged professor and the young student. Jed is clearly portrayed as a single man in this world of couples and the dominant image of him is as a lonely outsider. He is no longer the affluent man of the book, but an impoverished and solitary down-and-out; there is also little possibility in the film that Joe could be wrong about the threat that Jed poses.

To a greater extent than the novel, the film concentrates explicitly on the theme of letting go and holding on. This is developed from the opening balloon scene into a metaphor for the endurance or failure of relationships. As in the book, if success depends on all parties hanging on, the crucial question for Joe is who gives up first; but, at the end of the film this question seems less important to Joe than it does earlier. With regard to the accident, the question of who let go of the ropes first is answered slightly ambiguously in the film. The men hold on as the balloon ascends but they are shown to be loosening or releasing their grip one by one. This is presented in close-up such that only the hands individually releasing are apparent to the viewer, making it very difficult to know which individual lets go first. Despite this, the order in which the men hit the ground has Joe second, after the anonymous farmer, suggesting that his fear that he let go first is unfounded. However, the end of the film suggests that this entire question is one that has primarily arisen from Joe's self-obsession and self-doubt. His action in stabbing Jed appears to bring closure on this issue just as it brings an end to Jed's threat.

Perspective and miscommunication remain strong elements of the film as they are of the book. Joe and Jed's entire relationship appears based on Jed's misunderstanding of what happened in their first meeting and is made worse by their persistent incomprehension of each other's meaning. When Joe explains to Claire about his first meeting with Jed, she says: 'He sounds nice.' Soon after, Joe thinks Jed is talking about who let go of the balloon first when they meet at the bookshop and Jed insists that Joe 'knows' what has passed between them. At Joe's later meeting with Claire, she insists that 'you must have done something or he wouldn't be following you'. She concludes her comments with the half reprimand: 'Don't encourage him, okay?' Joe replies that 'Nobody understands', and Claire asks him if he is perhaps suffering from post-traumatic stress and so should 'see someone' professional. This chimes with the book's positioning of the narrative as 'talking cure', where Joe uses the reader as analyst as he confides his story.

A major theme of the book is the opposition between Joe's rationalising theories and his emotional concern over the balloon accident. When Joe tells Claire about his meeting in the bookshop with Jed and about his fears that he is responsible for Logan's death, she tries to convince Joe that he is 'a good person' and that she loves him. This is undermined in two ways. First, Joe remains exercised throughout the film by the possibility that he has let down John and Jean Logan. Second, Joe has already called the beliefs and values that underpin the concept of the 'good Samaritan' radically into question in discussion with his student Spud:

SPUD: So, we're saying art is just an evolutionary tool.

JOE: Perhaps all sorts of complex human behaviour serve the same purpose. Perhaps moral behaviour is another one. Fairness. Kindness. Self-sacrifice.

SPUD: So it's nothing to do with character or personality or simple goodness.

JOE: Maybe that's an illusion too.

This is an example of where the film tries to express through dialogue the evolutionary concepts Joe reflects upon in his narration. However, Joe in the film is not a scientist but a social-studies lecturer: his opinions are based on theorisation, reflection and conjecture. However, because his conclusions are unpalatable they have the effect of alienating those around him.

For example, at the three couples' get-together, Robin tries to ameliorate the impression made by Joe's bleak views on romantic love by saying that 'what he means' is that a rational analysis doesn't make the feeling 'any less fantastic'. Unfortunately, this is another case of misunderstanding, as Joe is saying nothing of the sort – he is arguing instead that the fact that humans are biologically driven ultimately makes all of their emotional experiences at best deluded and at worst meaningless. Similarly, when Joe meets with the television producer to discuss and sell his ideas, the dangers involved in applying his academic theories to his personal life are all too manifest to the viewer, though not to Joe.

> JOE: I'm saying all these things have meaning but they only have meaning because we as human beings give them meaning.
>
> PRODUCER: That's your theory? That life is a meaningless Darwinian expedient. Just biology, but humans struggle to give it meaning.
>
> JOE: Yes, that's what makes us human.

In the midst of this theorising, Jed appears almost as a monstrous personification of the theory, a parodic manifestation of all that Joe says about the delusion of love (pointing up his theory's inadequacy at distinguishing between Jed's and Claire's love for him). Ironically, while the zealot Jed appears calm throughout the film, even when violent, the rationalising intellectual Joe is the one who demonstrably seems emotionally unbalanced to those around him. Here, the film parallels the novel's interest in Joe's growing obsession but whereas the novel shows it from within the film shows it from without, through Joe's behaviour and the reactions of those around him.

Joe's theories about human meaning are later echoed in his conversation with Jed in the café. Jed explains that the purpose of the balloon accident was to bring Jed and Joe together and Logan to God.

> JOE: I think you think that there's this sort of special bond between us because of what we went through. You think it somehow means something.
>
> JED: Everything means something to someone. Otherwise there wouldn't be much point would there. Everything happens for a reason.

This exchange points up Jed's relationship to Joe's rationality more explicitly than the novel does. Jed is not just a physical threat but he epitomises everything in which Joe does not believe: faith, belief, purpose and, perhaps, love too.

Jed then describes how there is for him even meaning in the way that Joe opens and closes the curtains: '[S]imple but effective . . . loving.' To an extent this parallels the Romantics' pantheistic belief in nature as God's handiwork – every landscape and leaf is fashioned by the creator and is an expression of his love. What is also being explored here is the way in which humans ascribe meaning to a life that Joe has pronounced otherwise meaningless: how an understanding of the limits or boundaries of human meaning, interpretation and communication is integral to both emotional well-being (which Joe has lost) and sanity (which Jed has lost, though the film explains this more simply in terms of his extreme loneliness). The questions raised by the scene are also ones that are pertinent to, but seemingly unexplored in, Joe's academic work, such as: if everything is fundamentally meaningless but imbued with meaning by human beings then what regulates, dictates or decides particular meanings? Which is to say that the cultural dimension to Joe's theorising appears unexplored, leaving the accent on the genetic in his social-scientific work.

In the subsequent scene, back at the flat with Joe and Claire's friends, it becomes further clear that this is fundamentally linked to love as the ultimate test case of the differences between individual human perceptions, though Joe simply calls it 'biology' to 'ensure good breeding': 'We're just stupid organisms. It's meaningless. I don't even know why we fucking bother.' After further barbed discussion, Joe reveals that his intention of proposing to Claire was ruined by the balloon incident, which now appears as the interpolation of death and guilt into their untested love and comparative innocence. The conversation ends with Joe haranguing Frank: 'Do you never tire of letting your dick do the thinking?' Yet, this is precisely what Joe has argued love is: sexual desire predicated upon ideals of beauty that are themselves based on the visual signs of genetic health. As in the book, in the film Joe projects his own thinking onto others and finds his own faults in them because of the incompatibility he experiences between his rational and emotional life.

The film is also concerned with definitions of masculinity, and this is an aspect to his self-perception that seems to trouble Joe deeply. Robin says early on that in comparison with most people Joe behaved like an action hero at the balloon incident, but Joe is repeatedly self-condemning, wondering if he has been cowardly. The homosexual tension between Joe and Jed, who regularly appear as squabbling lovers, is also relevant here, as is Joe's sense of diminished potency beside Robin's growing family. When Joe visits Jean Logan, she says of her GP husband that he was 'always traipsing off somewhere having adventures', like going to conduct inoculation safaris in Uganda and to visit orphanages in Yugoslavia. Joe asks if this is 'instinctive', again wondering about whether he himself is innately far more cravenly self-preserving than generously altruistic. 'I need to find out who let go first,' he says. (Jean responds by talking about the picnic found in her husband's car and that she 'needs to know' about his supposed affair.) The next time Joe is with Claire he asks 'Have I let you down?' as he picks away at the scabs on his hand from the balloon accident. She does not know what he means but it is evident that for Joe the failure to save Logan and his social-scientific theories on the invention of love and goodness are interlaced. It is also significant to ask whether it is Joe's hands, as a metonym, that he feels have let Claire down: it is these that let go of the rope and that Claire is sculpting – she has earlier joked that his hands are all that interest her in Joe.

Like the book, the film of *Enduring Love* rarely features children, but they have key parts to play. The opening scene from the book remains of the stranded boy in the balloon for whom the adults risk their lives. Though the Logans' two children from the book, Leo and Rachael, are not retained, they have a daughter who plays with a friend in earshot of the adults when Mrs Logan vows to Joe that if her husband's putative lover comes near the house she will 'kill her'. Most importantly, the moment at which Joe turns away from his spiralling descent occurs when, soaked to his skin in the rain, he goes to visit Robin and Rachel with their young twins. Joe has destroyed his relationship with Claire and nearly assaulted Jed violently. The turning point in his emotional health seems to occur when he is handed one of the children to hold by Robin, who goes to phone Claire. Joe tries to make the baby smile and is evidently pleased when he succeeds. Observing them from the doorway Rachel remarks, 'It's biology remember.' Recanting the theme of his book ('love is just biology'), Joe replies: 'It's not biology. It's fantastic.' When Robin returns, Joe is able to acknowledge for the first time that he has foolishly ruined his relationship with Claire, as though the baby has reminded him of what he has lost. The next scene takes the narrative to the following morning and, in a slow dissolve, shows Joe waking in sunlight, reborn into clear-sightedness and proper perspective, determined to 'sort it all out'. Finally, before Joe and Claire's reconciliation scene at the end of the film, Joe has been talking to Jean Logan's daughter. Through explanation to her of the balloon incident he completes his own talking cure by recounting events simply and focusing on what is important (Logan's decision to hold on) rather than self-important (Joe's obsession over who let go of the rope first).

In the final scene, Claire asks Joe, 'How's the flat?' Illustrating his return to emotional health, he replies with a metaphorical description of how he feels about losing her: 'Small, dark, cold, damp, lonely.' Ambiguously she replies, 'Good, I'm glad', which might be taken to signal she is pleased either that he is suffering or that he misses her. Where the book is ambiguous about the share each partner has played in the breakdown of the central couple's relationship, the film squarely places responsibility on Joe's shoulders because he has been unable to deal effectively with the balloon incident or with Jed's stalking. 'I made it so complicated,' he says at the end, and this is the conclusion the film draws about Joe's response to all that has happened in the course of the narrative. Because of his academic theories and personal fears he has complicated simple events and dealt with them introspectively; like Jean Logan, he has made himself a victim of fabulation. By contrast to Clarissa, Claire is sympathetically drawn throughout, largely because the viewer sees Joe from the outside and not simply through his own words.

In conclusion, and arguably most importantly, it might be said that because the novel is presented almost exclusively from Joe's point of view, the film shows more graphically the effect of the central character's obsessive behaviour on those around him through its third-person perspective, especially in group scenes. The viewer thus observes the implications of Joe's disintegration from the outside whereas the reader infers it or speculates upon it. What both novel and film have in common is, *inter alia*, an interest in the morality of situations: Joe's responsibility for the balloon accident, his relationship with Claire/Clarissa, and his relation to Jed. As his fellow novelist, William Sutcliffe, observed of McEwan in 2005, he is now 'known above all else as a moral writer'.[6] This is a remarkable development for a writer whose debut fiction was almost universally greeted as macabre and sometimes as gratuitously shocking. It is one of the strengths of a novel like *Enduring Love* that it has the capacity to remind readers that McEwan has always been an ethical writer above all else, even though he explores moral questions through the proximity of unusual deaths and everyday loves, the intersection of the extraordinary with the ordinary.

Film credits [7]

Director: Roger Michell
Producer: Kevin Loader
Associate Producer: Ian McEwan
Screenplay: Joe Penhall
Director of Photography: Haris Zambarloukos
Editor: Nicolas Glaster
Production Designer: John Paul Kelly
Music: Jeremy Sams

Cast

Joe Rose: Daniel Craig
Jed Parry: Rhys Ifans
Claire: Samantha Morton
Robin: Bill Nighy
Rachel: Susan Lynch
Mrs Logan: Helen McCrory
TV Producer: Andrew Lincoln
Professor: Corin Redgrave
Grandfather: Bill Weston
Boy in Balloon: Jeremy McCurdie
John Logan: Lee Sheward
Farmer: Nick Wilkinson
Spud: Ben Whishaw

6   William Sutcliffe, 'Cracking Up', *The Guardian* Review, 11 June 2005, p. 37.
7   These credits are taken from Jessica Winter's review of the film in *Sight and Sound*, November 2004, p. 48.

5

Further reading and web resources

The most helpful and up-to-date bibliography on McEwan can be found at Ryan Roberts's Ian McEwan web site: <http://www.ianmcewan.com/bib>.

Books on *Enduring Love*

Clark, Roger and Andy Gordon, *Ian McEwan's* Enduring Love, London: Continuum, 2003. Useful primer that takes the reader through chapters on McEwan, the novel itself, *Enduring Love's* reception and its performance, concluding with discussion questions.

Books on McEwan's work

Malcolm, David, *Understanding Ian McEwan*, Columbia, SC: University of South Carolina Press, 2002. Studies all of McEwan's work chronologically up to *Amsterdam*. Very readable and student friendly, it offers a sustained critique that concludes by asserting that *Enduring Love* confirmed McEwan as a substantial writer.

Byrnes, Christina, *The Work of Ian McEwan: A Psychodynamic Approach*, Nottingham: Paupers' Press, 2002. More of a specialist work, Byrnes's book takes a particular approach to the study of McEwan's work alongside his life. Good on background and biography, the book contains a substantial chapter on *Enduring Love*.

Childs, Peter (ed.), *The Fiction of Ian McEwan*, Basingstoke: Palgrave Macmillan, 2006. A collection of critical reviews and readings of each of McEwan's publications, connected by editorial commentary. Covers all McEwan's fiction up to *Saturday*.

Ryan, Kiernan, *Ian McEwan*, Plymouth: Northcote, 1994. Excellent overview of McEwan's career up to *Black Dogs*. The first book devoted to McEwan, it is also one of the best. Ryan offers short essays on each of the books that preceded *Enduring Love*.

Schemberg, Claudia, *Achieving 'At-one-ment': Storytelling and the Concept of the Self in Ian McEwan's* The Child in Time, Black Dogs, Enduring Love, and

Atonement, London: Peter Lang, 2004. Closely argued analysis of four texts in relation to the struggle for integration of self.

Slay, Jack, *Ian McEwan*, Boston, Mass.: Twayne, 1996. Like Ryan's study, this book ends with the last novel before *Enduring Love*. One in a series of studies, it aims to offer a critical introduction to the life and work of the author.

Reviews on McEwan and *Enduring Love*

Bien, Peter, 'Enduring Love', *World Literature Today*, 72:4, autumn 1998, pp. 830–1.

Birkerts, Sven, 'Grand Delusion', *New York Times Book Review*, 81:2, 25 January 1998, p. 7.

Donahue, Deirdre, 'McEwan Conveys Power and Pathos of Enduring Love', *USA Today*, 29 January 1998, Section D, p. 5.

Eder, Richard, 'Twitching Curtains', *Los Angeles Times Book Review*, 25 January 1998, p. 2.

Goring, Rosemary, 'At 49, He's Fed up with the Trembling Psychopath Scowling behind His Glasses – but He Isn't Mellow', *Scotland on Sunday*, 10 August 1997, p. 3.

Lehmann-Haupt, Christopher, 'Science vs. the Divine, With Suspense and Passion', *New York Times*, 15 January 1998, Section E, p. 11.

Mars-Jones, Adam, 'I Think I'm Right, Therefore I Am', *The Observer*, 7 September 1999.

Reynolds, Oliver, *Times Literary Supplement*, 4928, 12 September 1997, p. 12.

Yardley, Jonathan, 'Pathological Lovers: From Ian McEwan, a Triangle With a Twist', *Washington Post*, 28 January 1998, Section D, p. 2.

Selected articles and essays on McEwan and *Enduring Love*

Bewes, Timothy, 'What Is "Philosophical Honesty" in Postmodern Literature?', *New Literary History*, 31.3, summer 2000, pp. 421–34.

Docherty, Thomas, 'Now, Here, This', in Roger Luckhurst and Peter Marks (eds) *Literature and the Contemporary*, Harlow: Longman, 1999, pp. 50–62.

Miller, Laura, 'Ian McEwan Fools British Shrinks', *Salon*, 21 September 1999.

Morrison, Jago, 'Narration and Unease in McEwan's Later Fiction', *Critique*, 42(3), spring 2001, pp. 253–70.

Moseley, Merritt, 'Recent British Novels', *Sewanee Review*, 106, 1998, pp. 678–82.

Ryan, Kiernan, 'Sex, Violence and Complicity: Martin Amis and Ian McEwan', in Rod Mengham (ed.) *An Introduction to Contemporary Fiction*, Cambridge: Polity, 1999, pp. 203–18.

Selected interviews

Cowley, Jason, 'The Prince of Darkest Imaginings', *The Times*, 6 September 1997, p. 9.

Daoust, Phil, 'Post-Shock Traumatic: Profile of Ian McEwan', *The Guardian*, 4 August 1997, p. 6.

Hunt, Adam, 'Ian McEwan', *New Fiction*, 21, winter 1996, pp. 47–50.

Leith, William, 'Form and Dysfunction', *The Observer*, 20 September 1998, pp. 4–8.

Reynolds, Margaret and Jonathan Noakes, *Ian McEwan: The Essential Guide*, London: Vintage, 2002, pp. 10–23.

Walter, Natasha, 'Looks Like a Teacher, Writes Like a Demon', *The Observer*, 24 August 1997, p. 2.

Writer's Talk: Ideas of Our Time, 'Ian McEwan with Martin Amis', Guardian Conversations, 69, ICA video, 1989.

General books that discuss McEwan and the British novel

Bradbury, Malcolm, *The Modern British Novel, 1878–2001*, rev. edn, Harmondsworth: Penguin, 2001.

Brannigan, John, *Orwell to the Present: Literature in England 1945–2000*, London: Palgrave, 2003.

Head, Dominic, *The Cambridge Introduction to Modern British Fiction, 1950–2000*, Cambridge: Cambridge University Press, 2002.

Contemporary reports of de Clérambault's syndrome

De Bruxelles, Simon, ' "Lady Chatterley" Stalker Believed in Secret Relationship', *The Times*, Section 2, 25 May 2006, p. 23.

Stuttaford, Thomas, 'An Obsessive Love', *The Times*, Section 2, 15 November 2000, pp. 3–4.

Index

In the index, real persons are listed alphabetically by surname (e.g. Turing, Alan); fictional characters are ordered by full name (e.g. Jed Parry).

Related titles from Routledge

Richard Wright's Native Son
Andrew Warnes
Routledge Guides to Literature

Richard Wright's *Native Son* (1940) is one of the most violent and revolutionary works in the American canon. Controversial and compelling, its account of crime and racism remain the source of profound disagreement both within African-American culture and throughout the world.

This guide to Wright's provocative novel offers:

- an accessible introduction to the text and contexts of *Native Son*;
- a critical history, surveying the many interpretations of the text from publication to the present;
- a selection of reprinted critical essays on Native Son, by James Baldwin, Hazel Rowley, Antony Dawahare, Claire Eby and James Smethurst, providing a range of perspectives on the novel and extending the coverage of key critical approaches identified in the survey section;
- a chronology to help place the novel in its historical context;
- suggestions for further reading.

Part of the *Routledge Guides to Literature* series, this volume is essential reading for all those beginning detailed study of Native Son and seeking not only a guide to the novel, but also a way through the wealth of contextual and critical material that surrounds Wright's text.

Hb: 978–0–415–34447–0
Pb: 978–0–415–34448–7

Available at all good bookshops
For ordering and further information please visit:
www.routledge.com

Related titles from Routledge

William Shakespeare's Hamlet
Edited by Sean McEvoy
Routledge Guides to Literature

William Shakespeare's Hamlet (c.1600) is possibly his most famous play, in which the motives of revenge and love are entangled with the moral dilemmas of integrity and corruption.

Taking the form of a sourcebook, this guide to Shakespeare's remarkable play offers:

- extensive introductory comment on the contexts, critical history and many interpretations of the text, from first performance to the present
- annotated extracts from key contextual documents, reviews, critical works and the text itself
- cross-references between documents and sections of the guide, in order to suggest links between texts, contexts and criticism
- suggestions for further reading.

Part of the Routledge Guides to Literature series, this volume is essential reading for all those beginning detailed study of Hamlet and seeking not only a guide to the play, but a way through the wealth of contextual and critical material that surrounds Shakespeare's text.

Hb: 0–415–31432–1
Pb: 0–415–31433–X

Available at all good bookshops
For ordering and further information please visit:
www.routledge.com

Related titles from Routledge

Jonathan Swift's Gulliver's Travels
Roger Lund
Routledge Guides to Literature

Jonathan Swift's Gulliver's Travels (1726) ranks as one of the most biting satires of British and European society ever published. Since first publication, reactions to the book have varied from delight to disgust, but Swift's powerful treatment of the issues of power, morality, colonisation, social conventions and human nature seldom fails to engage and challenge his readers.

Taking the form of a sourcebook, this guide to Swift's controversial novel offers:

- extensive introductory comment on the contexts and many interpretations of the text, from publication to the present
- annotated extracts from key contextual documents, reviews, critical works and the text itself
- cross-references between documents and sections of the guide, in order to suggest links between texts, contexts and criticism
- suggestions for further reading.

Part of the Routledge Guides to Literature series, this volume is essential reading for all those beginning detailed study of Gulliver's Travels and seeking not only a guide to the novel, but a way through the wealth of contextual and critical material that surrounds Swift's text.

Hb: 978-0-415-70020-7
Pb: 978-0-415-70021-4

Available at all good bookshops
For ordering and further information please visit:
www.routledge.com